POWERPLAYS

MIKE POOLE AND JOHN WYVER

POWERPLAYS
Trevor Griffiths in Television

BFI Publishing

First published in 1984 by the British Film Institute
127 Charing Cross Road
London WC2H 0EA

British Library Cataloguing in Publication Data

Poole, Mike
Powerplays.
1. Griffiths, Trevor – Criticism and interpretation
I. Title   II. Wyver, John
822'.914   PR6057.R/
ISBN 0 85170 152 3
0 85170 153 1 Pbk

Cover design by John Gibbs

Printed in Great Britain by Centurion Print Ltd of Hertford

Contents

Frontispiece: Trevor Griffiths

Acknowledgments

This book could not have been written without the assistance of many people. Trevor Griffiths himself has been consistently supportive and more than generous with his time and his ideas. For helping us with information, advice and encouragement, we would particularly like to thank Sue Birtwistle, Stuart Burge, Richard Eyre, Barbara Flater, John Fordham, Carl Gardner, Gill Cliff, Clare Paterson, Jonathan Powell, Philip Simpson and John Stewart (who organised the National Film Theatre season which this book is designed to accompany). We are also most grateful to our editors at the British Film Institute: Ed Buscombe, Geoffrey Nowell-Smith and David Wilson.

Acknowledgment for the stills reproduced in this book is made to BBC Television, Granada Television, Thames Television, Central Television and Paramount Pictures Corporation.

Front cover: Jack Shepherd in *Bill Brand* (Thames Television).
Back cover: Jonathan Pryce in the first production of *Comedians* (Nottingham Playhouse).

1 Introduction: 'Intervening in society's life'

'I knew from very early on that I wanted to work in television. Television seemed then and still seems a massively powerful means of intervening in society's life.'[1]

Trevor Griffiths' commitment to television over the last fifteen years has produced some of the medium's most important and critically acclaimed dramas. Remarkably, this substantial body of work has been consistently radical in character, directly engaged with *political* questions. As such, it has frequently occasioned contention, and at times censorship, within the institutions, not least because of Griffiths' continuing interest in working with popular forms. The attendant struggles over meaning, the powerplays which Griffiths himself quickly came to see as an integral part of television production, strikingly illuminate the practices and prejudices of the medium. Indeed, there is a sense in which Griffiths' work can be seen to define the limits of the possible within television. Consequently, he is the appropriate focus for a study which seeks to explore the relationship of the writer to the medium and to locate the ways in which the elements of that relationship produce the meanings within, or on offer from, finished texts. Griffiths' varied experiences in television have also produced a reflexive understanding of this relationship which makes him an aware and exceptionally articulate guide through the questions which surround it. In addition, his work itself is often a self-conscious critique of the main television genres. Thus, we hope, this is a study that will stimulate thought and discussion about television which is not limited by a strictly defined conception of 'an author and his plays'.

It will already be apparent that we are primarily interested in Trevor Griffiths' writing for television. To have excluded considera-

1

tion of his other scripts, however, would have been nonsensical. So this book provides a full exposition of all his theatrical work, as well as a detailed analysis of his single major cinema script to date, *Comrades*, which was filmed as *Reds*. Our concentration on the television texts, together with the plays that have 'crossed over' from the stage, is partly determined by our own backgrounds in television journalism. But the central reason for our emphasis is simply that we regard television as more fundamentally significant to our culture and the life of society than the theatre. Quantitative support for this assertion can be found in the relative sizes of audiences; qualitative backing is more subjective but, in our view at least, no less persuasive. It is a cliché, if not a truism, that television is our real national theatre. Yet the critical fraternity continues to privilege the proscenium over the small screen. Griffiths, perhaps more than any other writer of his generation, has challenged this prejudice and, although he began by writing for the theatre, in the last decade he has devoted the major part of his creative energies to television. Indeed by 1979, as he told the critic Edward Braun, he saw writing for the stage 'largely as the necessary means of sustaining a reputation which would enhance his bargaining power when dealing with television.'[2]

Griffiths' understanding of the medium underpins the strategies he has developed for working within it. And this understanding begins with that recognition of its importance: the theatre 'is incapable, as a social institution, of reaching, let alone *mobilising*, large popular audiences . . . there are fewer cinemagoers in Britain now than there are anglers; fewer regular theatregoers than car-rallyers. For most people, plays are television plays, "drama" is television drama.'[3] Such importance inevitably entails control. The system of control and its relation to those who benefit from it is complex, but what is important for Griffiths is that the control is not, and indeed cannot be, absolute. Drawing on the writing of H. M. Enzensberger, he sees television as a 'leaky' system which can be exploited to make and transmit works subversive of itself and of the understandings dominant within society. In part this 'leakiness' is due to television's size and scope, for it could only be rigidly policed by a censor's office larger than any other element within it. Moreover, 'direct leakage is not the only sort: for example, the "meanings" or "messages" of plays are often encoded in such a way that the controllers of television output are incapable of decoding them with any precision.'[4] We do not wish in this introduction to offer a substantial elaboration and critique of this, or of our own, theory of the media. Ours will be implicit in what follows: Griffiths' is essential to the plays, and his roles in their production. In particular, this last remark accounts for his obduracy in resisting imposed changes to his scripts and the importance he attaches to the resultant struggles. Closely related to this is his conception of an active, individuated audience. In a preface to two published television scripts, he admiringly quotes Raymond Williams: 'The "telly-glued" masses do not exist; they are the bad fiction of our second-rate social analysts. What the masses, old or new, might do is anybody's guess. But the actual men and women, under permanent kinds of difficulty, will observe and learn, and I do not think that in the long run they will be anybody's windfall.'[5]

Griffiths' recognition of television's importance, its 'leakiness' and its active audience is intimately bound up with the two strategies with which his work has become associated in media debates over the last decade: entryism or 'strategic penetration', and a continuing commitment to naturalism. We will return to both of these on numerous occasions in our analysis. Here it is sufficient to note their inter-connectedness. For the reasons suggested above, Griffiths has chosen to operate within the dominant forms of cultural activity: television, subsidised 'national' theatre companies, Hollywood cinema. Complementary to this has been the choice to work, for the most part, with the dominant mode of those activities: naturalism. His justification for this is pragmatic rather than theoretical: 'When you're trying to speak to large numbers of people who did not study literature at university, because they were getting on with productive work, and you're introducing fairly unfamiliar, dense and complex arguments into the fabric of the play, it's just an overwhelming imposition to present those arguments in unfamiliar forms.'[6] So he has consistently, although not exclusively, preferred to work with naturalism rather than risk alienating a wide, popular audience. Interestingly, in *Comedians*, at what we will argue was a critical moment in his writing, he began to move towards an anti-naturalistic mode. Yet this shift, together with a shift in the politics of his drama, has to date remained largely undeveloped in his subsequent writing.

Associated with this point, although importantly different from it, is Griffiths' conception of his own practice as 'realist'. Deriving the term from the critical theorist Georg Lukács and his *The Historical Novel*, Griffiths uses it to refer to his employment of *typical* characters representative of social, political and historical forces. Lukács identified this operation in certain nineteenth-century novelists such as Flaubert, Dostoevsky and Balzac. As Griffiths states it, 'It's the whole idea of a character working as a confluence of important social and political and moral forces within society, in real historical time . . . [so] my interest in character is not basically psychological but social, sociological and political.'[7] He recognises the twin dangers in the practice of schematism and of an audience's identification with a character submerging an awareness of history, so 'I have to find ways both of allowing identifications and establishing critical distances from characters in action.'[8]

We are aware that critical discourse about television drama in Britain, partly because of the early influence of the theatre, is organised around the writer. In the cinema there has been, until recently, an almost unchallenged parallel emphasis on the director. We recognise the problems surrounding these simplistic notions of 'authorship', particularly in media such as these where production is inevitably collective. Griffiths himself occasionally betrays a wish that this were not so: 'I think all plays have their best production in the head.'[9] Yet he is often generous in his praise for his collaborators. It is inherent in our centring of this study on a writer that we will neither give sufficient recognition to the creative contributions of others nor altogether escape a limited conception of authorship.

This book does work with, although often questions, a framework of ideas erected by Griffiths, but it is concerned to problematise the notion of authorship, and this is central to our adopted methodology. Our book is not a biography of Griffiths, nor is it an academic study of the texts associated with him. It aims simply to provide a critical introduction to that work and is informed by a journalistic approach. Indeed its origins lie in a journalistic project which we began with our separate writings for *Time Out* and *City Limits*. The impetus for its tentative completion was a season at the National Film Theatre which it is intended to accompany. Much of its character has also been the product of the (for us unaccustomed) opportunity to stand back from a close engagement with the work and to look at it more reflectively. This, coupled with our intent to problematise authorship, has led us to attempt to place the individual works against three histories: that of Griffiths himself, his class formation and subsequent translation; that of 'moments' and identifiable trends within British television; and that of general developments in the country's history, politics, culture and thought, particularly as these have been constructed by the Left. Obviously all three histories are closely intertwined, and we have reflected the connections throughout, trying to draw them together wherever this seems to be illuminating. On occasions this has necessitated temporary lacunae in our development of the separate histories.

Even so, it should be made clear that this study has a quite specific chronology. In the interests of a *thematic* exposition of Griffiths' development we have often grouped his works out of sequence. This is partly because his development is uneven, but also because it helps to

4

facilitate the kind of methodological approach outlined above. By identifying its broad thematic patterning we hope to be able to clarify the specific manner in which Griffiths' oeuvre registers and in turn reflects major aesthetic and political shifts in British cultural life since 1968. We have been greatly assisted here by the extraordinarily unified nature of the work itself. No critic has ever really had to construct a unity for Griffiths' output or 'auteurise' the texts themselves: they already contain a coherence virtually unknown elsewhere in television. An effect enhanced by the fact that in over a decade in television Griffiths has worked with a surprisingly small group of personnel. Just three directors have been responsible for realising all his major work: Michael Lindsay-Hogg, Stuart Burge and Richard Eyre. A 'protective repertory' of actors developed early on, centred around Jack Shepherd and Dave Hill, and at different times including Patrick Stewart, Bill Fraser and Lynn Farleigh, further contributing to the sense of a *continuing* project. Similar patterns of extended collaboration can be observed in other areas: Ann Scott, who is married to Jack Shepherd, has script-edited or produced no less than four Griffiths works; Sue Birtwistle, producer on *Oi for England*, is married to Richard Eyre; while most of the remaining production credits go to Stella Richman, Stuart Burge and Jonathan Powell.

This collaborative method of working, together with its underlying thematic organisation, has produced a body of drama of an immediately recognisable temper and character. Centrally concerned with the meshing of the private and the public, the personal and the political, it has invariably engaged with large issues, frequently situating itself at moments of historical crisis. Many of Griffiths' plays are quite literally set in the ante-rooms of history: a hotel bedroom on the eve of Turin's 'revolutionary moment' in 1920; the rented rooms and halls of London in 1903 as Lenin engineers the political schism that was to produce Bolshevism; the plush apartment of a radical intellectual desperately trying to make sense of May '68. Even more strikingly, the interest in the public and the private, the insistence on history as the prerequisite of politics, results in a typical kind of structure: that of the dialectical debate in which two dominant voices or points of view *dramatise* a synthesis. Griffiths' work is full of binary oppositions – revolution and reformism, authoritarianism and libertarianism, 'hard' and 'soft'; Lenin and Martov, Gramsci and Kabak, Scott and Amundsen. Oppositions, moreover, that reflect the blockages and contradictions of history and hence in the process of their attempted resolution complexly re-enact the political dilemmas which originally gave rise to them.

But Griffiths' concern with history has never been simply in what is

5

past. All his 'historical' work attempts to 'recover' the past for the present not only by offering counter-readings to those proposed by bourgeois historiography, but also by using what has previously been suppressed in the culture to provide unexpected contemporary resonances and parallels. Thus the depiction of Tom Mann in *Such Impossibilities* not only recovers a major working-class figure from oblivion but at the same time offers a number of pertinent parallels to the 1972 wave of industrial militancy that 'coincided' with its writing. Gramsci was similarly used in relation to May '68 in *Occupations*. Griffiths has also adopted a related strategy for literary texts. In both *Sons and Lovers* and *The Cherry Orchard*, conventional literary-critical readings are prised open to reveal much more radical works, rendering them, in the phrase of the historian Gwyn A. Williams that Griffiths is so fond of, 'usable' again. Needless to say none of this is achieved without a quite sophisticated degree of debate at the level of dialogue, and a willingness to deal in ideas that is wholly alien to the traditions of British theatre. Griffiths is one of only a handful of playwrights working anywhere in the culture who is, for instance, prepared to quote at length from other texts to support an argument or develop a scene.

Yet for all that it is unusually *wordy*, Griffiths' drama is also closely contoured round a carefully observed concern with the texture of day-to-day living. This is most obviously evidenced in its prominent treatment of sexuality, always a likely indicator in Griffiths of both a character's politics and psychic health. In this respect, of all his contemporaries, Griffiths is the dramatist who has most inherited David Mercer's concern with psychological alienation as an index of social alienation. Except that in Griffiths' case this is overlaid with a much more unequivocally Reichian understanding of sexual regulation as part of the massive inhibitory control system of late capitalism. Griffiths' project is, then, in a sense, nothing less than the exploration of human subjectivity in and through the collectivities of history. Its dramatic dynamic centres on those key moments of individual, group and class *resistance* that attempt to remake history in a genuine fusion of the public and the private.

As this brief characterisation of Griffiths as *auteur* suggests, a good deal of the impetus for his writing comes from the cultural configuration designated by that much over-worked phrase: 'the Sixties'. It is no accident that he began work on his first script in 1968. Nor that it should have so typically been called *The Love Maniac*. Nor, indeed, that he should much later have described 1968 as witnessing 'the most politically shapeable eruption of popular energy the developed world has experienced since the October Revolution'.[10]

Griffiths' early work very much bears the impress of the moment he describes here and might almost be accounted precisely an extended attempt to explore what was 'dramatically shapeable' in it. Certainly this aimed-for reciprocity would find parallels throughout a career as closely contoured by socio-political shifts in the wider culture as it is by changes within the institutions of television and theatre.

Griffiths began writing at a time of great optimism on all three fronts. Change was in the air. British theatre was benefiting from 'de-censorship' following the abolition of the Lord Chamberlain's office in 1968 and from a new input of energy from the burgeoning fringe. Television drama was enjoying its most socially influential period in the wake of the pioneering work of Garnett, Loach and others on productions like *Cathy Come Home*. Additionally, both the BBC and ITV companies were beginning to exploit a huge untapped overseas market for their programmes, accruing large revenues in the process which, for a few brief years, would be ploughed back into programme-making and thus help to create a protective environment for the highly costly business of producing drama. In politics, too, May '68 had given fresh impetus to those disillusioned with Wilsonism on the one hand and British far-Leftism on the other. Griffiths' first major work, *Occupations* (staged in 1970), very much reflects these conditions: produced at a fringe theatre subsidised by Granada Television as a means of recruiting writers for its expanding drama department, it examined the legacy of May '68 through the prism of Turin in 1920, specifically seeking a contemporary revolutionary model in the experience of Gramsci and the factory councils. Griffiths' move into television in 1972, with a popular drama series called *Adam Smith* for Granada, overlapped with a period of working-class militancy provoked by the industrial policies of the Heath government. Yet the 'liberal' structures of television were such at this time that Griffiths was still able to mount an uncompromisingly revolutionary stance in a piece like *Absolute Beginners*.

About this time, too, Ken Tynan commissioned Griffiths to write *The Party* for the National Theatre. The experience proved decisive. In attempting to explore the potential for a revolutionary politics in contemporary Britain, Griffiths was simply unable to find a credible dramatic form for what he was increasingly coming to see as no longer a credible political option. The result was his most unsatisfactory stage play. At this point, along with many others on the Left, Griffiths began to turn his attention again to the Labour Party, whose 1973 Conference had ratified the Party's most radical programme since 1945. Returning to work within television, he embarked on his long and detailed examination of Labourism in the single play *All Good*

Men and the drama series *Bill Brand*. Again his concerns reflected those of a wider moment: *Bill Brand* effectively dramatises almost as it was happening the Left-Right struggle that was to issue in the SDP breakaway. But here, too, Griffiths was to run into something of a political dead-end. Labour seemed unable to deliver a politics capable of dealing with the deep-seated changes in British society becoming apparent by the mid-70s. Griffiths' next work, *Comedians*, gave a voice to political constituencies Labour appeared intent on ignoring – the ethnic minorities, the youth subcultures. The political change of direction brought with it a formal change: *Comedians* is the least naturalistic of Griffiths' work and arguably the most major. Yet it was not a direction he chose to pursue, except abortively in *Oi for England* six years later. Instead he abandoned contemporary concerns altogether, scripting *Reds* for Hollywood and returning to Britain to work on two 'classical' projects: *Sons and Lovers* and *The Cherry Orchard*. What seemed like a retreat was partially halted with *Country*. But the fact that what was to have been the first of six *Tory Stories*, extending through to the present, ended up as merely a one-off tended to confirm the overall trend: Griffiths appeared to be experiencing real political difficulty in writing about contemporary Britain. The trajectory we describe in this study ends, more than a little symbolically, with *Judgement over the Dead*: an elaborate period reconstruction of Scott and Amundsen's race for the South Pole in 1911.

Views will vary over the relative merits of Griffiths' later work. Yet there can be little doubt about its changed character being the product of genuine political difficulties, difficulties far from confined to Griffiths alone. Indeed, with the Left in major disarray under Thatcherism, the television institutions steadily shedding themselves of their commitment to indigenous contemporary drama and Griffiths' generation of playwrights in the theatre – David Hare, Howard Brenton and David Edgar – apparently in related flight, his later work begins more and more to seem *symptomatic*. Edgar himself has talked about a drift in the theatre into the non-contentiously 'celebratory' on the one hand and into socially evacuated dramas of 'disability' on the other.[11] His own work during the period has contained examples of both in *Nicholas Nickleby* and *Peter Pan*, and *Mary Barnes*. Hare's retreat into history in *Plenty* and *Licking Hitler* has most recently been supplemented by a conscious attempt to break away from writing about Britain at all, issuing in the Third Worldism of *A Map of the World*. While in Brenton's case the 'archaeology' of *The Romans in Britain* has been followed by the 'classicism' of *The Life of Galileo* and *Danton's Death*. True, Edgar and Brenton have also produced in

8

Maydays and *The Genius* works that are of direct contemporary political relevance. Yet even here the writing retains a strong sense of crisis – in Edgar's case emerging in a revisionist stance, in Brenton's in a formal hesitancy.

In television, the retreat has been institutionalised. Tied to the regime imposed by co-production and its preference for period drama and 'internationalised' series, even the BBC is progressively with-drawing its support for the single play. *Play for Today*, connoting as it does expectations of contemporary, indigenous relevance, was dropped as a title for the 1983 autumn season of single dramas. The kind of habitat in which Griffiths' early and middle work had developed and thrived is, in short, in the process of being dismantled. The long-term prospects, with the advent of cable and satellite, are for the disappearance of any remotely protective environment as public service broadcasting makes way for the 'self-regulating' forces of the market. Within such a purview, tracing the parabola of Griffiths' individual progress through the changing institution of television inevitably begins to take on a certain finality, prompting the question: is 'Trevor Griffiths' repeatable, is a comparable body of drama likely to emerge again from inside British television? That the answer is almost certainly no gives Griffiths' achievement an added importance and is one of the principal reasons why we embarked on what follows. Furthermore, if we are indeed living through what Raymond Williams has described as 'an epoch's end'[12] in the broader political sense, then Griffiths' work – so clearly a product of that epoch (1968–83) and so scrupulously honest an attempt to map its shifting political terrain – may well come to be seen as something of an epitaph not just for a phase in television but for one in British society as a whole.

2 The Making of a Television Dramatist

Trevor Griffiths' writing project can be seen to be neatly encapsulated in the title of the work which first brought him to prominence: a stage play about the Italian Marxist revolutionary Antonio Gramsci and the Turin factory occupations of 1920, called simply *Occupations*.[1] Much of its author's subsequent career would be shaped precisely by attempts to occupy spaces – intellectual, theatrical and televisual – traditionally viewed as ideological no-go areas for the Left. Thus *Occupations* itself, originally staged in Manchester, was brought to London in a production by the Royal Shakespeare Company at its fringe venue The Place in October 1971, immediately ensuring that the political issues it raised were aired in the pages of the national press. By then Griffiths was at work on his first intervention into popular, primetime television drama, *Adam Smith*. His theatrical 'entryism' continued two years later when John Dexter directed Griffiths' most direct attempt to grapple with May '68, *The Party*, for the National Theatre, with Laurence Olivier playing an ageing Trotskyist; and again in 1975 with the extended West End run of *Comedians*, which also starred a household name in Jimmy Jewel as the disillusioned old comic Eddie Waters.

The critic Malcolm Hay has rightly pointed to something 'paradoxical' in what he calls this 'relationship between revolutionary playwright and theatrical establishment'.[2] Certainly in the case of *Occupations* it elicited a paradoxical response from the critics. Harold Hobson, at the time a key arbiter of mainstream theatrical taste, found that the play could not be 'too highly commended', while at the same time professing what appeared to be genuine surprise that a piece could be 'theatrical *as well as* politically serious'.[3] A number of other critics registered the same difficulty more sympathetically: Irving Wardle, in *The Times*, for instance, described *Occupations* as 'totally free from the intellectual poverty and good-guy emotions that beset British political drama';[4] and Helen Dawson began her *Observer* notice by contrasting Griffiths' political articulacy with the received notion that 'English writers are notoriously uncomfortable when they delve into politics'.[5]

What is interesting here is that all three critics instinctively sought to place Griffiths outside an indigenous, 'English' tradition, both as a dramatist and as an intellectual. In a sense, they were right to do so. The English theatre, like the English novel and so much else in the wider culture, often does appear allergic to ideas, particularly *political* ideas. Locked into those twin ideologies of Anglo-Saxon liberalism – 'experience' and individualism – it has significantly failed to produce any major explicitly political playwright. Yet, for all that he clearly intervenes from outside this tradition, Griffiths remains very much an English figure, both in his concerns as a dramatist and his formation as an intellectual. To mix Gramsci and Richard Hoggart for a moment: Griffiths is a classically 'organic' intellectual produced by a class and a region at 'the friction point between two cultures'.[6] Which is to say that his Englishness defines itself in relation to a highly specific tradition: Northern, working-class, socialist. A tradition, moreover, historically marginalised within English society as a whole and hence excluded from and oppositional to dominant versions of 'English' culture. It is as the product of this opposition and its lived experience that the crucial political component in Griffiths' work needs to be seen.

'SCHOLARSHIP BOY': EARLY BACKGROUND

Trevor Griffiths was born in 1935 in Ancoats, a working-class district of East Manchester close to where Engels had lived. The son of a chemical process worker from a Welsh Nonconformist background and an Irish Catholic mother, his early years were marked by the tail-end of the Depression: when he was still only two, unemployment forced the family to give up its home and go to live with various relatives, Griffiths himself being sent to stay with his maternal grandmother in the nearby district of Bradford. It was she who effectively brought him up, teaching him to read before he was four, when he was already attending the local Catholic primary school. (Much later he was to write many of her qualities into the minor character of Mrs Scully in *Through the Night*: 'a certain kind of unsentimentalised indomitability, resistance, will, all those qualities,' he remembers.[7]) This Irish-Catholic culture suggests close similarities with the kind of Manchester of the same period depicted in Jim Allen's 1983 BBC drama series based on his own childhood, *The Gathering Seed*.

Unlike his elder brother who went to state schools, Griffiths was educated entirely within the Catholic system and this, together with his experience of an extended family group as opposed to the more usual nuclear household, were the key influences on his early development. But these essentially local influences were soon superseded by national factors that brought Griffiths' experience into line with that of a whole generation: the class of '44, as it were, since he was among the first to benefit from the Butler Education Act which opened up secondary education to a new kind of working-class pupil. Griffiths won a scholarship to St Bede's, a Catholic grammar school in Manchester, in 1945. His subsequent development was very much that of Hoggart's 'scholarship boy'. Like so many of his own age, class and background, he experienced the education process as a class translation. There was an added tension in the fact that his brother Brian had missed out on the opportunities created by the Act by being just one year too old in 1944. Brian went to a technical high school, left when he was fifteen and got a job as a trainee shirt-cutter. After three years he went into the Army for his national service, and then returned to work making shirts. Griffiths would later describe their divergent paths as inducing a kind of 'schizophrenic' attitude in himself, and certainly from *Sam, Sam* through *The Party* to *Bill Brand* and *Comedians* the theme of two brothers separated by various distances – social, political, intellectual – has been a major one in his work.

In 1952 Griffiths went to Manchester University to study English on a state scholarship. The choice of subject is significant, not just because Griffiths' work is in some ways noticeably more 'literary' than that of any of the other post-'68 generation of dramatists he is associated with, but because of the peculiar status of English as a discipline at the time. In a culture which lacked any tradition of social science, English under the influence of F. R. Leavis had come to fulfil many of the functions of sociology and it is no accident that the two most influential books of social theory to emerge from the 1950s – *The Uses of Literacy* and *Culture and Society* – were both produced by critics working in university English departments. Unsurprisingly, also, the two teachers who most influenced Griffiths at St Bede's, in history and English, were both Leavisites.

Griffiths' course at Manchester included a substantial element of language analysis, especially in Anglo-Saxon and Middle English. But Griffiths was far more engaged by the literary components and was already writing his own poems. The poets Harold Massingham and Robin Skelton were on the staff and they encouraged him to publish some of his writing in a magazine called, prosaically, *Manchester University Poetry*. For his third year dissertation he chose

12

T.S. Eliot, taking a thoroughly traditional lit.crit. line through the work: 'that Eliot was major, that obscurity was very necessary,' he remembers; 'deeply elitist, mostly copied from other books; not an atom of originality in the whole thing.'[8]

Unusually, though less so then than now, Griffiths lived at home for most of his university career. He was present later when his father died of lung cancer. The strong local ties that characterise every stage of his early life continued the following year when, after completing his degree, he began his national service with the Manchester Regiment. There is something apt about the fact that Griffiths should have experienced 1956, the great post-war watershed year, from the sidelines, from the distance imposed by army discipline. For while he would undoubtedly have been engaged in debate about Suez, most of the other elements that went to make up the cultural climacteric that was 1956 – the Royal Court production of Osborne's *Look Back in Anger*, the Soviet invasion of Hungary, the advent of Independent Television – all occurred in areas that had yet to exercise Griffiths to any significant degree. Provincialised out of any involvement in the theatrical revolution being hatched in Sloane Square – though an avid listener to radio drama – he would only come to the theatre much later; and the intervening period of political activism that was in many ways to prompt him into writing had yet to begin; while television would only start to stimulate him post-1958, with the arrival of Sydney Newman's *Armchair Theatre*.

POLITICAL BEGINNINGS: MANCHESTER'S NEW LEFT

Griffiths' politicisation dates from 1957 and his entry into the job market – as a teacher, first of English and games at a school in Oldham and then of Liberal Studies at Stockport Technical College. As he told one interviewer: 'That's when I began to find myself. The responsibility of teaching made me realise that I didn't know anything.'[9] Having left the Army able to drive a truck but with few other skills, he had looked for employment without enthusiasm or direction. Then through a local newspaper advertisement, he was engaged to teach at a nearby private school, one of many opened in the early 50s for the not-too-bright children of not-too-rich middle-class families. Another of the masters there was Albert Smith, described by Griffiths as 'an old anarchist pacifist scholar . . . a very remarkable man.' Smith quickly interested his new colleague in the ideas of A. S. Neill and the related progressive education movement; and together they influenced staff appointments so that the school became increasingly 'experimental'. Yet the experience was clearly contradictory and Griffiths grew alienated from the privatised system. After just over four years he left in the autumn of 1961, intending to write an external MA thesis at Manchester University.

These final years of the 50s saw the beginnings of CND and the New Left, and Griffiths became progressively involved in both. In 1960 he was chairman of the Manchester Left Club, one of forty or so 'readers' groups linked to the newly formed *New Left Review*, which under the editorship of Stuart Hall was describing itself somewhat enigmatically as 'more than a journal, not quite a movement'. *NLR* had yet to espouse the kind of gnomic super-Marxism for which it was later to become notorious, but even so its instinctive orientation tended towards the academic and this, together with his deep involvement with teaching, gave Griffiths' politics a certain intellectualist stamp.

The Left Club attracted to their discussion centre in a Manchester café a remarkable list of speakers: Edward Thompson, Raymond Williams, Peter Worsley, Stuart Hall, John Rex, John Saville – many of the intellectuals whom Griffiths would later write of as 'involved in the long ideological struggle to deliver the 50s to the 60s'.[10] Complementary reading included not only *NLR*, but Thompson's book on William Morris and Williams' *Culture and Society* (1958) and *The Long Revolution* (1961). These latter works prompted Griffiths' choice of 'The Meaning of Culture' as his subject for the (eventually uncompleted) MA thesis, which analysed the writings of Lawrence, Leavis and Williams. During its preparation he met teachers at the rapidly expanding Stockport Technical College, where a new department of Liberal Studies was being established, and secured a full-time job there in 1962. His subject area was wide – although dominated by contemporary political history and 'civics' – as was the range of students, who included craft apprentices in decorating and bricklaying as well as students taking external degrees in science subjects.

At the same time, Griffiths was drawn into the Labour Party, and quickly began to write for and co-edit *Labour's Northern Voice*. This eight-page monthly was a constituency-level, left-wing paper published by a group which included the MPs Frank Allaun and Stan Orme. Griffiths contributed a good deal of political journalism in the months immediately before and after Harold Wilson's election, but like many others he became rapidly disillusioned with the Labour government and left first the paper and then the party in early 1965.

14

As indicated above, Griffiths cites Raymond Williams' *The Long Revolution* as a major influence during this phase: Williams' concern with examining the institutions of British cultural life, including the educational system, very much reflected his own experience as a teacher. But the book also offered an analysis of the institution of writing itself, surveying the social origins of British authors from the Tudor period through to the present day as a prelude to discussing the wider socio-economic shifts behind the late-50s emergence of a whole generation of working-class writers, journalistically hyped at the time as Angry Young Men. Williams discerned a 'characteristic pattern' in this development and its typical texts: 'the more freely mobile individual mocking or raging at the institutions which are made available for him to join, or else, if he acquiesces, suffering rapid personal deterioration (cf. *Lucky Jim, Look Back in Anger, Room at the Top*). There is a continuing sense of deadlock, and much of the experience generated within it seems sterile.'[11] In suggesting reasons why this should be so, Williams outlined a model of institutional *constraint* within the various cultural apparatuses that undoubtedly influenced much of Griffiths' own subsequent 'entryist' practice as a dramatist: 'The terms of mobility, thus conceived, are hopelessly limited. The combination of individual mobility with the stability of institutions and ways of thinking leads to this deadlock inevitably . . . There is an obvious danger of the advantage of individual writers drawn from more varied social origins being limited or nullified by their absorption into pre-existing standard patterns.'[12]

Griffiths' first experience of publication was with his poems at Manchester University. Then he had begun a novel, and had written a succession of intense personal diaries: 'long descriptions of emotional states,' he remembers, 'mendacious accounts of how good I was feeling about being rejected by a woman, and always with a kind of extreme involvement in style, in the form.'[13] Drama had always been an interest, and he recalls listening to the radio from the late 40s, discovering Shakespeare, Chekhov and Ibsen and finding that 'they nourished me . . . that I liked the sense of voices in conflict, of argument, of narrative through argument'.[14] This awareness of classical drama had been developed in his education, but the crucial shift to writing plays himself was prompted less by tradition than by 'the tremendous stimulation I got from seeing rough reflections of lived experience on television'.[15]

Until the late 50s television drama was dominated by a mix of classics and recent commercial hits from the West End. In 1958 the

Canadian producer Sydney Newman was brought over by ABC to enliven their *Armchair Theatre* series. Drawing on his experience of live drama in North America and recognising the British theatrical excitement of the time, he began commissioning new writers – Alun Owen, Harold Pinter, Clive Exton – for original scripts about contemporary issues. Sensing that the country was experiencing radical social changes, he determined that his plays 'were going to be about the very people who owned TV sets – which is the working class'.[16]

In 1963 Newman crossed over to become Head of Drama at the BBC, where the following year he initiated the influential drama slot 'The Wednesday Play'. Under its regular producers James Mac-Taggart and Tony Garnett, this series developed Newman's tradition and, with the popular series *Z Cars*, introduced a further wave of new talent: John McGrath, Troy Kennedy Martin, Ken Loach, Dennis Potter, Jim Allen. Recognising in their work how drama could deal with the lived experience of his own class and background, Griffiths began to write television scripts. One dealt with life in the Army and another was about a homosexual; a third (like the others, unperformed and now lost) was *The Daft 'Un*, which explored Raymond Williams' theme of social mobility and was loosely based on Griffiths' relationship with his brother. These three scripts were written in Manchester and were completed before Griffiths and his wife Jan, a social worker whom he had married in 1961, moved to Leeds, where he took up a post with the BBC as a Further Education officer.

Griffiths' involvement with television now became intensive. An element in the Corporation's substantial expansion of broadcasting for the further education sector, his role was to evaluate and report on the educational effectiveness of television and radio trans-missions. He was assigned to cover the North of England, Scotland and Northern Ireland, so he inevitably travelled a great deal and spent a considerable amount of time watching BBC programmes with their target audiences: trade unionists, owners of small businesses, pensioners. In 1968 he was attached for six months to the production department in Manchester, where he worked on a series called *Something to Say*. An adult education class in a studio, the programme featured writers and critics discussing with a small audience extracts from literary texts. Griffiths was most pleased with the programme in which E. P. Thompson analysed William Blake's *London*, and he has spoken of how valuable the experience of a production process was.

Before that attachment he had sent an idea for a television series to a producer in Newcastle who suggested that he should submit it to

Tony Garnett. The outline was based on his contacts with trade unionists in industry while working on *Labour's Northern Voice* and explored the relationships between three sides of industry: the management, the union bureaucracy and the shop stewards. Garnett met Griffiths, and commissioned a script from him, but recommended that he should write from more direct personal experience. Consequently Griffiths began his real television writing apprenticeship with a play about education, *The Love Maniac*. (The outline for the programme about industry, called *The Big House*, was never developed as a television series, but Griffiths reworked it as a radio play in 1969, and it was produced in December of that year, directed by Alan Ayckbourn.)

The Love Maniac opens on the first day of term at a recently built comprehensive school. A new teacher, Jake Mortimer, is late for the staff meeting and the script cross-cuts the drab discussion there with his arrival on horseback: 'The horse is pure white Arabian, fantastically tripped out. The rider is dressed in a heavy Mexican poncho, silk denim trousers and calf-high highrise boots. His long blond hair streams behind him.' To the established teachers, Jake's opinions are as outlandish as his dress, since he immediately challenges the basis of streaming and of the prefect system.

As the term progresses, it transpires that Jake has been deliberately 'bequeathed' to the school by the departing Director of Education. He has a brilliant mind and is an excellent teacher, fully engaging the pupils' interest and stimulating them to take up many new activities. And when his wife Su ('a cool, slim, beautiful Indian') says offhandedly, 'Teaching's fine,' he exclaims, 'It's not fine. It's the greatest, the best, the worthiest thing a man can do.' 'What about loving a woman?' Su asks. 'Teaching *is* love,' Jake replies. 'Can't you see it. It's that simple.' Parents, however, are less responsive to his 'love' than are his kids.

Hostility from the PTA is eventually focused round the suspicion that Jake has seduced a girl pupil, but the misunderstanding is sorted out by the intervention of George Noble, Chairman of the Education Committee. When Jake and Noble first meet, the elder man grins at the teacher and says, 'You've got trouble written all over you.' 'I'm a teacher –' Jake says simply. 'No, not a teacher,' Noble decides. 'A saboteur. A revolutionary. An idealist.' 'Same thing,' Jake affirms. 'That's what a teacher is.'

They discuss the school and Jake contrasts Noble's radical past with his support for half-hearted comprehensive measures. 'It's all the old toffee served up in different wrappers,' Jake says of the school, 'class, privilege, segregation, deference, repression. It'll train human

17

beings to be fodder as effectively as any grammar or secondary modern school I know.' Noble recognises his own short-sightedness and begins to institute changes. As the next term opens, Jake, in a Mao tunic, addresses the school with 'Guantanamera' coming from speakers behind him. He commits the school to a different direction, and to a representative students council to decide on that direction.

Although this bald summary necessarily renders the text more schematic and simplistic than it is, the play does read today more as a naive fantasy than as a serious engagement with the politics of education. Clearly developed from the 'experiments' tried by Griffiths and Albert Smith at the private school in Oldham, the text has elements of an exercise in wish-fulfilment. Equally clearly the ease with which change is effected reflects the optimism of the moment of its writing – early 1968. None the less the anticipations of Griffiths' future work are obvious: the strong dialectical structure; the integration of public and personal politics, of education and sexuality; the explicit debate of a contemporary issue; and quotation from a wide range of cultural references (including the Beatles, Blake, Orwell and Woody Guthrie).

Commissioned by Tony Garnett for the BBC, *The Love Maniac* script was completed (in May 1968) after the producer had already left to set up Kestrel Productions for the newly formed London Weekend Television. Apparently Griffiths gave the BBC a 'substitute' instead – a copy of *The Daft 'Un*, which was promptly rejected by Garnett's successor – and took the original commission over to Kestrel. According to Griffiths, they were still searching for the resources to make it and a 90-minute slot, which the play would require, when the LWT-Kestrel relationship broke down in early 1970.

As with *The Big House*, Griffiths then reworked the idea as a shorter radio play, *Jake's Brigade*, which was transmitted in December 1971. The compression increased the schematism, especially as the drama was structured around the education committee considering Jake's suspension; and as one critic has written, 'This version is considerably inferior to the original.'[17]

STRANGERS AND BROTHERS: THEATRE DEBUTS

Griffiths' apprenticeship in television was to continue with his work on *Adam Smith*, but this was after he had had success in the theatre with *Occupations*, his first truly accomplished drama. Despite the fact that the script had not been produced, Garnett's enthusiasm for *The Love Maniac* gave Griffiths the confidence to continue writing and he embarked on a parallel theatrical apprenticeship with *Sam, Sam*

18

(scripted 1968–9 but not produced until 1972) and his one-act 'exercise play' *The Wages of Thin* (scripted and first performed in 1969).

Sam, Sam is a three-acter about the contrasting lifestyles of two brothers from a Northern working-class background. The one still lives in the family home; the other has been recruited into the professional classes. Transparently autobiographical, it was to be the first of many dramatic excursions through which Griffiths would attempt to explore his own experience of class translation. Like its title, *Sam, Sam* has a schizophrenic structure – the two brothers share the same name and their parts are written to be played by the same actor – the aim being, as Griffiths' stage directions put it, to describe 'the pyrrhic victory of environment over genes'. Sam One is a savagely comic creation who introduces us to a number of 'scenes' from his 'environment' in the manner of a stand-up comedian. They range from the petty to the tragic, from domestic disputes to the death of his father (like Griffiths' own, a chemical process worker). Together they form a portrait of a stifling, brutalised existence – 'authentic working-class drudgery' as Sam puts it in his typically ironic, embittered fashion. The ironic mode is the key to the play's cultural provenance, since what Griffiths seems to be saying via his character is that the working-class chic associated with the Angry Young Men of the 50s and accentuated by the 'egalitarian' pop culture of the 60s has made it almost impossible to represent working-class life except in a self-deflating way. The point is reinforced by an elaborate literary joke: a sequence of dialogue from D. H. Lawrence's *Sons and Lovers*, featuring an unpleasant, violent domestic squabble, is dramatically 'quoted', and Sam offers a gloss on it by citing an absurdly inappropriate passage from F. R. Leavis to the effect that 'Lawrence is more authentic than life itself'.

The contrast around which the whole piece is built is achieved through a short transitional act establishing Sam Two as a university-educated teacher and Labour Party activist. But both his assurance and his radicalism in this glimpsed scene – where he is seen practising a speech on education policy – evaporate in the third act when he emerges rather as a classic study in bad faith. Sam Two is, in fact, a deliberate parody of Osborne's Jimmy Porter, but in love with the very people and things he professes to despise: his middle-class wife, her family and their bourgeois values. Even when his mother – putting in a reappearance from the first act – is horribly shunned by his wife, he does not seem able to react. It's no surprise when the piece ends in a masochistic sex act, with Sam on the receiving end of his wife's class-inflected erotic abuse: 'You . . . dirty little nobody. Snot-

19

eating also-ran. You should have stayed with your own kind . . . down *there*. Where you belong.' Griffiths would develop this use of masochistic sexual preference as a metaphor of class betrayal in his television play about a Labour politician, *All Good Men*. Here it is merely an index of Sam's confusion and psychological stress – on a par, as it turns out, with that of his brother, despite the huge difference in their material conditions.

Like much of Griffiths' early theatrical work, *Sam, Sam* is marked by the Fringe fashionableness of performance-as-shock. But whatever the frisson generated by Charles Marowitz's Open Space Production in 1972, it now reads as somewhat naive and not a little unpleasant. Significantly perhaps, it has never had a major revival, suggesting that its concerns have become damagingly dated. Certainly, its principal interest now would seem to lie in the way it looks forward to Griffiths' later development as a dramatist. There is a real sense, for instance, of its form being determined under the pressure of a specific content – particularly the way the dominantly ironic version of working-class life produces a resort to play-within-a-play devices and the direct address of Sam in his guise as a stand-up comic. Both of which, of course, along with much else here, anticipate Griffiths' most mature work to date, *Comedians*. It is also worth noting that Griffiths is, somewhat paradoxically, often at his most non-naturalistic when writing about his own experience.

Griffiths has explained in some detail how he came to write the rather curious *The Wages of Thin*. Trying to characterise the difference between his own writing and that of his friend, the novelist Stan Barstow, Griffiths apparently said that he could not imagine Barstow writing anything which did not come from his own lived experience. Griffiths was confident that he could: 'And I said, for example, I bet I could write a play about three men in a public lavatory.' Which is indeed what *The Wages of Thin* is about. 'This came from fifteen years earlier when I was at university and we had meetings of would-be and quasi-poets. Robin Skelton would set a little exercise, a subject, and the next week we would all see what we'd come up with.'[18]

In this case Griffiths came up with a mysterious, threatening interrogation of a mild businessman. Two policemen accost him in an underground lavatory, accuse him of the murder of the body in one of the cubicles and then extract a simpering confession of his incest, homosexuality and association with known European sex criminals. At the end they let him go, and reveal themselves as intelligence agents setting up Mr Thin so that later he can perhaps be intimidated into becoming a spy. The text's most noticeable aspect is

20

Griffiths' evident relish for words, particularly insults, which are spun into crackling exchanges.

'The odd thing was,' Griffiths admits, 'that I found after it had been produced for three nights at the Stables I had to construct a meaning for the play. It had been so much of an exercise that I hadn't really worked out what it was about or for. In a sense it wasn't about or for anything except somebody trying to write . . . Then right through the 70s I wrote plays as if I was Stan Barstow; with the exception of *Occupations*, most of the things I wrote were carved from the life I'd been living.'[19]

Through Tony Garnett, Griffiths had met his agent, Clive Goodwin, who was also prepared to take on the eager writer. Goodwin suggested *The Wages of Thin* to the newly established Stables Theatre Club in Manchester, where it had three late-night performances in November 1969, and this led to the commission which was to produce *Occupations* almost a year later. Although it would be a further four years before Granada produced it for television, *Occupations* caused sufficient interest for Griffiths to be offered scripting work on the television series which would complete his apprenticeship. By early 1972 he was confident enough to leave the BBC and take up writing full-time.

WRITING FOR TELEVISION: 'ADAM SMITH'

Adam Smith, a drama series about a Church of Scotland minister, was the brainchild of Granada's Denis Forman, who seems to have conceived it as a sort of homage to his father, also a Church of Scotland minister. As a BBC employee, Griffiths was unable to write for an ITV company under his own name: for the purposes of *Adam Smith* he became 'Ben Rae'.* The pseudonymity of the project accurately reflected the essential anonymity of the kind of writing process in which Griffiths now found himself involved: writing to someone else's brief. All television drama tends to replace the writer with the collective author that is the production process. But series drama problematises the whole notion of the 'writer' at the *script* stage: authorship always resides elsewhere in the overall conception of the series, which predates the recruitment of individual writers to work on it. That Griffiths should from the outset have encountered television as a set of structural, institutional *constraints* rather than

---

* 'Ben Rae' is given the writing credit on 9 of the 12 episodes produced in the first series of *Adam Smith*; the three other segments being credited to Tom Gallacher.

21

simply as an 'expressive' medium has an obvious bearing on his subsequent development. It marks him in important ways, making him highly self-reflective about writing for television – the perfect subject, in fact, for a study of how the medium itself works and, moreover, how it works to *form* those who write for it.

Adam Smith cannot be understood outside the conditions that shaped it. Designed as a popular drama series with a contemporary setting and aimed at the same kind of audience that had turned the A. J. Cronin adaptation *Dr Finlay's Casebook* into a surprise ratings success in the 1960s, *Adam Smith* was given an additional scheduling function by being earmarked for transmission early on Sunday evenings in what is colloquially known within the industry as the 'God slot'. The intention was clearly to offer the ITV network a sort of secularised religion, a series that would sweeten the religious pill sufficiently to provide a scheduling block on which to build a primetime Sunday night audience. The series was, in fact, to offer the same kind of ethical framing of contemporary day-to-day living that *Dr Finlay* had provided in a period format. That the similarity was intentional is confirmed in a remark made by the series producer June Howson about the village where it was filmed. 'Gifford was our eventual choice,' she told *TV Times*. 'We decided to rename the village Lammerton, and we hope it will become as famous as Tannochbrae in *Dr Finlay's Casebook*.'

Not surprisingly, both in terms of structure and geographical setting the two series had a common literary origin: in the kailyard tradition of Scottish writing. 'Kailyard' literally means 'cabbage patch' and is used to denote the peculiarly shrunken, inward-turning quality of Scottish literary culture in the late-nineteenth and early-twentieth centuries: its typical product being the regional novel, the narrative of life in an isolated rural community morally and socially centred on the kirk and its minister. The Cronin stories on which *Dr Finlay* was based drew heavily on this tradition, while modernising it to the extent of replacing the kirk with the surgery and turning the two doctors into surrogate ministers by giving them strong pastoral roles within the Tannochbrae community. *Adam Smith* continued this bifurcation of kailyard by supplementing the minister, its central character (Andrew Keir), with a doctor figure, Calvi (played by a very young Tom Conti). Partly designed merely to extend the available storylines, this device also assumed a *dramatic* function by setting up a dialectical conflict at the very heart of the series between the competing claims of religion and science, as represented by the two men.

Adam Smith provided Griffiths with an unusually wide thematic scope. The setting – the semi-rural, semi-urban community of Lammerton, a small town within commuting distance of Edinburgh – enabled the scripts to explore a wide social mix, from middle-class professionals and businessmen at one end to trade unionists and council house tenants at the other. A further dimension of available social reference was created by making one of Adam Smith's two daughters a student at an English university, active in radical campus politics. Indeed, while the class composition of Lammerton, its peculiar stresses and 'Scottish' contradictions, frequently hint at an oblique commentary on Britain in general in the early 1970s, the only direct references to contemporary politics as such in the series tend to stem from her experience. Watching *Adam Smith* one could be unaware that Britain had a Tory government, but not that there was radical unrest in the universities. None of this is particularly surprising, of course, since Griffiths had no brief to take the series into directly political areas. And yet his scripts clearly do address issues at the very least not traditionally associated with popular series drama. They do so by using the series concept – and its literary and televisual antecedents – to operate a strategy of *displacement*. Thus the strong pastoral role passed on to the eponymous central character from both kailyard and *Dr Finlay* becomes greatly extended, turning him into a kind of social worker complete with 'casebook'. The welfare of the *whole* local community becomes the series' legitimate terrain of concern. A specifically religious discourse is noticeably absent, except as a means of distinguishing Adam's broadly humanist values from those of the other clergymen he comes into contact with. In one episode, for instance, he is seen to disagree profoundly with the other members of a church board over their administration of slum tenancies. Religion does enter into the key relationship with Calvi, the town's other focal figure, but again largely in terms of contrast: the doctor represents the rationalism of 'science' while Adam, in an opposition frequently encountered in the Victorian novel, represents the ethics of 'feeling'.

What, following on from this, we might call an affective discourse can be said to dominate *Adam Smith*, subsuming both politics and religion to a concern with the 'personal'. Adam's 'interventions' in the life of Lammerton are both prompted and bounded by the individual – often emotional – problems of his parishioners or their friends. Significantly, the locus is almost always sexuality, and specifically female sexuality. The two most important narrative strands in the first series involve respectively a young woman who has become psychosomatically asthmatic after an unhappy affair with the manager of a factory where she once worked; and the alcoholic wife of a local businessman who confides in Adam when her marriage breaks down. At one level, both strands (extending, incidentally, over many weeks) are attempts to dramatise a notion of the personal as political through a Reichian understanding of how capitalism's social relations deform its sexual relations. And, if one includes the transparently repressed sexuality of Calvi, the 'liberated' lifestyle and attitudes of Adam's student daughter and the fact that he himself is crucially defined by the *absence* of a woman (the opening segment makes it clear that the death of his wife and the subsequent break-up of the nuclear family are what propel him towards his new pastoral role), it becomes tempting to see *Adam Smith* as as much about a sexual economy as a social or political one. Yet the fact that the series also relies heavily on representations of 'neurotic' female sexuality – which mark out and define women almost exclusively in terms of a disturbed and disturbing sexuality – begs a number of important questions. It is not just that women are only allowed an identity through their sexuality, with all that that implies for other aspects of the way they are represented – notably a tendency towards *iconic* framing which fixes them voyeuristically for the camera. They also seem to exist principally *for* men and, moreover, for men as 'problems'. 'Problems' which, significantly, only men in the dual guise of priest and doctor can solve.

Women in *Adam Smith* seem to exist principally as 'problems' for men: Adam (Andrew Keir) comforts Elizabeth Crichton (Janet Munro).

This frankly phallocentric structure makes it difficult to read *Adam Smith* as a straightforwardly 'progressive' text. Griffiths' claim that he conceived of the series as being predominantly 'about social and political issues' also needs to be approached with some caution. It is true that *Adam Smith* contains political concerns not normally found in popular drama series. Yet its purchase on contemporary Britain remains necessarily oblique, a prey to both culturalism and peripheralism. Thus what gives the series its sense of time and place tends to be references to then fashionable *cultural* figures and events – the radical psychiatrist R. D. Laing, say, or the stage musical *Hair*, and more indirectly, quotations from the visionary poetry of William Blake and the utopian writings of the seventeenth-century revolutionary Gerald Winstanley – rather than to the politics of the Heath government, for instance, or internment in Northern Ireland. (One of the segments scripted by Tom Gallacher manages to explore the differences between Adam's Presbyterianism and the Catholicism of a visiting priest, while at the same time comprehensively suppressing any allusion to or resonance from the situation in the North.) The series' fractured political perspective is well illustrated by the narrative strand involving Adam's bedside visits to the dying ex-miner, Jack Ross. Like the huge mining lodge banner draped across the whole of the one wall that forms the backdrop to their meetings, the former pit activist is an iconographical rather than a political presence: there is no attempt to connect him with developing militancy in the coalfield in the run-up to the 1972 miners' strike. Even allowing for the constraints of the series format and the possibility that Griffiths may well have been deliberately low-key here – promoting identification with a 'sympathetic' militant at a time of legislative and ideological assault on the trade union movement – *Adam Smith* still comes across as politically *decentred*. It is no accident that the second series left Britain altogether, with Adam taking up a missionary post in South Africa. Yet this decentring process would itself have to be seen as reflecting a certain immobilism in Left politics in Britain at the time: already on the slide into culturalism and academicism after the heady days of 1968.

A FIRST ENCOUNTER WITH CENSORSHIP

Trevor Griffiths' experience working on *Adam Smith* was troubled and he has spoken with some bitterness about it on several occasions.[20] In particular, he has pointed out the direct censorship of episode twelve, an incident which caused him to leave the second series. This blunt constraint was clearly significant and was to be only the first of a

25

number of such incidents in Griffiths' engagement with television. But it is important to recognise that the creation, and alteration, of meaning in television is far more complex than such limiting incidents might suggest. As Griffiths learnt, and as *Adam Smith* now usefully illustrates, meaning is produced by television as an institution, as a collection of contributing individuals and as a set of practices and relationships. The writer is one element within that, but his or her meanings will be overlain with many others in the creation of a final text. As Griffiths has said, 'I had no automatic right of entry into the production process and I found that so many ideological insertions were being made from producers, directors, actors that in a way I felt like somebody making wallpaper.'[21]

An example of this can be recovered by a comparison of a script from the first series with the final visual text. In episode two Griffiths wrote a scene in which Adam's student daughter Annie goes to visit Dr Calvi. She has come with the excuse of returning his prescription book but actually to satisfy her curiosity about him and to flirt. In the rehearsal script, Griffiths' stage directions for the scene read in part: 'The room is handsomely furnished (leather chesterfield and chairs, good carpets, heavy oak desk, etc). A hi-fi set plays the Bartok 6th string quartet very quietly. Despite everything, the room is a very obvious tip.' In the margin on the MS in the British Film Institute collection is the scribbled note 'Beethoven 5th' and in the later rehearsal script this alteration has been typed in. On screen the most obvious feature of the room is some reproductions of modern paintings (not mentioned by Griffiths), including a Modigliani; the room is appropriately 'masculine' but also immaculately tidy, and Beethoven's 5th Symphony is coming from the record player. A little later in the scene the camera script indicates that Annie changes the record to Miles Davis' 'Someday My Prince Will Come'. In the episode itself she puts on 'The Age of Aquarius' from *Hair*. In the rehearsal script the scene begins with Annie and Calvi sitting across a table, with the doctor studying a book and a chessboard in silence. 'At length Calvi turns to the book then back to the board, moves a rook to the seventh rank, and sighs an amazed and wondering sigh.' 'Do I take it,' Annie asks, 'you have . . . reached your climax?' The scene in the later camera script and as recorded starts with Annie's arrival; chess is referred to subsequently but the 'climax' line was cut.

Each of these changes inflects in a small but significant way the meanings and resonances of the scene. As in other scripts, Griffiths was using cultural references with quite specific purposes, and the substitutions undermined them. The structure and dialogue changes could be said to strengthen the conversation dramatically, but they certainly drain a significant element of sexual tension from it. The point is not that Griffiths' intentions were just inadequately rendered or that others in the production process deliberately subverted them; rather it is that similar changes are inevitable in any realisation and that the producer (who probably substituted the records) and the designer (who added the pictures and 'tidied up' the room) and many others contributed, as their counterparts will always contribute, meanings to the final text. What Griffiths learnt was that the writer must endeavour to increase his or her power, which may be based on contract or stature or personality, to limit the inflections and to make them productive. But as a new writer on a low-prestige weekly series, his control on *Adam Smith* was minimal.

Repression and 'liberation' in the sexual economy of *Adam Smith*: Dr Calvi (Tom Conti) with Annie Smith (Brigit Forsyth).

This lack of control was most starkly evidenced in a cut made in the last episode of the first series. Adam is considering a move to a new parish and is 'auditioned' at a church in an affluent area of Edinburgh. Reacting against the congregation's complacency, he preaches a powerful, political sermon about the exploitation of the many by the few and the importance of retaining Christianity's relevance to social questions. The speech seems completely out of character, a grand 'Sermon on the Mount' and a spectacular example of a kind of 'religious entryism'. Unsurprisingly, Adam does not become the new vicar and the series ends with him being offered a temporary post in South Africa. Griffiths had researched and written these later programmes when episode twelve went out on Easter Sunday 1972. Then he discovered that Granada had taken out a brief section from the sermon. In part this had read: 'Six days of the week we pillage and plunder, extort, manipulate, *use*. And on the seventh, we worship. And the Church – the whole Church – condones . . . no, connives at it.' The writer was greatly angered by the cut and parted company with the series, having already contributed six further scripts and the basis of two others. Two of these were transmitted with his pseudonym on them, four others – those set in South Africa – eventually carried a credit to John Hardiman and Susi Hush (who had previously been listed as researcher and then script associate) and the final two were billed without a writer.

The first pair of these second series episodes wrap up a number of storylines from the previous series, including Calvi's reconciliation with his until-now absent wife. They also bring home to Adam an awareness of racism in Britain. In episode fifteen (the script of which, in common with those for episodes sixteen–eighteen, carries the name Ben Rae) Adam arrives in Johannesburg to take up a temporary ministership at a white church, with an unofficial black 'garage church' attached. The political and social situation is more complex than he had thought, and he encounters two responses to apartheid: a white, voluntary organisation offering free legal advice to Africans, and a radical, Abbas, who argues for the necessity of fundamental change – 'a miracle. Or a revolution'. Adam is placed in the position of witness, not activist; it is a marginal role which Abbas underlines in his question: 'How can you feel that a few liberal European churchmen can change anything?' Abbas acts as guide to the appalling conditions of Soweto, which are contrasted later in the episode with the comfort and ease of the white community in Adam's parish. There Adam discovers that his African congregation has been 'removed', and in his search for them he encounters Abbas a second time. Together they find a women's camp of extreme poverty; the men

28

have been taken away for contract labour. Adam tries vainly to interest the white authorities, but succeeds only in being sent back to Edinburgh. On his final night in Johannesburg he reflects on his failure to make any impact on this 'huge, monolithic giant of a society – the great oppression'. He is consoled only by the thought that he has learnt from his experience and may now be qualified to make a protest.

So Adam returns to Scotland, to a poor, inner-city parish; and the series continued without Trevor Griffiths who, in his own way, was impotent in the face of a monolith. *Adam Smith* continued for a total of thirty-nine episodes and drew variously on writers who included C. P. Taylor, James MacTaggart, Barrie Keeffe and Peter McDougall. Griffiths too moved on, since he had already written two major scripts which used history to engage with contemporary politics in a far more direct manner than had been possible on *Adam Smith*. One of these, *Occupations*, had been a considerable success in the theatre, and both it and the other script, *Such Impossibilities* (commissioned by the BBC), were soon to be not just inflected with different meanings by the production process of television but, in different ways, to be all but destroyed by the medium.

3 'Lessons to be learnt': *Occupations* and other dramas of revolution

Soon after winning his best actor Oscar for *Gandhi*, Ben Kingsley gave an interview in which, somewhat bizarrely, he cited *Occupations* as a major influence on his performance in Richard Attenborough's film: 'I believe that I started to prepare for *Gandhi* when I did Gramsci in Trevor Griffiths' *Occupations* ten years previously.'[1] He never made it entirely clear in what this preparation consisted, but significantly he went on to describe Gramsci as 'the Italian communist *non-violent revolutionary*.'[2] This (mis)reading of the play – which recruits Gramsci as a pacifist on the basis, presumably, of his refusal to countenance an insurrectionary course in 1920 – highlights in how maverick a way dramatic meaning often circulates: a problem Griffiths would encounter again and again in his involvement with television. Not least in the case of *Occupations* itself, which fared spectacularly badly in the translation from stage to small screen – especially disappointing after the original Manchester and London productions had been so successfully supplemented by a 7:84 touring version that brought the play to audiences up and down the country in 1973.

Occupations is set in a hotel room in Turin during the 1920 metal-workers strike. Kabak, a Bulgarian member of the Communist International (based on a real Comintern agent of the period called Kabakchiev), has recently arrived, apparently with a brief to discover whether the widespread occupation of factories throughout Italy constitutes a revolutionary moment. To this end he arranges a number of meetings with Gramsci, the theoretician of the factory council movement and who, as a leading member of the leftist wing of the Italian Socialist Party (PSI), was also heavily involved in the day-to-day running of the occupation of the nearby Fiat Centro, Italy's biggest industrial complex. Their political exchanges, which give the play its celebrated dialectical structure, oppose two different kinds of revolutionary ideology: Kabak's Leninist rigour, with its cool and distant appraisal of the masses merely as a 'machine' for making revolution, versus Gramsci's libertarian project, with its emphasis on 'love' and concern with the 'masses as people . . . in their particular, detailed local individual character'. This fatally schizophrenic split in revolutionary consciousness – neither position is in itself adequate – recurs throughout Griffiths' work and is given ironic inflection here by being acted out before Kabak's mistress, an ex-Romanov aristocrat now bedridden and dying of cancer like the old order she represents. In many ways, *Occupations* is about the consequences of this split. It ends with Gramsci admitting defeat on behalf of the assembled Fiat workers, belatedly quoting Trotsky to the effect that revolution is like war: 'We shall not enter into the kingdom of socialism with white gloves on a polished floor.' Kabak, meanwhile, responds to the same defeat, in unashamedly Stalinist fashion, organising a meeting with a Fiat director to arrange a plan for cars to be made under licence in the Soviet Union.[3]

CONTEMPORARY PARALLELS

Nearly four years separate the original stage production of *Occupations* from the television version directed by Michael Lindsay-Hogg for Granada in 1974. Four years of Tory government which effectively sealed off any lingering vestiges of the historical and political conjuncture of which the play was so obviously the product: 1968. This gap between text and context is characteristic of television 'adaptation' in general, and *Occupations* focuses all the attendant problems – around meaning and history – associated with it. But there is a more important reason for seeking to situate *Occupations* in this wider conjuncture: Griffiths' text, written in 1969, is quite simply and at almost every level a response to that particular historical moment. Europe and North America had recently been convulsed by a revolutionary protest movement. Universities and factories had been occupied; street demonstrations on a scale unprecedented in the post-war period had regularly ended in violent confrontations with the forces of order; and in one country, France, the state itself had been momentarily threatened. In choosing to foreground an earlier revolutionary moment – the occupation of the factories in Italy in September 1920, arguably the last time socialist revolution had seriously been on the agenda in Europe – Griffiths was clearly offering certain parallels with the contemporary situation.

The very title *Occupations* carried a heavy freight of associations,[4] industrial as well as political: the RSC's London production of the play

31

opened just three months after a work-in at Upper Clyde Ship-builders had developed into the full-scale occupation that was to last some sixteen months and inspire similar initiatives at Meriden and elsewhere. In general, a new militancy and self-confidence character-ised the whole trade union movement during this period. The traditional repertoire of industrial action was being supplemented by the development of new tactics: sit-ins, work-ins, mass picketing and the use of the so-called 'flying' picket. Prompted by the 'modernising' policies of successive Labour and Tory governments – exemplified by the attempt of both the Labour policy document 'In Place of Strife' and the Heath Industrial Relations Act to find a way out of economic crisis by disciplining the trade unions – this new militancy has been described by one commentator as 'unparalleled since the 1920s'.[5] And it is perhaps worth noting here that 'mass action' was also beginning to assume a prominence on the agenda of 1970s' British Communist Party Congresses not seen since the 1920s.

GRAMSCI AND MAY '68

It was against this background, particularly in the immediate aftermath of May '68, that the 'rediscovery' of the revolutionary thinking of Gramsci – which *Occupations* also, and perhaps predomin-antly, reflects – took place. *The Little Prince* had appeared in English as early as 1957, but Gramsci remained just another obscure continental Marxist until the May events focused the need for an understanding of the new kind of political perspective which was opening up. Typically, the task of unearthing Gramsci's theoretical writings from 1920 fell to *New Left Review*, whose whole project by this date had largely become precisely the importation of key texts from the European Marxist tradition Britain never had. In September 1968 *NLR* published a selection of Gramsci's political articles culled from the Socialist Party journal *L'Ordine Nuovo*, of which he was editor during the period of the formation of the factory councils and the September occupations themselves. *NLR* described them as 'the only sustained theoretical contribution in the West on the political problems posed by factory occupations and councils – the central drama of the French events. These texts of Gramsci represent a crucial moment in the development of revolutionary thought: their relevance has never been greater than today.'[6]

Published as *Soviets in Italy* with an introduction by Perry Anderson, the nine *NLR* articles were both the main inspiration and source material for *Occupations*. Nor was this just a case of overall orientation: many of the long political speeches which give the play its peculiar character are closely modelled on the English translations of the *L'Ordine Nuovo* pieces. Compare these two passages, for instance. The first from one of the *NLR* texts, written the day the occupations finally ended; the second from *Occupations*, in which Griffiths' Gramsci tries to salvage something from defeat after the referendum vote for a return to work:

> . . .the working class can register a great step forward. As a mass guided and disciplined in the factory by its direct representatives, it has proved itself capable of industrial and political self-government. This fact, which should be elementary for revolutionary Communists, has consequences of incalculable social importance. The middle classes of the population have compared the strength of the proletariat with the inadequacy of the entrepreneurial class. Half a century ago, the proletariat was still, as Marx put it, a *sack of potatoes*, a generic imponderable, an amorphous conglomeration of individuals without ideas, without will, and without a unitary perspective. Today it is the entrepreneurial class that has become a *sack of potatoes*, an aggregate of the inept and the imbecile, without political capacity, without internal power. The revolutionary events of the past few days have illuminated this position.
>
> This new political situation has definitely put forward the proletariat as a ruling class; it is a spring that drives it irresistibly towards the conquest of power.[7]

> It might be that the working class can chalk up a great leap forward. Certainly as a mass, shaped and disciplined in the factories by its *direct* representatives, it has shown itself vibrantly capable of running its own affairs. And that, *as a fact*, may have consequences of incalculable social importance. Only half a century ago – a single tock of time in the long history of class struggle – that same class was still, in Marx's phrase, a sack of potatoes, a . . . generic unknown, a . . . shapeless gathering of individuals, without ideas, without will, above all without perspective. It was, if you like, comrades, a blind boil on the arse of capitalism: annoying, but hardly fatal. (*Pause*) Today, it appears to be the entrepreneurial class that has become a sack of potatoes, an aggregation of the useless and the idiot, powerless, nerveless, will-less. (*Pause*) If we find this; if we find that *this* action, these occupations, have advanced the proletariat as a ruling class; if we find, too, that this new political situation is a spring driving irresistibly towards the conquest of power . . .[8]

What is interesting here is not just that Griffiths *dramatises* Gramsci – by turning his phrasing into a speaking register and dressing it up with English colloquialisms – but that he changes Gramsci's sense. The introduction of a phrase like 'it *might be that*' to describe the possibility of revolutionary change is symptomatic of a thread of political pessimism running throughout *Occupations* and marking it off sharply from both the *NLR* texts and Anderson's accompanying commentary on them. Whereas Gramsci in defeat was, to borrow one of his own famous formulations, all optimism of the will, and Anderson rather naively full of what Turin's 'Red Days' could contribute to a revolutionary way forward in 1968, Griffiths is attempting first and foremost to account for a *failure*, for what went wrong in 1920 and why the process seemed to repeat itself in 1968.

TURIN'S 'RED YEARS': 1919–20

The occupation of the factories in September 1920 was the culmination of two years of intense political activity on the Left in Italy. The *biennio rosso* or 'red years' saw the tentative development in the spring of 1920 of a system of factory councils or 'soviets' – inspired by the *L'Ordine Nuovo* grouping within the PSI associated with Gramsci – followed by a four-month wage dispute in the metallurgical sector. The factory councils, which bypassed traditional trade union structures and their corporatist tendencies, helped to turn what had initially been an 'economic' dispute into a political one by channelling growing militancy at shop-floor level. A go-slow throughout the summer escalated when Confindustria, the employers' association, panicked and attempted to instigate a lock-out at the end of August. Between 1 and 4 September, Italy's 400,000 engineering workers occupied their workplaces in factories, dockyards and steelworks. In the great industrial triangle of Turin, Milan and Genoa, they were joined by other groups of workers in what amounted to a general strike. This was how *Il Corriere della Sera* described the scene outside one factory:

> . . . the factories yesterday evening presented a singular spectacle. One reached them through crowds of women and children, coming and going with dinners for the strikers, voluntary prisoners of the factories. Nearer to them, here and there, on the pavement or on the grass, were the debris of the day's bivouac. Entrances were strictly guarded by groups of workers. Not the ghost of an official or police officer in sight. The strikers were complete masters of the field. Whoever passed, in car or cab, was subjected to control as if

he were crossing the frontier, control exercised by vigilance squads of workers and their enthusiastic companions.[9]

Italy was at a standstill for nearly a month and for a while, with the state seemingly teetering on the edge, the revolutionary card seemed possible. With hindsight, however, it is clear that too many factors were militating against its being played.[10] The striking workers' strength was also their weakness: by occupying the factories, where they maintained production, they isolated themselves. As a result, there was very little coordination between plants or effective contact from city to city, region to region. The support of the peasantry, so crucial in a predominantly rural society like Italy, was never secured. However, the overriding factor was the divided leadership of the PSI, historically split between reformists and communists and which now offered a confused lead to its militants, eventually allowing the employers and the Giolitti government to impose an economic solution to the crisis by appealing directly to the workers through a referendum. The historian Gwyn A. Williams has described their leadership failure as an act of 'historic renunciation', 'a species of "revolutionary reformism"', which later experiences in France and elsewhere have made familiar.'[11] In Italy in the 1920s the pay-off was unequivocal: fascism.

'A REVOLUTIONARY DUTY TO TELL THE TRUTH'

Hardly surprising, then, that much of *Occupations* should pivot around the question of organisation: the need to reconcile the socialist vision of a more humane world with the ruthless discipline required to achieve it; the importance of not underestimating the sheer resilience of capitalism and its ability to adapt and survive; and, looming behind it all, the need to guard against Stalinism, the spectre of which, it is suggested, haunts all revolutionary failures:

> When you have a failure like May '68 there's often only one image of revolution left . . . From the ashes of every failure or disaster there is the image of a Kabak or a Stalin saying we *will* succeed. Psychologically, the authoritarian and the libertarian live very close in my Left sensibility and in most Left sensibilities that I've encountered, and that is also an important dimension in *Occupations*.[12]

Writing in reply to an attack on the play's political 'pessimism' by Tom Nairn (a member of the *NLR* editorial board) in the now defunct magazine *7 Days*,[13] Griffiths described writing *Occupations* 'as a sort of Jacobinical response to the failure of the '68 revolution in France. *What it asserts* is that courage and optimism do not, of themselves, ensure the success of revolutions, unless they are harnessed, disciplined, tightly organised; in a word, *led*. And what it *asks* – because it's a play that, characteristically, asks rather than asserts – is whether the courage and optimism aren't in some way necessarily damaged, distorted, in that disciplining process.'[14] Griffiths was obviously surprised that Nairn should have queried his right to pose such questions and quotes Gramsci back at him on it being 'a revolutionary duty to tell the truth'. It is worth pausing for a moment here to consider Griffiths' defence of his play. He began by distinguishing between 'art-works' and what he called 'documentary accumulations . . . evaluable largely in terms of a "known" historical and political reality', citing Lukács in support on *typicality*: 'assimilating into each individual type the most characteristic and central features of a social crisis'. This, Griffiths claimed, made a nonsense of Nairn's 'it's-either-historically-"accurate"-or-it's-purely-and-only-"symbolic"' argument, which he described as 'crude'. Interestingly, Griffiths still chose to meet the charge that the play was inaccurate, claiming the right to 'conflate' material for dramatic purposes, while admitting that in the case of Kabak and his *bon viveur* aura he had probably gone over the top, inviting a cynical reading of the role of the Comintern that ran counter to his overall intentions in the play. But he rejected entirely the claim that the characterisation of Gramsci himself was ahistorical.

Nairn had found Griffiths' Gramsci too romantic and sentimental a figure, when 'all accounts agree . . . Gramsci was a hard, even a harsh figure in most public situations'. Moreover, this 'sinewy intolerance' was according to Nairn 'inseparable from Gramsci's particular form of greatness'. This staggeringly spartan assessment was vigorously contested by Griffiths: 'It's this myth that's damagingly romantic, sustaining, as it does, the notion that rebarbative personality is a necessary . . . prerequisite of serious revolutionary activity.' This in essence, of course, was the message of the play, and drawing on his own research in Turin prior to writing it – when, among others, he interviewed Umberto Terracini, who worked with Gramsci in the 1920s before later going on to become leader of the Italian Communist Party himself – Griffiths spelt it out. In personality Gramsci was 'certainly "hard" . . . but rarely ever *only* that'. Politically, he had maintained a long dialogue with the anarchists, conducted a policy of 'openness' towards non-communists and even appointed a liberal, Gobetti, as *L'Ordine Nuovo*'s theatre critic.

Finally, and in terms of his own future development crucially, Griffiths cited Gramsci's

> preoccupation with the relationship between public and private forms of experience, there is no doubt that 'love' was a basic reference for much of his social thought. He it is (not me) who asserts: 'One cannot divide oneself into fragments and make only one part function; life is a whole, and each activity is strengthened by all the others; love strengthens the whole of one's existence . . . it creates a new equilibrium, a greater intensity of all other feelings and sentiments.' Mucking about with love and Revolution?[15]

Griffiths might almost have been writing about himself. Certainly these are concerns which run like an arrow through all his work right up to *Reds*, where we find him precisely mucking about with love and Revolution.

In addition to its contemporary resonances, *Occupations* can also be seen to graft a number of longer-standing, specifically British concerns on to its historical subject. The debates between Gramsci and Kabak, and Gramsci and the moderate leadership of the PSI, for instance, though they take place in a revolutionary framework, clearly echo traditional conflicts within the Labour Party around notions of pragmatism, gradualism and reformism, particularly as accentuated by Harold Wilson's two administrations of the 1960s. The problems of Labourism were, significantly, to become Griffiths' major thematic in the mid-1970s, producing not just the premonitory TV series about a Labour MP, *Bill Brand*, but also the 1974 TV single play, *All Good Men*, a sort of contemporary reworking of Howard Spring's novel *Fame is the Spur*, in which a Labour peer is forced to confront the shabby compromises that have cut him off from his working-class roots. A similar continuity of concerns can be observed in the much later *Country* (1981), where capitalism's ability to adapt and renew itself – represented in *Occupations* by the Fiat management's vision of company welfarism – is developed in the specifically British context of the post-war reconstruction and, notwithstanding 1945, its hijacking by and in the interests of capital. At a more general level, *Occupations* might also be said to reflect some of the incipient difficulties facing the non Labour left in Britain, notably its chronic factionalism and inability to unite around a common strategy, let alone programme. The television version of the text would suppress all these resonances in an interpretation which reduced the play to little more than a historical chamber piece.

Occupations was originally written for the Stables theatre club in Manchester, a small venue which had been set up by Granada Television. Granada had undertaken to fund a company to mount a new production each month, to be done first for the stage but with a good chance of a transfer to television. Part of the brief of the Stables was the encouragement of new writers and, in line with this, Griffiths' *The Wages of Thin* was given three late-night performances there in November 1969. Granada's backing for the theatre, however, lasted only two years and had ended just a month before the premiere of *Occupations* on 28 October 1970. None the less it was Granada which subsequently mounted the television version, almost four years after that first opening.

In those four years the play had been staged with considerable success by Buzz Goodbody at the Royal Shakespeare Company's smaller London theatre, The Place, where Ben Kingsley played Gramsci to Patrick Stewart's Kabak, and had subsequently gone on tour in a 7:84 company production. Later it was to receive major productions throughout Europe, and for several of these Griffiths sat in on rehearsals and reworked elements of the text.

'All my theatre plays, in so far as they're produced at all, become sites for new work and new thought,' he explained in 1983. The three early British productions of *Occupations* had shown him how valuable this could be. 'In eighteen months I'd had three opportunities to see the play acted, and to see it with different sorts of audiences. There were areas that were impenetrable, that were over-wordy, and I think that's still the case. It has a sort of very creaky form, parts of the debates are people in chairs – but in some ways that was its fresh-ness . . . But stitched into that, almost seamlessly and almost irremovably, were also very old and very arid forms of presenting material in theatre . . . the brandy and cigars and matches and portfolios, all the naturalistic business. The literalism of naturalism is very painful when you have to sit through it.

'One production in Holland was particularly important as it turned out. Sater (a Dutch socialist theatre collective) did a fantastic production in 1980 in the course of which they raised many interesting questions about the form of the play. That moment enabled me to come out with a new printed edition, to bring these revisions together.'[16]

The 1980 text is more concise, particularly in the closing moments, with the Countess' previously lengthy dying speech pared back to essentials. Such concision tightens the play, whereas the considerable

38

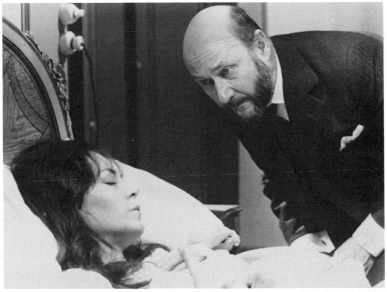

The death of the old order in *Occupations*: the Countess (Natasha Parry) attended by Kabak (Donald Pleasence).

cuts imposed by the slot-length of the 1974 television production went a long way to emasculating it. Productions of the play in the theatre invariably run over two hours, but the Granada version clipped this time to just 78 minutes. Although stage drama can be played faster on screen, this still meant substantial deletions had to be made. One scene between Kabak and the hotel manager Libertini was omitted and the two central factory speeches were heavily cut. The dramatic action in the hotel room was recorded in a studio with four videotape cameras, but the speeches were filmed in black and white in a disused warehouse. An unvarying medium shot of Jack Shepherd as Gramsci (imposed by the budget and time constraints – both speeches were shot in a single afternoon) eliminates any sense of the huge meetings he is addressing, apart from reactions on the soundtrack and glimpses behind his head of one or two workers – one dressed in a very English Northern working-man's cap and another looking like a mafioso. The cuts are made by freeze-framing the picture, carrying over and editing the sound, and then picking up the image again. The effect is odd, distancing the speeches but not in a productive or meaningful way. The delivery of these crucial speeches also indicates how television as a medium diminishes *Occupations*. In the theatre, slides, a lectern and the singing of 'Bandiera Rossa' transform the auditorium into the site of the meetings; Gramsci speaks to the audience *as the workers*. On the small screen this dramatic effect cannot even be approximated.

This transformation is one element in the play's exploitation of the techniques of 'epic' theatre, as developed by Erwin Piscator and later used extensively by Brecht. In Berlin in the mid-20s, Piscator staged plays and revues which integrated films and projected pictures, as well as direct addresses to the audience, within conventional dramatic action. Titles and explanatory texts were also used to break with the dominant conventions of naturalism. Brecht worked with Piscator at this time and continued to use such techniques in his own works. As John Willett writes, 'Piscator's aim was to make the theatre into a mixture of lecture hall and debating chamber, where the audience would see a socially relevant play supported by a wealth of documentary material and so be inspired to argue the issues out. Though more than one of his productions ended with the singing of the Internationale by the cast (and sometimes by the audience too) he claimed not to be aiming at a simple revolutionary impact . . .'[17]

Occupations actually begins with the 'Internationale', and both it and *The Party* make extensive use of these devices, to situate the specifics of the drama within historical, political and cultural contexts (*Occupations'* stage directions feature a wide range of iconography, including a painting by Lissitsky). Brecht could well have been writing of either play when he paid tribute to Piscator's experiments:

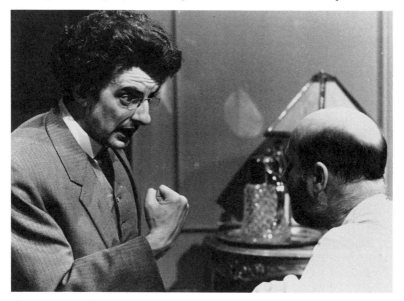

'A revolutionary duty to tell the truth': Gramsci (Jack Shepherd) engages with Kabak (Donald Pleasence).

'They turned the auditorium into a meeting hall. For Piscator theatre was a Parliament, the audience a legislative body. Before the body were visibly set the great public questions that demanded decisions . . . The stage set itself the task of prodding the audience – the parliament – into making political decisions.'[18] This 'epic' dimension is completely eliminated in Granada's production, so that even the play's final recognition of how the events depicted have opened the door to Fascism – slides of Mussolini and Hitler – is omitted. And indeed more than one of the generally enthusiastic newspaper reviews picked up this point, but ascribed the fault to the play and not the production.

The Granada adaptation (which was produced by Jonathan Powell and directed by Michael Lindsay-Hogg) subtly inflects the meanings of the play in other ways. As always, design was a critical element. Griffiths is quite specific in the stage directions: 'Hotel Fiorina: good, solid, tasteful, bourgeois. The set represents these values without fully realising them through committedly naturalistic design.' Television, however, is nothing if not 'committedly naturalistic' and *Occupations* reflects this. The single room is also transformed into a lavish suite and the Countess – who should lie in bed stage-centre – is banished to an adjoining room. Kabak is thus presented from the start as a lover of comfort and luxury and his revolutionary sentiments are undercut. Equally the power of the Countess as a symbol of the dying order is much reduced. The strangest aspect of the production is that Jack Shepherd plays Gramsci on his knees. Gramsci, according to the text, is 'of dwarf-like stature . . . seriously hunchbacked' though 'in spite of his deformity, he moves with grace', and Griffiths recalls that this way of playing him was decided upon only two days before recording. The result looks absurd. Despite this, Shepherd gives an impressive performance, matching Donald Pleasence's forceful Kabak. In contrast, several of the minor characters are stiffly, unconvincingly played.

As already indicated, the reviews were unanimously positive, whereas critics of the previous stage productions had been divided. Even so, the enthusiasm with which the Stables' original presentation had been greeted suggested the arrival of a major new playwright and brought Griffiths to the attention of metropolitan producers. He was approached for an idea for a projected BBC drama series on 'The Edwardians' and, in July 1971, suggested a play about the working-class leader Tom Mann. Also intrigued by the press notices, Kenneth Tynan, Literary Adviser at the National Theatre, asked to see a script of *Occupations* and some months later he too commissioned a new work. At the time Griffiths was planning another drama set in the historical period of *Occupations*, which would deal more directly with the Revolution in Russia and be centred on Kronstadt. That remained unwritten and, after two years, the National mounted its controversial production of *The Party*.

FRINGE INTERLUDE: 'LAY BY', 'APRICOTS' AND 'THERMIDOR'

Griffiths' positive response to television and to a large, subsidised theatre company illustrates his concern to work within the dominant cultural structures. During 1971, he continued his engagement with fringe theatre by contributing to the collectively written text *Lay By* and by writing *Apricots* and *Thermidor*. All three works were performed that year on the Edinburgh Festival Fringe (after *Apricots* had been premiered in London in June), but Griffiths was quickly to move on to initiate his practice of cultural interventionism. As he would later put it, 'I'm not interested in talking to 38 university graduates in a cellar in Soho.'[19]

Lay By's curious history apparently began at a writers' meeting at the Royal Court in 1971. Among the many topics discussed was the possibility of group writing, which David Hare raised. Griffiths had arrived after the meeting's start and a year later remembered that 'the dominant mood was that this was the worst weekend any of them had ever spent – the pubs aren't open, let's for Christ's sake do something! And we filed off rather doggedly into the closed bar, on a cold Sunday afternoon, and talked.' Collaboration was mooted again. 'I'd got the *Sunday Times* out,' Griffiths recalled, 'and on the back page Ludovic Kennedy had been doing a piece on this extraordinary case. And I said, Does that switch anybody on? And – erections were palpable!' From then on we were into it.'[20] Hare and Griffiths were joined by Brian Clark, Stephen Poliakoff, Hugh Stoddart, Snoo Wilson and Howard Brenton. As Brenton remembered it, 'We had great rolls of wallpaper, and big children's crayons and the seven of us crawled around on the floor scribbling a continuous text, and you looked down and saw the latest line, and there'd be an argument about the next line.'[21] The article was about a possible wrongful conviction for rape and the final text built a collage of scenes around the reported incident. The Royal Court itself rejected the play, but the Portable Theatre Company mounted a production in Edinburgh, in conjunction with the Traverse Theatre. Later it came back to the Court for Sunday night performances and had a short season at the Open Space.

The Portable Theatre Company had been set up three years earlier by Brenton, Hare, Snoo Wilson (who directed *Lay By*) and others as a touring group committed, in Brenton's words, to 'anarchic, antagonistic theatre'. 'Political' awareness came gradually. 'If you set up an antagonistic theatre,' Brenton later explained, 'touring to people who have never seen the theatre before, it transforms itself into political theatre.'[22] Portable Theatre was passionately dedicated to the idea of fringe, oppositional work. At the end of the 60s the fringe was seen by many as the central site for committed drama which sought to break with the established forms and concerns of current theatre and, importantly, with its traditional audiences. Drama had to speak directly to working-class audiences. Hence Portable's concern to tour, even if many of the working-class audiences it encountered were no more than ambivalent about the shows on offer. It was precisely this conception of drama which Griffiths was to reject in his move to and continued involvement in television. The audiences were too small and too narrow, and they were not being appropriately addressed, Griffiths felt. 'One of the reasons I wrote such a short time for the fringe is because I realised how impotent it was as a mouthpiece to the whole of society,'[23] he has said.

Lay By created something of a stir, and prompted much passionate criticism for and against. Yet in Edinburgh and in London it could hardly be said to have addressed a broad swathe of society. Read today the text betrays the prurience and incipient voyeurism in Griffiths' remark 'erections were palpable'. A succession of scenes feature the three people involved in the alleged rape – the man and his mistress, both around forty, and a young girl to whom they give a lift on the motorway. The scenes cut across each other and include a pornographer's lengthy photo session (during which 'hardcore photos of gang-bangs, sodomy, fellatio etc.' are handed out to the audience) and a reconstruction of the incident. The final sequence has two orderlies in a mortuary washing the corpses of the three protagonists in blood.

An intention to shock is apparent throughout, together with a certain concern that the man was wrongfully imprisoned, since the girl consented. Dramatic treatment of the associated issues is superficial, and analysis of the complex sexual politics is minimal. Brenton justified the piece in a subsequent interview: 'In a way it could be read as a manifesto of that group, for that kind of theatre, when the two hospital attendants are washing the corpses of the three main characters, and pulping their bodies in a huge dustbin into jam, we tried to put every phoney humanist statement that you could hear in the theatre from our elder playwrights into that. It was a total piss-take – the end.'[24]

Portable went on to a further collective show, *England's Ireland,* in

43

which Griffiths was not involved. He has, however, worked on two other collaborative dramas, *Don't Make Waves* (1975) and *Deeds* (1978). As with *Lay By*, which seems closest to other plays by Brenton, his own contribution appears dominated by the distinctive voices of those with whom he is working.

Seemingly as uncharacteristic as *Lay By*, the short plays written at the same time, *Apricots* and *Thermidor*, can in fact both be seen as sketches for still unwritten dramas. For Griffiths has spoken of wanting to write a rigorous examination of human sexuality, and also of having always wanted to write about Stalin. *Apricots* is a graphic attempt at the former; *Thermidor* an oblique approach to the latter.

In three brief scenes *Apricots* presents the conversation of Sam and Anna, a couple in their mid-thirties, after a dinner party they have hosted. As they sit in their garden, drunk and tired, they bicker about other sexual partners and Sam recalls their early love-making. In the second scene they fuck, and talk about fucking others. Sam withdraws, Anna goes casually to make some tea and Sam masturbates listening to a tape of their conversation. During the final exchange Sam reflects 'that once . . . it used to be . . . graceful. Full of grace'. Anna disparages his sentimentalised memory and talks of her recollection of the first time they made love: 'I was, to you, a face and a hole. That's all. I don't think I've ever known such absolute fear in anyone. And now you have the . . . nerve to call it holy.' She asks him 'to fuck me hard and strong and long'. He declines.

Written very quickly, the play came directly out of Griffiths' personal experience and was, he has said, a response to his relationship with his wife. In her introduction to the published text, Catherine Itzin writes (after an interview with Griffiths): 'He says that he had swallowed whole the myth that women are romanticists and men are realists, that he realised in his own life the reverse was true. That discovery in part prompted the play. . . He did not intend the play to be a study of sexuality *per se*, but to use "perverted", thwarted sexuality as a metaphor for a whole socially conditioned relationship.'[25] Analysing the text, Catherine Itzin concludes that, 'Implicit in the play is the impossibility of considering personal relationships as autonomous – they take their meaning from the conditions of reality, of society and the world . . . The play is a metaphor of life in capitalist, bourgeois society.'[26]

Written in spare, sometimes brutal language, this play's personal introspection contrasts with the more familiar historical dialectic of *Thermidor*, with which *Apricots* was paired in performance at Edinburgh (sharing the two actors and director Robert Walker). Cast in the form of an interrogation, *Thermidor* is set in Moscow's police headquarters during the purges of 1937. A party official, Yukhov, charges Anya with having associated with Trotskyists. She demonstrates her superior grasp of the realities of the revolution and refuses to accept that the description Trotskyist applied to Volsky, one of her former colleagues. 'Since Volsky is a convicted Trotskyist traitor,' Yukhov insists, 'objectively, therefore, you knew the Trotskyist Volsky.' Anya rejects this forcefully: 'There is no power in the world that can give you the right *to tell me what I know* . . . *I* am the *only* subject of *know*. You cannot *tell* me I knew the Trotskyist Volsky. I knew Volsky the father of two teenage daughters. I knew committeeman Volsky. I knew Volsky the husband of fat-faced Katya with the red hair and bad teeth. *That* Volsky I knew. No other. No other.' This central exchange reflects the split between the concerns of the individual and the requirements of the revolution which underpins *Occupations* and which recurs throughout much of Griffiths' later work. As in *Occupations*, the revolution is shown to have failed because these elements were not united; ten years later, *Reds* was to engage with a parallel dynamic.

In 1971, *Thermidor*, like *Occupations*, was specifically addressed to a contemporary failure. Writing in 1978, Catherine Itzin explained: 'A critical approach to socialism must be historical rather than philosophical, says Griffiths. And sometimes we must necessarily address our comrades rather than a wider audience. This was the case with *Thermidor*, written in 1971, set in 1937 and deliberately intending to parallel the situation in the 1970s, both in the USSR and the UK. If anything Griffiths feels the play is more topical now, with the recent spate of dissidents' trials in the Soviet Union and the hypocritical banner-headline hue and cry about it all in the West. *Thermidor* puts this lingering Stalinism in its historical perspective.'[27]

TELEVISION HISTORY: TOM MANN AND 'SUCH IMPOSSIBILITIES'

Griffiths' next work was to be a more ambitious attempt to develop parallels between past and present. With 'The Edwardians' commission from the BBC, he shifted his frame to Britain, but continued to explore the basic strategy and philosophy of revolutionary politics. Developing an idea for television, he was faced with a quite different performance context from the fringe. And two years on from the writing of *Occupations* he was confronted by a changed political context in Britain. The outcome was the script of *Such Impossibilities*, intended for 'The Edwardians' series but ultimately never produced.

45

Set in the summer of 1911, *Such Impossibilities* focuses on Tom Mann and his leadership of the Liverpool dock strike. The growing labour movement mounted several strong, effective attacks on capital in that year, including major strikes in the ports and a national rail stoppage. Mann, who Griffiths has described as 'the most important and able working-class leader this society has thrown up',[28] was at the centre of these activities, tirelessly speaking and organising for the transport workers. The Liverpool dispute was to establish a number of fundamental union demands, including a minimum wage and the fixing of hours of labour and rates of overtime. Mann co-ordinated it successfully, having just won a similar fight in London.

Such Impossibilities chronicles the strike and Mann's organisation of it, and culminates in the massive peaceful and disciplined public meeting which was brutally broken up by the police, despite previous assurances of non-intervention. The play ends with Mann in jail, defiant, triumphant. A final title quotes his words: 'Actions that aim only at securing peace between employers and men are not only of no value in the fight for freedom, but are actually a serious hindrance and a menace to the interests of the workers. Political and industrial action direct must at all times be inspired by revolutionary principles. That is, the aim must ever be to change from capitalism to socialism as speedily as possible. Anything less than this means continued domination by the capitalist class.'

Throughout the debates on strategy, two requirements are stressed as necessary for effective industrial action: organisation and solidarity. 'Strikes aren't won by public sympathy,' Mann asserts, 'they're won by ruthless organisation, concerted action, and understanding between leaders and led.' Mann is presented as a hard and obsessive leader, but Griffiths is careful to include scenes to show his 'human' face, his personal warmth. As the strike builds to the edge of insurrection, Mann's stress on discipline recalls the debates in *Occupations*, but *Such Impossibilities* employs a less complex, linear structure, dispenses with a fundamental dialectic and has far less time for the personal aspects of revolutionary politics than it does for the public ones.

Presenting an outline to a BBC script editor in a letter in July 1971, Griffiths wrote: 'I don't think it's difficult to see where one finds relevance for today in the events of summer, 1911.'[29] A Conservative government had been returned in June 1970, and had immediately faced a succession of strikes which were settled by tribunals sympathetic to the workers. Having initially adopted a policy of distancing itself from individual disputes, Edward Heath's government moved quickly to tactics of confrontation, and the consequent

46

ill-will from the trade union movement grew alongside anger at the proposed Industrial Relations Act.

Debated in Parliament during the summer of 1971 and passed on 6 August after 450 hours of heated debate, the Act has been described by a contemporary historian as 'one of the most significant measures of the century. It had a number of admirable qualities but it seriously misread the signs of the times and did more to undermine the rule of law than any Act of Parliament of modern times. The rule of law in a democracy rests ultimately on consent . . . The Heath government challenged the unions in such a manner that the unions not only accepted the challenge to the point of breaking the law, but did so with a good measure of popular support.'[30]

The Act's measures were designed to reduce fundamentally the rights of individual members and the overall power of unions. And as Griffiths conceived it that summer, *Such Impossibilities* was directly addressed to this question: 'Under [the Act] workers will lose important, hard-won rights. "Militants" will risk imprisonment for "incitement to unauthorised industrial action". It remains to be seen what the precise response of organised labour will be, but it is not impossible to see ourselves on the threshold of a new era of grassroots agitation and action. Men will go to jail. Police will be once again squarely in the middle of industrial activity.'[31]

Early in 1972, as Griffiths was finishing the script, the miners rejected a National Coal Board offer and came out for most of January and the whole of February. With widespread public backing, they organised massively successful pickets at many power stations and were supported by the railwaymen, who refused to move trains. Eventually the Wilberforce Inquiry recommended pay increases three times the size of the Coal Board's offer. The NUM Kent Area organiser, Malcolm Pitt, later wrote: 'The 1972 strike was a dramatic demonstration of working-class power and revealed to everybody what united working-class action could achieve.'[32]

As already indicated, an emphasis on the need for organisation and solidarity is central to *Such Impossibilities,* as is a discussion of the role of the police in industrial disputes. But Griffiths was not solely preoccupied with the concerns of the moment, and had a wider aim in writing the play: 'to restore, however tinily, an important but suppressed area of our collective history; to enlarge our "usable past" and connect it with a lived present; and to celebrate a victory.'[33]

In the creation and circulation of 'our collective history', television has assumed a central place. Expansive documentary series appear to offer the impersonal 'facts' while seductive costume dramas flesh out the past with human 'fictions'. Yet as Colin McArthur has demonstrated in his important study *Television and History, all* television and *all* historiography is ideological, constructed within fundamentally political frameworks of thought. *Such Impossibilities,* even – or perhaps especially – as an unproduced script, must be seen against this electronic tapestry and specifically against the moment of the early 70s. For like Griffiths' subsequent scripts *The Silver Mask* and *Absolute Beginners*, it was very much shaped by the imperatives of television drama at that time.

In January 1967 BBC2 transmitted the first episodes of *The Forsyte Saga*, a 26-part adaptation of Galsworthy's Edwardian *roman fleuve*. An enormous success, it was to be repeated on BBC1 in 1968, 1970 and again in 1974. It also sold exceptionally well abroad and in 1969 was picked up by National Educational Television, the public broadcasting network in the United States. Strong ratings there prompted NET in January 1971 to launch an anthology slot for prestigious British serials under the title *Masterpiece Theatre*.

In Britain, the late Victorian and Edwardian years became the favoured settings for costume drama, and were rivalled only by the Tudor age, the attraction of which was first proved by *The Six Wives of Henry VIII* (January 1970) and a year later by *Elizabeth R*. McArthur offers an explanation: 'To be speculative, it seems reasonable to suppose that a society going through a period of historical transition and finding it immensely painful and disorienting will therefore tend to recreate, in some at least of its art, images of more (apparently) settled times, especially times in which the self-image of the society as a whole was buoyant and optimistic. For post-war Britain, faced as it is with adjustment to being a post-colonial power, a mediocre economic performer, a multi-racial society in which the consensus of acceptable social and political behaviour is fragmenting . . . what better ideological choice, in its art, than to return to the period of the zenith of bourgeois and imperial power.'[34]

So popularity, critical prestige and, perhaps most importantly, foreign sales – in particular the ready market at NET – prompted further imitators, and 1971 saw the debut of London Weekend Television's Edwardian saga *Upstairs, Downstairs*. It too was soon bought and shown on *Masterpiece Theatre*. And that year 'The Edwardians' must have seemed an attractive concept to BBC producer Mark Shivas (who had co-produced *Henry VIII* and produced *Elizabeth R*). Scripts were commissioned from regular episode writers like Ian Curteis, John Prebble, Alan Plater and Keith Dewhurst, as well as the one from Griffiths, and other subjects in the series were to include Rolls and Royce, Horatio Bottomley, Conan Doyle and Lloyd George.

48

Griffiths' script, however, was rejected and the text – which would require considerable resources to be produced properly – has not been filmed. (After a 1979 reading, the writer resisted the Royal Shakespeare Company's interest in a stage version – the script was specifically written for television.) Several critics have subsequently implied that the rejection was the result of overt political censorship, and when the script was published in 1977, Griffiths wrote in the introduction: 'the ostensible grounds were cost – they often are – but it's at least as likely that the play offered too brutal and too overtly political a contrast with the remainder of the series . . . Tom Mann might well have roughed the series up a bit, but it's arguable he might also have done something towards redressing its "balance" too.'[35]

Asked to explain, Mark Shivas responded in a letter to the present authors that 'one of the points of commissioning the piece was to have a play or plays in this series of biographical plays showing the harshness of life for much of the working population'. He confirmed that *Such Impossibilities* would have cost too much: 'The series nearly ran out of money totally. The Lloyd George play by Keith Dewhurst, the last to be commissioned and recorded, was deliberately kept without film inserts or large cast.' Shivas also resisted the view of the series as cosily nostalgic and middle-class: 'Alan Plater's *The Reluctant Juggler* in large part dealt with the grim working conditions of people low down on the billing in Edwardian music halls and the formation of a union to protect them. Horatio Bottomley started life as a journalist before he became a notable fraud. Mr Royce was a mechanic who joined up with the upper-class Charles Rolls, and the Nesbit story was partly about women in bourgeois society. *Baden Powell* debunked a myth . . . And the Lloyd George play was thought to be so damaging to his reputation by his descendants (supported by Huw Wheldon!) that it was the subject of an injunction (which failed, though it didn't stop Wheldon refusing to repeat the play later).'[36]

The ascription of the charge of censorship is frequently as problematic as the conflicting statements from Griffiths and Shivas suggest, but in any case the playwright failed in his attempt to celebrate a major working-class victory, and to disrupt – to however limited an extent – television's portrayal of history. For none of the plays which Shivas outlines represents anything close to the uncompromising challenge of *Such Impossibilities*. Indeed television as a whole rarely recognises that challenge.

After the disappointment of *Such Impossibilities*, Griffiths wrote his next two television scripts for London Weekend. One of these was a further historical play, as was his next piece for the BBC, *Absolute Beginners*. After that he moved into the present or near-present and did not engage with history again until *Country* in 1981. His feeling was rather as Tom Mann expresses it in *Such Impossibilities*: 'I'm not a great one for the past. It's what we do now that counts. But there's one or two lessons to be learnt.' Certainly there were lessons to be learnt in *Absolute Beginners*.

'ATTACKING COMFORT': 'THE SILVER MASK'

Griffiths' first script for LWT was an adaptation of a Hugh Walpole short story for the 1973 showcase drama series 'Between the Wars'. Produced by Verity Lambert (later to be responsible for commissioning *Bill Brand*) and screened in the late spring and early summer, the six-part series aimed to refract the inter-war period through some distinctly minor literary texts of the 1920s and 1930s. In addition to Walpole's 1930 psychological fable, *The Silver Mask*, these were: Osbert Sitwell's marital thriller, *The Greeting*; *Mr Loveday's Little Outing*, an Evelyn Waugh story about a mental patient who everyone thinks is sane; *Voyage in the Dark*, Jean Rhys' short story about a young actress drifting into prostitution; and two stories by Richard Aldington, *Now She Lies There*, about a sexually predatory heiress who runs away with a lion tamer, and *Yes Aunt*, a comedy about an irresponsible bachelor. John Bowen, Brian Clark and Willis Hall were among the adapters, but although the series won plaudits for its production values, it was also widely seen as an instance of the growing trend towards what Sean Day-Lewis in the *Telegraph* called 'television-as-nostalgia'. Another critic described it as a 'competent philistine job, which appears not to notice that the stories aren't good enough to be pulled out of oblivion'.

The material on which Griffiths had to work was certainly no exception, though Walpole's story about a wealthy society hostess offering assistance to a destitute young artist and then finding him taking over her home was a cut above the romantic excess of the historical romances for which he is best known. Walpole, in fact, claims to have 'dreamt' the whole thing 'from the first word to the last' and a certain Gothic-like element in the use of the central motif of the silver mask generates a sense of menace more in keeping with the work of another Walpole – the eighteenth-century author of the celebrated horror prototype *The Castle of Otranto*. Predictably, Alastair Reid's direction uses television's visual advantages over print to exploit this element, focusing repeatedly on the sinister silver *objet d'art* hung on the wall of the Mayfair house and heavily underscoring its role in the mock-Gothic final scene. Light and dark spots, silvers and blues in the design greatly aid the atmospheric effect.

Griffiths' main interpretative contribution is to draw out something that is latent in both Walpole's text and, to some extent, the series as a whole (*The Silver Mask* was transmitted last): a deep-seated and widespread fear of social upheaval. What Walpole's story does, in effect, is to dramatise subconscious anxieties about proletarian revolution through its account of how Sonia Herries' house is invaded by the young artist and his family and how she herself becomes a prisoner under the new regime they impose. Griffiths makes this *conscious* by playing down Walpole's somewhat prurient stress on the ageing Miss Herries' sexual interest in the young man, and emphasising his phrase 'I *have* to attack your comfort' by using it as a kind of verbal motif throughout, a social complement to the psychological motif of the mask. Apart from offering this 'symptomatic' reading of the story, which in any case remains understated, *The Silver Mask* contains very little impress of specific 'authorship'. True, Sonia Herries, dying on her bed in the final scene, recalls another threatened member of the old order, the Countess in *Occupations*, but otherwise *The Silver Mask* appears to have been very much a journeyman piece of work, highly competent but still that of a writer mostly interested in perfecting the *craft* of scripting for television.

Not so *There*, also commissioned by LWT in 1973 but, perhaps significantly, never produced. Here Griffiths clearly was writing about something close to him since this was a piece that picked up the theme of *Sam, Sam* to tell the story of two brothers, one a shirt-cutter, the other a television producer, who meet up for the first time in five years to spend an uneasy day together in Manchester. The fact that the textile worker is called Ged and that he is trying to borrow money from his brother in order to set up a business looks forward to both Ged, the milkman-half of the brother duo in *Comedians*, and Eddie, the working-class brother in *The Party*; and this suggests that both these later plays may represent reworkings of this now lost script.

'MAKING REVOLUTION': 'ABSOLUTE BEGINNERS'

Still looking for subjects set at the turn of the century, the BBC had initiated the historical drama series 'Fall of Eagles'. This was to relate the collapse of the nineteenth-century European dynasties – the Romanovs, the Hohenzollerns and the Habsburgs – to the outbreak of World War I and the rise of revolution. An outline had been prepared and several scripts written before Stuart Burge was brought in to produce the series. He was concerned that it should not emerge simply as a romantic, nostalgic and spectacular celebration of the autocratic families. 'I needed a demonstration somewhere in the series of what was happening in the undergrowth, in the revolutionary world,'[37] he recalled.

Prior to this, Stuart Burge had been running the Nottingham Playhouse, where Richard Eyre had now taken over as director. Eyre had introduced him to Griffiths and they commissioned the play which eventually became *Comedians*. Burge was impressed by the writer and so went to him now with a loose brief for a play about the Russian revolutionary movement. Griffiths immediately recognised the opportunity to extend further his attempt to write for the mainstream forms of a dominant medium. '*Absolute Beginners* is my most popular play,' he has said, 'having been seen in sixty-five or seventy countries. That was a great decision; I'm glad I had the wit to see it. What was good was that I didn't have a head cluttered with notions of high art and popular art, nor did I have a sense that my career rested in the high art direction rather than in a popular direction. I was committed to communicating across as wide a societal band as I possibly could. And I was just eager and excited to get something said that was complex and severe and entertaining.'[38]

Eventually transmitted in April 1974 as episode six in a series of thirteen, *Absolute Beginners* details the conflicts within the Russian Social Democratic Workers' Party before and during their 1903 Congress in Brussels and London. Earlier programmes, by John Elliott and Hugh Whitemore, had concentrated almost exclusively on the dynastic courts, but subsequent episodes, from among others Jack Pulman, Troy Kennedy Martin and Keith Dewhurst, detailed certain stages in the later progress of Bolshevism. Griffiths' script, by contrast, concentrates single-mindedly on it, and in particular on Lenin. At one point Lenin travels to Switzerland to consult the revered Marxist theoretician Plekhanov on preparations for the Congress. Half-admiringly, half-warily, Plekhanov says to him, 'I've always been fascinated by your hardness'. And so is the play, which reflects Plekhanov's ambivalence in its account of Lenin's ruthless drive to organise the party round a tight-knit core of professional activists.

1903 was the formative moment of Bolshevism and a key point in the development of the revolutionary movement. The Russian Social Democratic Workers' Party, one among several Marxist groups, had held a small initial conference in 1898, and had organised since then around the weekly paper *Iskra*, published in Munich by a group which included Plekhanov and Lenin. In Russia, from 1902 onwards, a forceful campaign of police repression was initiated by the new Minister of the Interior, Von Plehve, and *Absolute Beginners* has a prologue in which Plehve urges an uncertain Nicholas II to be coherent, ruthless and intelligent in a total war against anarchists and revolutionists.

Lenin had recognised a similar need for the Social Democratic Party if it was to grow and be finally effective. Arriving in London in early 1903, he was distressed to find the party's organisation there was dominated by individuals like Martov and Zasulich whom he saw as intellectual dilettantes. Griffiths sketches this recognition in the early scenes, and indicates the conflict to come as these émigrés suggest in discussion the need for a wider membership of the party. The author's confidence in carrying an audience through a dense political discussion can be seen in the brief exchange which encapsulates one of the fundamental theoretical issues of the Russian revolutionary experience. Zasulich objects that the peasants should be included within the movement. 'They have revolutionary potential too,' she proffers. 'They need . . . organising too.' Lenin dismisses the thought: 'They won't make the revolution. The question of the peasant arises after the revolution, when they are forced to bow to the dictatorship of the proletariat. We'll see then how revolutionary they are.' To which Zasulich responds with one of the play's suggestions of the problems which the revolution, organised on Leninist principles, will eventually face: 'It seems a bit late leaving it till then, comrade. What do you propose to do about it *then*, may I ask? Shoot them all? There are millions of them.'

Lenin's position is further contrasted with the vision of the young Trotsky, who dreams of the revolution as 'the boundless horizon of beauty, joy and happiness'. As Trotsky reads a florid account of his utopia to Lenin's wife Krupskaya, Lenin himself writes more letters about *organisation*. Only organisation, he impresses on Trotsky, will make the revolution, and anyone who hinders that organisation is an enemy. 'The real battle for now is not with the Tsar, Comrade Trotsky,' he says, 'it's with ourselves.'

This 'battle' is highlighted by Lenin's clash with Martov and Zasulich over an issue of personal morality. A comrade wishes to address the London group to lay a serious accusation against one of their agents, Bauman; Lenin refuses even to see him. Clearly sharing concerns with *Occupations*, this scene in *Absolute Beginners* lays out a further analysis of the ideas which were later, historically, to produce Kabak. The 'fatally schizophrenic split in revolutionary consciousness' identified earlier recurs in Martov's outburst to Lenin: 'You can't separate private from public like that, can't you see it man! We are what we do . . . you, me, Bauman, all of us. Party morality is more than just loyalty to the party . . . it's the highest level of ethical

Absolute Beginners: a drama fascinated by the hardness of Lenin (Patrick Stewart).

consciousness yet afforded the human species . . .' Lenin scorns him: 'Metaphysics, Julius. Another time, perhaps, we may speculate. Just now we're trying to make the revolution *possible.'*

Lenin's purity and rigour emerge not only through his words and speeches, but through the images of the play. As it opens, he is completing fifty press-ups before a frugal breakfast. And at the critical moment of the Congress, he caucuses with his 'hards' in a small, bare room to which Martov – presented throughout as a weak, dilettantish émigré – is forcibly and illegitimately denied entry. But like Tom Mann, Lenin is presented with a 'human' face, at least in his relationship with Krupskaya. Drawn largely from Krupskaya's own

54

Memories of Lenin, these domestic scenes show her working alongside him as a colleague, comforting him in his illness and living with him in a relationship of, as the script's final image has it, 'two simple bourgeois'. Yet, on the basis of Lenin's documented decision as a young man to repress his love of music, Griffiths has him refuse a song from her. 'No more music,' he says gently. 'It's too . . . moving. It softens.' The next shot has him writing at his desk, at 3 a.m., while Krupskaya sleeps. He remains totally resolute, even with regard to his closest personal relationship.

The growing disagreements on party policy and membership are crystallised in debates at the Second International Party Congress

Dreaming of revolution: Michael Kitchen as Trotsky.

55

which was held first in Brussels, where the police disrupted it, and then reconvened in London. A scene in Brussels illustrates the growing gulf between Lenin's supporters and Martov's; on a crucial procedural point, Martov's group is in the majority. Party membership is then discussed in London. Martov argues for a party of a *class*: 'the more widespread the title of party member, the better.' Lenin objects that Martov is confusing party and class. He presses the Congress to 'vote for coherence, organisation, discipline, above all power at the *centre* . . .[to] make the necessary distinction between an entire *class*, shaped by capitalism, and its *vanguard*, the party.' In a stormy vote, Lenin loses.

That evening Lenin again caucuses with his 'hards' and unconstitutionally bars Martov from the meeting. Lenin then completely outmanoeuvres Martov, forcing him to support the 'hards' the next day on the question of expelling the Jewish Workers' Alliance. The Workers' Cause group withdraws in protest against 'the dictatorial tendencies that are emerging within the party apparatus' (a further suggestion in the text's vocabulary of the totalitarianism to come). Martov is now in the minority, and Lenin uses his new strength to dispose of Zasulich from the *Iskra* board and so force Martov also to resign. Trotsky follows him. Lenin is calmly triumphant and the party is irrevocably split between the Bolsheviks (the majority) and the Mensheviks (the minority).

The play's coda is set around Marx's grave, with the new factions clearly illustrated in director Gareth Davies' compositions. (This scene, like the opening and two early exteriors, is shot on film, and carries a greater impact than the tightly shot bulk of the play, which was recorded on videotape in a studio.) Plekhanov speaks with irony of 'this great unifying congress' and in a final exchange with Trotsky, Lenin reiterates the importance of his stand. He refers to the Tsar and Von Plehve's organisation (as glimpsed in the opening scene) and stresses the importance of elevating the ultimate end above transient means: 'the success of the revolution is the supreme law' (actually a translation of a Latin text used by Plekhanov at the congress).

Partly as a consequence of the style of the series, *Absolute Beginners* is unable to accommodate the implications of Lenin's victory. Unlike *Occupations* on stage, a peak-time drama series like 'Fall of Eagles' cannot easily integrate stills and photos within the action to illustrate both the Revolution's triumph (this in any case will come in a later episode) and the spectre of Stalinist totalitarianism. These larger events must lie outside the narrow scope of a single series episode. But as already suggested, there are hints throughout, and especially in the final speeches of Zasulich and Trotsky as they recognise how they have been ruthlessly rejected. 'You're not a comrade, you're a dictator,' Zasulich screams, 'You're a bloody *Tsar*.' Trotsky is more measured, but he forcibly attacks 'the insatiable lust for power of one individual'. 'Comrades,' he concludes, 'we are privileged to be listening to the sound of party debate – new style.' As Griffiths has explained: 'I was getting at something important in me, but also very important in terms of social and political process, to do with commitment to a revolutionary perspective which will inevitably eliminate humane considerations – of relationships, sympathy, care – and that seems to me to be a problem that we face all the time.'[39]

So although there is a reading of *Absolute Beginners* which sees it as a celebration of Leninism, with a recognition of the October Revolution's dependence on this, the play is more complex. This reading is certainly strengthened by the forceful performance of Patrick Stewart (who had played Kabak in the RSC *Occupations*) as Lenin, which dominates the production. But again like *Occupations*, the play is addressed to making sense of failure – the failure of the Soviet Union to emerge as a truly Communist country and the failure of the revolutionary movements of May '68 in the West. *Absolute Beginners* dissects the genesis of the split which, Griffiths persuasively argues, was to contribute to these historical failures. Here again are one or two lessons to be learnt.

WANTING TO SAY YES: 'THE PARTY'

Four months before the transmission of *Absolute Beginners*, the National Theatre had premiered *The Party*, Griffiths' first full-length stage play since *Occupations*. The National, then at the Old Vic, was a new space for the writer to 'occupy', and since it was the pinnacle of the traditional English theatre, a production there marked the fullest achievement of Griffiths' cultural entryism; especially as the play was mounted with the most revered of British actors, Laurence Olivier, playing a committed Trotskyist.

Although inevitably 'translated' in production by this treatment, *The Party* as a text is structured around the same concerns as *Occupations* and both *Such Impossibilities* and *Absolute Beginners*. This time, however, its analysis of revolutionary strategy is not refracted through history but presented straightforwardly, laid out in the living room of a London house on one evening in May 1968. The 'events' in Paris are a constant presence, witnessed at a distance by television (images from which are at moments projected on to a screen above the action), by newspapers and by voices on the telephone. But it is a strategy for 'revolution' in England that is sought by those brought together by television producer Joe Shawcross. Griffiths has said that the play grew from meetings held at Tony Garnett's house in 1968 when sixty or seventy people gathered with a sense of the need 'to do more, to get it right, to be correct, to read the situation as a first step towards changing it utterly'.[40] Yet he remembers being aware, as is the play, of the distance between the mundane realities of the participants' lives and their stated revolutionary sentiments. The play's observation of this is not cynical, but the contradiction is laced through the writing and finds one focus in an exchange about radical television drama. Sloman, a left-wing writer who seems to be permanently drunk, is staying with Shawcross, who is trying to wring a new play from him. After a mention of this as yet unwritten script, Sloman turns on Shawcross and says quietly, 'It's a sort of . . . presumption you have that you're different, Joe . . . And you're not . . . You occupy the same relationship to the means of production as every other . . . producer in that golden hutch at Would Not Lane you call the Centre. Socialist? A socialist producer? What's that? It's irrelevant.' Sloman's continuing criticism prompts a lame response from Shawcross which is, in many ways, at the heart of the play:

Shawcross: I know all this, Malc. I'd just sooner do a play by you
             than . . . you know. You know?
Sloman: Yeah, I'd sooner play chess than draughts. So what?
Shawcross: I just once . . . want to say yes to something.

By the end all he will be able to say yes to is a minor act of capitalist investment.

Shawcross' choice has been characterised in the play up to his argument with Sloman by two remarkable speeches presented to 'the party'. Early on, as host, he explains the rationale for the small, private gathering, called by the Revolutionary Socialist Party: 'I'm not a member of the Party, but I'm convinced that what the Left in Britain needs now more than ever is a united and coherent focus for its efforts. But above all, we need theory. Not necessarily the RSP's but a genuine socialist analysis of our situation that will give us a rational basis for political action beyond the single issue activities that have kept us fragmented and . . . impotent . . . in the past.' The first speech is delivered by Andrew Ford, an LSE academic and a contributor to *New Left Review*. (Griffiths has even referred to the character as 'Perry Blackburn', yoking together the names of two prominent *NLR* editors.) Ford's line is that traditional Marxism is obsolete, but that 'revisionism' of Marx's ideas can be productive. Lenin used one understanding of Marx to fashion the revolution in Russia, but it is fruitless to look to that 'revision' today; the European proletariats have been assimilated into 'the institutions of the reformed and superadaptive bourgeois state'. The only hope, the only positive element now, lies in movements in the Third World: 'China, Cuba, Vietnam: these are the new centres of the world revolutionary struggle. The national liberation movements in the colonial enclave are probably the sole and certainly the principal revolutionary forces at work in the world today . . . Our function . . . is to assist, however we may, the final victory of these anti-capitalist, revolutionary movements. Whether we are blacks in Detroit or white proletarians in Manchester, that is our sole remaining revolutionary purpose and duty.'

Ford's framework is immediately questioned by the listeners who represent specific groupings within the Left – blacks, students, women, even social democrats. But it is the Trotskyist working-class leader John Tagg who attacks the fundamentals of his analysis. Elaborating what is effectively the position of the Workers Revolutionary Party at that time, he rejects the assertion that the working class has lost its potential for revolution, although he foresees the overthrow of capitalism being brought about by an alliance with other groups. None the less the working class must be the base of this struggle, and he despairs of intellectuals who have lost, or never had, contact with that class. Ford's contribution was 'simply part of an elaborate game he enjoys playing and plays well'. What must be recognised, Tagg argues, is that European and American proletariats have been consistently betrayed by their leaders, particularly within the Communist parties of Eastern Europe: 'If we are to change all this, if we are to put proletarian revolution back on the agenda of European history, we are going to have to replace those defunct and corrupt leaderships with vital and revolutionary ones. But those leaders will emerge not as loose coalitions or spontaneous coalescings, but as a result of patient organisation and disciplined effort. That's to say, those leaderships will develop from new revolutionary *parties* which in turn will base themselves in and on the class they lead.' Tagg knows all too well that this strategy runs counter to 'the traditions and values of Western bourgeois intellectuals'. But intellectuals, even those on the streets of Paris, will not bring about the revolution.

Ford's and Tagg's closely argued, demanding speeches last over ten minutes each in performance and represent the most uncompromising instance of 'pure' dialectic in Griffiths' writing. They strain the play's naturalism, which is in any case fractured by the prologue in which a Groucho Marx figure lectures the audience on revolutionary theory with lengthy quotes from Marx, Lenin and

Shakespeare. Act Two reasserts a naturalistic style, as the guests leave gradually and Tagg talks on the phone to Paris. His Trotskyist comrades there are watching, but not participating in the fighting. He explains to Shawcross that the insurrection is romantic, leaderless and ineffective. The next morning, Sloman proffers a third understanding of revolution, which is not presented as didactically as Ford's or Tagg's, but is no less persuasive. Drawing on memories of his father, Sloman argues that the working class does not need the voice of Trotsky to lead them to the barricades. Revolution in Britain will come when the *masses* are ready. The germ of struggle is there, and capitalism's ability to absorb it is not infinite. Eventually the working class will rise spontaneously, 'and the class will throw up its own leaders and its own structures of leadership and responsibility.'

Griffiths did not intend that this third contribution to the debate should be regarded as a definitive statement. Sloman's view, the writer said later, is 'a very imprecise and to some extent a romantic formulation of the revolutionary process, but at least it is pointing to an argument which says that the working class itself has got to clean its house before it can relate to leadership, create leadership that *is* vital and that will change the situation. It is still a misreading of *The Party* to see Sloman as the author's point of view, because that isn't the way the play characteristically works at all.'[41] However, the ideas attributed to Sloman continued to preoccupy Griffiths, and were further developed in the character of Gethin Price in *Comedians*. Rather than making a statement, then, *The Party*, like all Griffiths' mature work, is a debate, with Shawcross at its centre endeavouring to draw out a form of action. As Griffiths has explained, 'I wanted to set one person in the centre of all that reverberance and resonance, set a life in that, and a set of relationships and see what happened.'[42] Yet 'what happens' is that Shawcross is reduced to impotent inaction. As when he numbly answers a question from his wife, Angie, in the closing moments of the play, 'Is it what I want? I don't know how to answer that.' All he is able to do is agree to give his working-class brother Eddie three hundred pounds to set up his own business. Earlier in the play he could not decide about this; filial loyalty contradicted a political stance: 'It seems illogical to use my surpluses to help set up a capitalist enterprise.' After 'the party' is over he agrees immediately. But even this action is ambivalent, since Sloman had previously taunted him gently with the suggestion that, 'P'raps you need a brother . . . down there . . . with the workers, eh?'

In the first National Theatre production, this political uncertainty was paralleled, as later in *Bill Brand*, by Shawcross' sexual impotence. A Reichian thread about the deformation of personal relationships

60

under capitalism ran through the play, just as it does in, among others, *Apricots*, *Brand* and even Griffiths' reading of *Sons and Lovers*. But the writer removed all suggestions of sexual impotence when he reworked the text for a touring production, without Olivier, directed some months later for the National by David Hare. Other peripheral elements and characters were also cut out, and Griffiths felt that this second version, and its staging, was considerably more successful. Even so, the dramatic form of the play is far less accomplished than that of either *Occupations* or *Comedians*, although its very unwieldiness seems to be one further reflection of the impotence it identifies.

On its opening, the play was strongly attacked by most of the mainstream critics. There is a sense in which, despite the touring production, the play has never recovered from this – it has not been staged professionally in Britain again* and it is the only one of Griffiths' major works for the stage not to have been transferred to television. Nor was there much enthusiasm from many elements on the Left, who criticised the play for its pessimism. Griffiths was additionally reproved from the Left for the strategy of attempting to work through the National Theatre. John McGrath later summarised this view: 'The character of an old Marxist revolutionary from Glasgow was taken over by Lord Olivier, and became a vehicle for a star to communicate with his admirers; a juicy part for the artistic director. The process, the building, the wages structure, the publicity machine, the free interval drinks' budget, all these can turn opposition into novelty; but it would be short-sighted to deny the value of trying.'[43]

Griffiths remained adamant about the value of his 'entryism' and regretted that the play had been seen as simply negative. *The Party is* a pessimistic drama, but to see it as solely that is as much a misreading as to interpret *Absolute Beginners* as a celebration of Lenin. As has been suggested already, both plays are addressed to the failure of 1968. Like Griffiths' other work since *Occupations*, they identify the failings of revolutionary parties in the early years of the century and illustrate how those failings were reproduced in 1968. *The Party*, set at that moment, in England, and in Griffiths' own milieu, confronts those failings most directly and most painfully. Yet it still represents an affirmation of a continuing struggle. If one route towards radical social change is blocked, then others, it suggests, must be found, explored, criticised and understood. For Griffiths himself, as for many

*In January 1984 the Royal Shakespeare Company announced that a re-worked version of the play would be produced later in the year at their small Stratford theatre, The Other Place.

on the Left similarly disillusioned after 1968, there was now a new route opening up away from radical groupings no more effective than the parties at which they met. This route lay with the party with which Griffiths now engaged as a dramatist, the Labour Party.

4 'Now and in England': *All Good Men, Bill Brand* and Labourism

In December 1973, television unexpectedly found itself caught up in the problems of the increasingly beleaguered Heath government. An overtime ban by miners, supported by the railwaymen of ASLEF and workers in the electricity supply industry, panicked the Tory administration into a series of draconian measures ostensibly designed to conserve energy stocks. As well as the three-day week and extensive power cuts, these included broadcasting restrictions. From 17 December, the BBC and ITV networks were instructed to end transmissions early at 10.30 p.m. every night.

Variously described in the press as a 'TV blackout' and even a 'TV curfew', the early closedown was claimed to save 600 tons of coal a day. However, Labour's opposition spokesman on broadcasting, John Grant, described the nightly shutdown as a deliberate attempt to 'create the maximum psychological impact as part of an overall campaign by the government to turn public opinion against the trade unions, even though this may involve an unnecessary degree of hardship or discomfort for the public.'[1] Certainly there was disruption, with for example *Match of the Day* – bound by contract with the Football League to go out after 10 p.m. – being hit, and programmes generally subject to cuts and schedules to rejigging. 'Play for Today', the BBC's prestige drama slot, was particularly badly affected. With a 9.25 p.m. start time, its maximum length was reduced to 63 minutes and the transmission tapes simply had to be edited down to fit. One such victim was Griffiths' debut single play for television, *All Good Men*, which went out in a truncated form at the end of January, minus 12 of its original 75 minutes. Ironically, given that an all-out miners' strike was now under way, Griffiths' dramatic exploration of Labourist ideology centred on a leading party member and ex-government minister who had betrayed the miners in the 1926 General Strike.

Despite the uncanny appropriateness of the context in which *All Good Men* went out, its origins were a good deal more contingent. Griffiths had been approached by 'Play for Today' script editor Ann Scott in the summer of 1973 for a script at short notice after another commissioned project had fallen through. The budget was to be skimpy, so it would have to be made without film inserts. The constraints involved were familiar from his work on series and Griffiths completed the script in six weeks, the quick turn-around neatly exposing the mythology of 'art' that generally accompanies a writer's transition from drama series to the more prestigious single play. Yet *All Good Men*, in truth, makes few concessions to populism, mobilising *ideas* in as complex a way as, say, *Occupations*, the work through which Griffiths had originally established the dramatic viability of ideological debate in the theatre. During the writing of *All Good Men*, he happened across Eric Rohmer's *Ma Nuit chez Maud* and this, he has said, reinforced his belief 'that people could actually talk and yet still hold interest'[2] (Rohmer's 1969 film interrupts a sexual encounter with a lengthy and involved discussion of Pascal's theory of probability). *All Good Men* is additionally complicated by the fact that it attempts to incorporate a commentary on television itself. This double focus, on a Left critique of Labourism and television's understanding of it, turns out with hindsight, like much else in the piece, to have been uncannily prescient in the light of what would become Labour's post-1979 preoccupations.

In line with its place in a broader writing strategy aimed at recovering the past for the present, Griffiths initially called the script *History*, since it was intended to provide just that: an alternative, anti-consensual reading of Labour Party history. The eventual choice of a typing 'exercise' ('Now is the time for all good men to come to the aid of the party') was, however, much happier. Full of the kind of ironies and plays on meaning one has come to expect from a Griffiths title, it usefully drew attention to the text's central dialectic: the contending claims of Labour's Left and Centre-Right to represent the party's 'soul'. *All Good Men* opens with a long scene (cut in the 63-minute transmitted version) in which Edward Waite, one of Labour's ageing elder statesmen and a casualty of the 1970 election defeat, is being interviewed by a television producer preparing a profile of him for a series called 'Living History'. The scene takes place in the conservatory of Waite's comfortable country house, where he is to be filmed the following day, and it immediately establishes the familiar class trajectory of the typical Labour politician: working-class background, trade union involvement, long parliamentary career, culminating in ministerial office. During the course of this exchange with Massingham, the producer, we learn that Waite is to be made a peer in the forthcoming New Year's Honours' List. On the face of it, a successful end to a successful career – and soon to be celebrated as such on television. But there is more than just a hint of unease. Something in Massingham's public-school manner smacks of the kind of class condescension Waite has had to deal with all his life – not least in a failed second marriage to the middle-class Ann, who seems to have specialised in humiliating him sexually. After Massingham has left, Waite goes into a kind of reverie in which private memories of this unhappy sexual past mingle with public memories of key moments in British political history: Ann's sneeringly erotic voice-over being mixed with recordings of Chamberlain's 'Peace with Honour' speech, Attlee promising 'responsible government' in 1945, Bevan's 'naked into the conference chamber' about-face, and Gaitskell's 'we will fight, fight and fight again to save the party we love' pledge. The highly emotional experience of reliving the past proves too much for Waite, however, and he suffers a mild heart attack. The suggestion, metaphorically at least – and it is greatly underscored by Michael Lindsay-Hogg's direction – is that Waite is weighed down by the memory of a whole series of personal and political betrayals. In the moments before he collapses, the camera rushes in and out in a staccato sequence of jerky, violent close-ups that crudely approximate this accumulated pressure from the past.

Waite recovers sufficiently for Massingham to get his interview. But not before a small gathering to celebrate Waite's 71st birthday – attended by his daughter Maria, an art teacher at a comprehensive school, his son William, a research student at Manchester University, and Massingham himself – has ended in the set-piece political confrontation that forms the play's core. During a conversation designed to 'prepare' Waite for his in-depth interview, William asks his father to justify Labour's record in office: 'Given the power that you and your party have from time to time exercised in the last fifty years, and given the fact that your rhetoric is invariably radical in temper, how do you explain the extremely modest nature of the changes you have managed to effect?' Waite responds by disputing that Labour's achievements have been 'modest': 'There isn't a part of this society, top to bottom, that hasn't been profoundly affected by what we have done, in office and out. The record speaks for itself, but I'll speak to it if you like.' And speak to it he does, running through the reformist catalogue – and creed – in far too well-practised a manner to be anything like convincing. Bill Fraser's wonderfully mock-avuncular performance manages in the process to allude to the idioms and idiosyncrasies of a number of leading Labour politicians: George

The Labour Party as an unhappy 'family': William (Jack Shepherd), Maria (Frances de la Tour) and Edward Waite (Bill Fraser) in *All Good Men*.

Brown, Lord Robens and, through a very familiar pipe mannerism, Harold Wilson. (The pipe, it later emerges, is in fact merely a prop: like the passion that has long gone out of Waite's politics, it too hasn't been lit for decades.)

Although utterly unconvinced by his father's attempt to make shabby pragmatism in office seem heroic, William none the less decides to defer to him on the grounds that he is ill and that he is, after all, his father. But buoyed up by his own rhetoric, Waite insists that they continue, and like any family row – and Griffiths clearly intends us to see the broad coalition that is the Labour Party as an unhappy 'family' – the confrontation proceeds to get more and more bitter. William, played with a dishevelled intensity by Jack Shepherd, immediately resumes his attack, condemning the seemingly fatal desire of Labour leaders to 'prove the papers wrong', to show that they are 'responsible' men. And being 'responsible' generally amounts, of course, to not rocking the boat. Thus, 'in the likes of MacDonald and Snowden the capitalist system found two of its ablest and most orthodox defenders in this century'. Pursuing a line of argument that suggests a fairly close acquaintance with *Parliamentary Socialism*, Ralph Miliband's classic study of Labourism (which had been reissued in 1973 with an appended postscript on the Wilson years), William continues by accusing successive Labour leaderships of a purely *rhetorical* commitment to socialism that has very little to do with what in practice they set out to achieve in government:

> . . . the rhetoric you never lost. So that you can describe the Attlee legislation as a *social revolution* as though what happened during that time was what socialism is all about. A *real* social revolution would have committed you to the destruction of capitalism and the social order formed and maintained by it . . . It wasn't a social revolution you achieved, it was a – as it turned out – minimal social adjustment. You drew a section of the working class into the grammar schools, and allowed the public schools to continue training upper and middle-class élites . . . You created a *national* health service and allowed doctors to practise privately. You created municipal housing and left the building industry in the hands of the capitalists. You nationalised ailing industries and services and allowed the strong to be run privately, for private profit. (*Pause*) You didn't create a new social order, you merely humanised an old one.

In a typically dialectical piece of writing, Griffiths allows Waite to come back with some accusations of his own: such as that his son's socialism is the product of a theoretical 'ivory tower', remote from anything resembling a political base. 'You read your Marx and your Trotsky' he tells him, 'and you get your slide rule out and do a couple of simple calculations and you have your blueprint. Revolution. Total change. Overnight. Bang. Especially bang. You have to have your bit of theatre as well, don't you? Reality isn't like that. Reality is . . . taking people with you. Arguing with people who disagree, passionately.' Adopting this kind of stance on the *practicalities* of working within a mass party committed to an electoral form of politics

– in effect, an avowal of the acceptable face of Wilsonian 'pragmatism' – might have been expected at least to form a useful counterweight to William's Left critique. In the event, the rug is almost immediately pulled out from beneath Waite's argument when William, incensed at what he calls this 'shabby definition of reality', decides to confront his father with the damning evidence of his conduct as a National Union of Mineworkers' area official in 1926. Access to NUM files for his university research has enabled William to establish how his father spoke and voted on the crucial issue of the General Strike: the record shows that he not only opposed it originally, but voted for a return to work on no less than six occasions and was prominent in negotiating pay reductions and blacklists with the owners after the strike had been broken. Waite's response is subdued, weary in the extreme. He tamely quotes Beatrice Webb, of all people, on 1926 as 'a proletarian distemper that had to run its course', before going on to inform William of the 'one more betrayal [he] should know about': his decision to accept the peerage.

The fact that William's maximalist position is never tested against a cogently argued revisionism means that at the level of political discourse *All Good Men* lacks the dialectical sophistication of, for example, *Occupations*. Yet it does retain a broad structural dialectic in keeping with its attempt to dramatise the tensions and contradictions inherent in the Labour Party's politically federated nature. Thus, at the level of both dialogue and direction, Bill Fraser's Waite is an engaging, emotionally warm presence, in contrast to Jack Shepherd's rebarbative, taciturnly intellectual manner as William. Equally the single-minded pursuit of the narrowly 'political' in both men registers important differences between them and Frances de la Tour's Maria, who as both a single mother-to-be and a teacher in a large London comprehensive school represents a broader conception of struggle. Unlike them, she has retained real contact – as opposed to her father's nostalgia and her brother's theoretical commitment – with working-class culture and working-class lives. Refusing to attend Waite's investiture as a peer, she tells him: 'It wouldn't be right, Dad . . . I couldn't keep faith with the poor kids I teach, if I did that. I spend most of my life battling against privilege . . . sooner or later we've got to stop being picked off. Sucked in one by one, patted, flattered. We've got to stay with the class, Dad.'

Much of the 'meaning' of the Waite figure is carried in his psycho-sexual characterisation as an individual who has been massively inculcated with an inferiority complex of class origin. Voice-over snatches of his second wife's mock-dominatrix bedroom style – which hint at the same kind of master-slave sexual relationship explored

68

more explicitly, through another cross-class marriage, in *Sam, Sam* – were withdrawn, even from the 75-minute version. But enough resonances remain to establish Waite's sexual submissiveness as deeply symptomatic of his politics, which as William is pleased to point out are the politics of accommodation. 'If there's one thing marks you all out – Labour leaders – it's this desperate need to be accepted. You . . . efface yourselves until there's nothing there. You all want to prove you can "do the job as well as they can" . . . It's a sort of masochism you all have. It's not there in the Tories, no fear. When a Tory minister calls at his favourite whorehouse, he doesn't go to be beaten, he goes to beat. He's used to it. You never will be.' What this account leaves out of course is the lived experience of all this, the existential *ambivalence* of the world Waite has had to inhabit, a world the middle-class-by-adoption William simply has not had to deal with. For all his political astuteness, William is short on imaginative sympathy and, like the politically related figure of Ford in *The Party*, his politics somehow lack any emotional charge. He is, in short, very much the middle-class Leftist. The kind of figure who became more and more vocal within the Labour Party in the 1970s and who helped move it leftwards at constituency level without ever really successfully squaring accounts with the old-style activists. This unresolved conflict at the heart of contemporary Labourism is also at the heart of *All Good Men*. Griffiths attempts no false resolution. So, while there is little doubt that he shares much of William's analysis, the text makes it clear that without the bedrock of a mass base – which is to say without Waite's Labour Party, warts and all – it can never come to any kind of political fruition.

Given that even the 75-minute version of *All Good Men* was pruned of its Bertoluccian psycho-sexual discourse for censorship reasons,* it is ironic that much of the play should have been taken up with a critique of television's narrow construction of the political. Massingham, the Wykehamist producer, is a walking embodiment of bias. It is not just that Ronald Pickup's oily performance oozes class superiority, but that professionally he hides behind a myth of 'impartiality' which is contradicted by almost his every move. When William puts it to him that he 'must have some framework, some point of view, attitude' to bring to the interview with his father, Massingham's reply is terse: 'The conventional rules of biography

---

* Interestingly, the censored voice-over bedroom scene was replaced by a fragment of overheard dialogue which offered a more abstract, *metaphorical* connection between sexuality and political compromise: 'Ann: Jesus – God, I only slept with him. He didn't take my soul.'

and historiography will be observed.' Later, he talks simply about 'making good programmes' as if it were self-evident what he meant, and it is again left to William to point out to him that you can't make a programme, particularly a political programme, *without declaring an interest*. Further on into the evening it emerges that Massingham has a reputation for right-wing tele-journalism and that consequently he is probably setting Waite up for some kind of hatchet-job, dangling the carrot of a sympathetic interview-profile for a wholly fictitious series while all the time planning something altogether different. This is perhaps too Machiavellian, too much a product of the conspiracy theory of media bias, to be entirely convincing, but it does provide *All Good Men* with a powerful dramatic climax. William decides to make the NUM files detailing his father's record in 1926 available to Massingham, knowing that he will use them in the interview. In the final scene, the producer is seen to begin the filming session by asking a question about the General Strike. Waite's face is caught in whited-out big close-up. As his lips start to mouth a response, we pull away slowly to an overhead shot of him sitting alone in a room emptied of all the filming equipment. He is draped in the ceremonial robes of a baronet. 'There'll Always Be an England' plays in the background as the titles go up.

All Good Men clearly anticipates Griffiths' more extended attempt to deal with Labourism in the eleven-part Thames series, *Bill Brand*. Thematically, both are obviously concerned to measure the extent to which Labour has reached a parliamentary dead-end. The Right leadership in *Bill Brand* proves more durable, if no more persuasive, than in *All Good Men* – reflecting Left setbacks in the mid-70s – but both single play and drama series for the most part occupy the same *political* problematic. There are other links, too. Most noticeably the repertory effect: the fact that Jack Shepherd appears in both, playing a character from a broadly Trotskyist background who comes into close contact with members of the Labour establishment. A number of textual references forward almost suggest an unconscious *roman fleuve* motivation on Griffiths' part. As, for example, when Massing-ham tells William: 'Perhaps you should go in for politics. You seem to have all the answers.' Or when Waite warns him: 'One day you may find yourself doing something really serious like running a ministry and then you'll see where dreams get you.' While in *Bill Brand* itself there is an unmistakable reference back to *All Good Men*, when Bill (short for William) leaves a message of support for leftist David Last's leadership push which reads: 'Now is the time for all good parties to come to the aid of the man.'

There is, however, one crucial difference between *Bill Brand* and *All Good Men* and it is this: *Bill Brand* differentiates much more sharply between the Labour Party and groupings to the left of it. The central character unequivocally rejects British Trotskyism as a way forward and, unlike his namesake in *All Good Men*, he remains theoretically committed to the belief that Labour can be won for socialism. There are a number of reasons for this apparent political realignment on Griffiths' part. *All Good Men* was written before the publication of *Labour's Programme 1973*, the most radical policy document the party had produced since 1945 and, potentially at least, a genuine blueprint for socialist transformation which confirmed Labour's steady move leftwards since its 1970 election defeat. A Labour government, albeit a right-wing one with a slender majority, had been elected on the basis of *Programme 1973*. The rank-and-file militancy of the late 60s and early 70s had subsided, drawing many activists back into the ambit of the Labour Party – this is the period in which 'entryism' gets under way again in earnest. Moreover, *Bill Brand* was conceived as a popular drama series in a primetime slot, so in television terms there were obvious pressures on Griffiths to contain his leftist perspective within a Labour Party framework, and hence within the parliamentary parameters of electoral politics.

'BILL BRAND': GENESIS OF A SERIES

All Good Men was transmitted in its truncated form on the evening of 31 January 1974. The following day the result was announced of the crucial miners' ballot about stepping up the overtime ban which they were then enforcing. 81 per cent authorised the National Union of Miners Executive to call an all-out strike, promptly scheduled to begin a week later. Within those seven days, Edward Heath was forced to set an election for 28 February.

Political debate was defined, on television as elsewhere, by the question of a 'strong' Government versus the demands of the unions. 'The choice before the nation today, as never before,' the Tory manifesto asserted, 'is a choice between moderation and extremism.' Constructed from an opposing viewpoint, with a different vocabulary, this was also to be a central dynamic of *Bill Brand*. As Brand says, 'I have these two voices . . . They say: might, right; power, principle; pragmatism, precept; slow, quick; one day, now . . .' Such was the choice before at least part of the nation. That February, however, 'the nation' found it hard to make up its mind. For the first time since 1929 no party gained an overall majority. A weekend of talks between the Conservatives and the Liberals failed to bring forth a coalition and

Harold Wilson formed the first minority Labour government since 1931.

On election night, Griffiths met for the first time the independent television drama producer Stella Richman, in the bar of Mayfair's 'White Elephant' restaurant, which she owned. They watched television coverage of the results together, and she later told the *Daily Express*: 'Suddenly the idea came and I asked him if he would like to do a series about the beginnings of life of a Labour MP.' 'We sat up until three in the morning,' she explained, 'trying to get the bones of something. Within a week he had the notes on paper. The man has the mind of a filing cabinet. It is the equivalent of a novel.'[3]

Griffiths himself has remembered the series' genesis in different terms: 'Stella Richman had seen *The Party* and wanted to talk to me . . . She met me in a restaurant-club of hers on the river, which I'd never been to before, and it was full of those reactionary showbiz people, who'd all had a bet with Ladbrokes on the Tories pulling it off. And, as the evening progressed and the results came out, it was amazing to watch these fuckers break down in tears and begin wailing. It was remarkable. I remember Stella said, would you consider doing an extended series for television? And I said, yeah. Then I went for a piss and listened to a couple of guys moaning about the political future, came out and said, what about something on politics, in Parliament? She said, great idea, and commissioned the pilot.'[4] The subsequent detailed research and writing of the eleven hour-long episodes were to occupy Griffiths for much of the next two years, and the scripting continued well into the production process.

In 1971 Stella Richman had been appointed Controller of Programmes at London Weekend Television after Michael Peacock, the company's first Controller, was fired by the board. This was a particularly difficult time for the company and she too left a year later. Backed by money from a former LWT partner, David Frost, she then established herself as an independent drama producer, investing in and packaging projects which she later sold to the TV companies to be made by their production staff. Her series *Jennie*, a costume drama about Lady Randolph Churchill, had been a particular success for Thames Television.

'Stella was going to do *Bill Brand* as a kind of independent production,' recalls Stuart Burge, who became the series' producer, re-establishing a working relationship with Griffiths forged on *Absolute Beginners*. 'But in those days that never worked out, with the complete dominance of the big companies. So I was brought in when some of the scripts were there and we all went to Thames with it. And Stella sold the whole idea to Verity Lambert.'[5]

After a successful career herself as a drama producer, Verity Lambert had recently been appointed Thames' Controller of Drama by Jeremy Isaacs. Isaacs, as Director of Programmes, and Lambert began with a long-term strategy. In Isaacs' words, 'She and I said let us do drama in the next couple of years that will make everybody sit up and take notice.'[6] Ratings and advertising revenue in the early 70s were both buoyant and a company like Thames could afford to take some risks, even though the executives were certain that demanding contemporary drama would not pull high peak-time ratings. When Verity Lambert started at Thames she made two important decisions: no costume drama in the first eighteen months, and a commitment to drama with a London base. She wanted 'a kind of style and a kind of feeling about our drama which meant it couldn't have come from any other company, it had to come from a London company.'

'I don't know whether that entirely worked,' she admitted three years after the event. 'But what those two decisions did bring forward in the first year was the first series of *Rock Follies*, *Bill Brand* and *Plays for Britain* (six single plays written by, among others, Stephen Poliakoff, Roy Minton and Peter Prince), which were attempting in one way or another to tackle modern problems and life.'[7]

Griffiths saw the project as a clear complement to his writing on revolution: 'It seemed an important thing to do, if you're talking about politics in Britain now, to examine and to explore social democracy as well as revolutionism. What I've tried to do is present as full a picture as I can of a Member's life in all its complexity and its density. So I spend quite a lot of time in the constituency, quite a lot of time in Parliament, in committee, in the desk room, the bar, wherever. We're investigating the stuff, the actual tissue and texture, of the social democratic processes within a major party. About which people know next to nothing. They really don't.'[8] (It is worth bearing in mind that Griffiths was once a teacher of liberal studies in a technical college and that this involved taking courses in what was then known as civics: the study of the constitutional and institutional workings of democracy, including the operations of Parliament.)

Stuart Burge is certain that Thames were surprised by this educative function and the density of the drama and that these factors accounted for the series' rather more stormy than usual production period: 'Thames took it on, typically I believe, thinking it was going to be a series about a politician in the same way that they'd just had a series about a private detective . . . So it was a nightmare getting it through. I'd spend a great many days quite acrimoniously saying you bought the series, we cannot cut it to this kind of budget. It's terrible

73

working under those kinds of conditions.' The series was also one of the first to be shot with a location video camera, and this caused frequent technical difficulties. 'But those were minor problems,' Burge says. 'And I must say the Thames staff absolutely adored doing it. It was such a change for them to do something really quite serious like that. All the crew was excellent.'[9]

Griffiths, too, feels that the production experience was one of the most fruitful that he has encountered within television: 'Something very important occurred on *Bill Brand*. Partly because we were in production for so long – we were rehearsing *Bill Brand*, thinking *Bill Brand*, acting *Bill Brand*, it was *Bill Brand* and nothing else, week in and week out . . . There was a very collective shape to the whole enterprise.' He also feels that the unconventional production arrangement worked, in the end, to the series' advantage. 'There was conflict between the Stella Richman organisation and Thames and we sheltered under that conflict, so while they were working out their problems, we were able to work out ours. And there was just extraordinary purchase on the imagination and spirit of the people who were involved.'[10]

While the series was in production, in the late autumn of 1975, Granada transmitted *The Nearly Man*, a series written by Arthur Hopcraft which also dealt with the life of a Labour MP. *The Nearly Man* had different concerns and a different politics, since Hopcraft's Member was on the right-wing of the Party. And in a later review, the then Labour MP Christopher Price wrote, 'Hopcraft took a snapshot: Griffiths has tried to portray a political odyssey.'[11] None the less the similarity was close enough to threaten *Bill Brand*'s chances of a primetime network slot. The ITV Controllers' committee wanted it to go out at 10.30 p.m. in the summer. The production team were adamant that it had to be shown at 9.00 p.m. Usually the Controllers would have overridden this wish, despite Jeremy Isaacs' passionate backing for the series. Then, as Griffiths recalls it, 'We put the word out and something like seventy people turned up for this meeting with Isaacs on the rehearsal room floor and he got a lot thrown at him . . . He took an hour or so of verbal punishment and he went back and fought for 9 o'clock, which we got, in the summer.'[12]

So eventually episode one of *Bill Brand* went out on Monday night 7 June 1976 in a slot previously occupied by an American thriller series, *Manhunt*. Preceding it in the schedule was *World in Action*; and directly after it came *News at Ten*, which it was to parallel fortuitously on several occasions in the coming weeks.

The decision to write an extended drama series about a newly elected left-wing Labour MP immediately provided Griffiths with a ready-made dialectical structure. Brand's parliamentary career brings him into conflict with the party establishment and its bureaucracy at virtually every level: in his constituency; in the trade union movement; and at Westminster. His differences are less marked, but no less forcefully expressed, with those on the Left: the 'Journal' group; his would-be mentor, David Last; and even his closest ally, National Executive member Winnie Scoular. Brand is, in other words, the classic loner, a cross between the alienated protagonists of the European novel tradition and the laconic heroes of Hollywood cinema. He is described both by his friends and his enemies as a 'maverick' – he comes, as it were, out of left of field in every sense. His actions are thus always open to a purely 'psychological' reading, and it was the combination of this sort of conventional television storytelling technique with a fairly sophisticated level of political debate that gave the series its highly distinctive stamp – and, its critics would argue, its limitations. From the opening scenes, which establish Brand as a husband and a father, there is a determination to use elements of the TV family drama to sugar the pill of politics in primetime.

Brand is presented as operating out of a recognised domestic context: he has a wife, two young children, a mortgage on a semi-detached house in a modern suburb and an extended family group in the old inner-city area of the Greater Manchester constituency of 'Leighley'. On polling day of the by-election that takes him to Westminster, we see him moving from the family breakfast table to his parents' terraced house, to a meeting with his brother (a local textile worker). We know next to nothing about his politics at this stage but already we are identifying with him *personally*. Critics of *Bill Brand* are quick to point out that this tends to mean that Brand's politics always remain essentially peripheral to the dramatic experience offered by the series – 'my hero right or wrong' as David Edgar put it.[13] This is to underestimate the problems involved in attempting to reach and hold a mass audience familiar with these kinds of conventions, and probably poorly disposed to the idea of a series about politics in a slot normally occupied by 'entertainment' drama: crime series, love stories, thrillers. It is also to fail to recognise that Brand's home life – his rocky marriage, his complicated relationship with his lover and his feelings of guilt towards his brother – though clearly the stuff of family drama and an important element in the series' ratings appeal, does not just supplement his political activity but offers parallels that comment on it. Griffiths is, that is to say, again in the business of exploring a 'personal politics'. The connecting link through which this parallelism is articulated is Alex, Brand's feminist lover. It is through her that Brand begins to embrace a political perspective that extends beyond the narrow confines of parliamentary Labourism. Indeed, it is one of the series' great weaknesses that this strand, and its contradictory links back to Brand's domestic arrangements, should have been phased out – leaving many of the issues it raised unresolved – to make way for the dramatic climax of the Labour leadership struggle and Brand's role in it.

What is perhaps most immediately striking about *Bill Brand* over and above its blending of the personal and the political, genre television and documentary realism, is its *contemporaneity*. Written in 1975–6, it contours itself closely on real events both inside and outside the Labour Party during the same period. Its eleven parts span just over one year – from the late winter by-election in Leighley, through the summer recess and autumn party conference, to the leadership battle in the spring of the following year – and a number of 'references' make it clear that the year in question is 1975–6: the reduced size of Labour's majority, the resignation of the Prime Minister, the IMF crisis. Griffiths himself, however, no doubt partly for legal reasons, denied any specific contemporary parallels. In an interview in *Streetlife*, he described the series as a 'fictional meta-world, where you can identify, not so much people, as stances. Which are much more important than people. For example, there might be what is now called a Wilsonian stance, or a Michael Foot stance, or a Roy Jenkins stance. But the people who occupy those stances in the series are not those people.'

Yet, *pace* the author's understandable reticence, there are clear *roman à clef* elements in *Bill Brand*. And because ideological differences within the Labour Party tend to find expression – or at least a public profile – through personalities, they are in many ways indispensable to an understanding of the series. Brand himself represents a current rather than any individual: the new wave of younger, broadly Marxist, Labour leftists who began to win seats in the 1970s. Something about him, though, intermittently suggests one of the great backbench mavericks of the 1974–9 Labour government: Jeff Rooker, the MP for Birmingham Perry Barr. David Last, on the other hand, doyen of the left-wing 'Journal' group – for which read Tribune group – is unmistakably a Michael Foot figure. A man of letters (the author of books on William Morris and Tom Mann) with thirty years experience on the Left of the Party and a home among the Hampstead literati, he is – just to clinch the parallel – a somewhat reluctant Minister for Employment in the Watson government. Watson himself, of course, with his brusque style and pragmatic stewardship of the Party is not a million miles removed from Harold Wilson, although Arthur Lowe's comically bluff playing of the part undoubtedly is. Alan Badel's Last is equally removed from its obvious model – too svelte and cynically astute by half. Not so Peter Howell's John Venables, Watson's Home Secretary and a cross between the two figures who represent the Party's Gaitskellite revisionist wing: Tony Crosland, its ideologue, and Roy Jenkins, its electoral heir apparent. Howell's mincing Home Counties intonation and the odd highly distinctive inflection on words such as (ironically) 'party' are more than accidentally redolent of the former Home Secretary, and like Jenkins also he is a part-time historian. On the other hand a certain steely resolve in Venables' pursuit of the revisionist grail – Labour transformed into a cross-class Party of the social democratic centre – plays with an image of Crosland. This leaves the much more sketchily drawn Denis Healey figure of Kersley, the belligerent Foreign Secretary, to represent the last major element in Labour's political coalition: the Right.

Other figures are less easy to identify or decipher as composites, though on the Left it is possible to see something of Tony Benn in leadership contender Trevor Brent; of Frank Allaun and Ian Mikardo in Reg Starr, Chairman of the Journal group; and of Joan Maynard, Joan Lestor and perhaps even Jo Richardson in Winnie Scoular. On the Right, the Jim Wilks figure seems to approximate to that of James Callaghan, even though his 'compromise' candidacy for the leadership fails. Interestingly, although Labour's actual leadership election following Harold Wilson's 1976 resignation took place in March, only three months before the series went out, Griffiths made no attempt to incorporate the result. Time was obviously a factor. But even if rewrites had been feasible, it seems unlikely that Griffiths would have scuppered his own very different scenario of a victory for the 'Jenkinsite' Centre-Right. And in this sense one sees why in interviews at the time he sought to play down the more immediate contemporary resonances: the latter half of *Bill Brand* is an elaborate attempt to dramatise the deep-seated contradictions within the Labour Party that would eventually give rise to the breakaway Social Democratic Party.

This remarkably prescient structure – which in many ways takes over and reroutes the whole series in the final episodes – helps to give *Bill Brand* a weight and substance far in excess of Granada's superficially similar saga, *The Nearly Man*. Even with hindsight, *Bill Brand*'s central political concerns do not seem dated. Griffiths' alternative title for the series had, in fact, been *Towards the Recent Future*. As he explained in the *Streetlife* interview: 'Out of the recency [sic] of political events, you can actually project a certain line through into the future.'[14]

BRAND: HIS POLITICS AND HIS PARTY

As a character, Brand's background is hazy, but there are clearly elements of autobiography in Griffiths' portrayal: the dying father (a chemical process worker like his own), the older, unreachable brother (a shirtmaker like his own), and Brand's background in Liberal Studies. In these and other senses, Brand's Leighley constituency is very much a *personal* fiction, an imaginative projection of the East Manchester in which Griffiths grew up, and the references suggest a familiar 'structure of feeling' being articulated alongside the more obviously public concerns of the series. In this respect, it is surely significant that Brand's wife is called Miriam: the name of Paul Morel's first girlfriend in Lawrence's *Sons and Lovers*, perhaps the classic fictional expression in English of working-class family life and a text that seems to be never very far away from Griffiths' concerns, from which he 'quoted' liberally in *Sam, Sam*, and which he would adapt for BBC2 in 1981.

Brand has been a Trotskyist, a member of the International Socialists in the days before the grouping became the Socialist Workers Party. But in episode eight he makes it clear that he has decisively rejected their politics (IS formally abandoned work inside the Labour Party in 1965). Griffiths' portrayal of Brand's former colleagues is far from sympathetic; at a constituency social evening they are depicted as beer-swilling louts. Before his selection Brand has been active but not particularly prominent within his constituency Labour Party. Projecting a history for him, it seems certain that he would have been a supporter of the comprehensive and radical statement of Party policy, *Labour's Programme 1973*. Devised by the Organisation Sub-Committee of the NEC and by leading members of the TUC, this left-oriented document was built round a call for the nationalisation of twenty-five major companies. Soon after its publication, Harold Wilson decisively rejected this call. But Brand, in his first 'political' statement of the series – to a radio interviewer on polling day – is unequivocal on this point: 'I'm a socialist, of the sort that Bernard Levin and his trail-blazing claque would describe as reactionary. I actually believe in public ownership of the means of production, distribution and exchange.'

It was the rejection by the leadership of *Labour's Programme* which prompted many activists to begin work within the Party for constitutional change, work which was to culminate in the 1979 Conference victory on mandatory reselection and the changes in the leadership election system decided at the Wembley conference in 1981. Indeed, the overall project of *Bill Brand*, with its concern to *understand* the Party, can be seen to emerge from the same fundamental frustration which prompted the activities of the Campaign for Labour Party Democracy (founded June 1973) and other groupings, with their intention to *change* the Party.

Brand, however, is not aligned with those campaigns, although his repeated rebuffs can be read as illustrating the paramount need for change. At the end, he is pushed towards a wider conception of struggle than constitutional tinkerings, or even the parliamentary process. 'It's not what's going to happen here,' he tells a despondent Journal group meeting, after Venables' win. 'It's what's going to happen – and we can help make happen – out there, that's going to make the difference as far as our new leader is concerned.' Throughout he represents a 'pure' radicalism, the uncompromised core of socialism with its long tradition of struggle. References to this tradition recur: William Morris, Tom Mann, the 1889 Dock Strike, Spain, Nye Bevan. As his name suggests, Brand carries the torch of such men and their victories.

On each episode the opening titles hammer this point home: a fast track in to the Labour Party symbol above the door of the Leighley HQ; newsreel scenes of industry and militant action inside the symbol's circle culminating in a shot of Brand with Big Ben behind him; back to the symbol, then in again on the flames of the torch which blaze up and mix to a close-up of Brand. The 'brand' association is exceptionally literal.

The tight structure of the series, as already observed, spans and reflects a single calendar year in the life of the 1974–9 Labour government. Beginning with a mid-session by-election, which records a 5 per cent swing against the government, it takes us through Brand's initiation into the Westminster round – finding desk space, learning to cope with the Whip system, arranging a 'pairing', acclimatising to the atmosphere of forced bonhomie in the tea-room. Later we see how Parliamentary sessions are wound up and how they resume with the Queen's Speech; we are shown the workings of the Left-caucus Journal group; the mechanics of how bills pass through committee stages; and how Party conferences and leadership elections are organised. There are also glimpses of the Cabinet at work, though the floor of the House of Commons itself remains off limits throughout.

At the constituency level, we are taken inside the less glamorous workings of the local Party machine: the role of the agent, the function of the General Management Committee, the logistics of getting the vote out on polling day. Leighley's inner-city demographic mix gives Brand and Alf, his long-suffering agent, a number of headaches which neatly illustrate how specific electoral politics at a local level can be. Brand's stand on abortion in episode four, for instance, has to be toned down because the Leighley electorate contains a large Catholic component. On the other hand, the fact that the constituency also contains a number of textile mills threatened with closure helps Brand to take a radical stance on the government's failed industrial policy.

Brand's odyssey through the series can profitably be seen as a progress through distinct layers of the Labour Party. He starts in his constituency, then moves to the back-benches and on to the Journal group and, in a different direction, to contact with the Party's industrial base. Drawn up to ministerial level, he witnesses the leadership contest, and then returns to the constituency with an understanding of the new connections to be made. At each stage he is preoccupied by his ineffectualness and ultimately he recognises the inadequacy, and yet paradoxically also the necessity, of his actions. The strands of drama associated with each of these layers intertwine in a complex pattern and are temporarily fixed at specific moments in the life of the Party: a factory occupation, Conference, the committee stage of a bill. Additionally, threaded among these are his relationships with his family and with Alex, this latter carrying the series' central metaphor of impotence.

The series begins with his family but, from the opening frames, Brand is defined as apart from them, literally *outside* the home of his wife and children. The first shot of episode one has him sitting in his car listening to the local radio station setting the background to polling day. He looks towards his house, sees signs of activity and goes in to breakfast. Conversation with Miriam (played by Lynn Farleigh) is tense, but he is obviously close to his children, Jane and Michael. A frosty exchange with Miriam ends with his request for her to 'put in an appearance later on'. She promises nothing.

Communication with other members of his family is similarly distant. Looking for more transport to take voters to the polls, he visits his brother Eddie, who has forgotten that it is polling day. Eddie offers no help. 'It's hopeless tonight, Bill – we're playing top of the league at snooker, Conservative Club.' Nor is he closer to his mother, who has also forgotten about the by-election, as she looks after her dying husband. Only with his father does Brand establish an intimacy. As he lies in bed, he quietly exhorts his son, 'Do someat *good*, won't you.'

At the Party election HQ, Miriam does turn up and for the evening a closeness grows between them, which Brand destroys when, after he has won, he phones Alex. Miriam enters the room as he is on the phone, and explodes at his selfishness. Later, as they drive home, she says that she wants a divorce and tells him not to come in. Consequently he spends the night with Alex, and asks her if she would marry him. She declines. Several days later he is driving down to London with the car radio on. The local station is carrying an interview recorded with Miriam on polling day, in which she praises Brand's qualities. 'It's very difficult to put it into words without sounding pompous – he's trying to be a good man.' The irony is underlined with a brisk cut to the end credits.

As well as sketching the necessary background, establishing Brand as a 'human' figure and exploiting the conventions of primetime family drama, these scenes in the first programme also introduce a theme which remains oddly undeveloped in subsequent episodes: Brand's guiding rationality and his repressed emotionalism. His mother observes that he never was an emotional person, and as he argues with Miriam he accuses her of not being interested in rational solutions. 'Rational solutions,' she responds. 'Oh my God – life isn't a series of resolutions to National Conference.' She also says he suppresses his feelings. Brand's passions, it seems, are channelled into his politics. Only once is the point referred to subsequently. In episode four, he and Alex make love, after which she says: 'You never make a sound; you should read some Reich.'

Brand's relationship with Miriam remains a constant counterpoint to the political drama of the series. In the second episode he is jealous at the thought of her sleeping with someone else; in the fourth he reluctantly submits to the instigation of divorce proceedings. But he remains devoted to Jane and Michael, takes them to the summer school at Ruskin College and encourages their non-formal education. (Episode seven, in a slightly arch comment on gender roles, has Brand helping Jane to mend her bike while Michael is baking tarts for tea.) His protectiveness towards the children, and to Miriam, is seen in his rapid response when their house is attacked after his controversial 'terrorism' speech. In the final two episodes, he has accepted that Jane and Michael will be happy with a step-father, and he and Miriam have made their peace.

The other familial ties feature less prominently, as his father dies at the end of episode two and is buried in the subsequent programme. Recognising the imminence of his death, Brand speaks admiringly about him to Winnie Scoular, and reflects that he refused to talk politics. 'Probably votes Conservative out of respect,' Brand says. His stoical mother does not reappear until the penultimate episode, when she remarries.

Eddie has a more significant role in the drama. Made redundant from his job as a shirt-cutter – even as Brand is fighting to prevent closures in the textile industry – he, like his father, appears to lack a politics. At the end of episode eight, Bill goes to see him, and finds him playing cribbage at the Leighley Conservative Club, where he is a member and on friendly terms with the barman. Although he has almost automatically always voted Labour, Eddie is now deeply disillusioned. 'There are blokes round here who've been unemployed for two years or more,' he says. 'They won't be voting Labour next time, I can tell you. Neither will I.' He sees himself as powerless and the unions as useless. Bill responds that he has to struggle, for example by joining the Fight for Work campaign. 'Struggle?' Eddie laughs. 'What good would that do? I mean when it comes down to it we're just a bloody rabble, aren't we?' But Bill stresses that he needs the power which Eddie and others can give him. Two episodes later, Eddie almost sheepishly admits that Bill's arguments won him over and that he was on the recent Fight for Work demonstration. At the march he met a friend of Bill's, the regional organiser Albert Stead, who fought with the Republicans in Spain. 'And he's still bloody fighting, isn't he?' Eddie says with respect and a new self-confidence.

'WE'RE ALL YOU'VE GOT, COMRADE': LEIGHLEY

Albert Stead, as his name suggests, is the solid base of the movement, 'still bloody fighting' within the Party and outside; as is the more central character, Brand's lugubrious and pragmatic agent Alf Jowett, the heart of the Leighley CLP. On polling day, he takes complete charge; Bill's presence is merely jovially tolerated. But his initial wariness of Brand gives way to a respect which the MP fully reciprocates. Jowett, after all, is enormously experienced, has written a book on the conduct of elections, has given his life to the Party. He offers his support for Brand's principled positions, as long as he feels such support is reflected within the constituency. Early on, he 'rigs' an extraordinary CLP Executive meeting, which is called to consider a vote of censure on Brand for voting against the Government. The constituency, Jowett feels, favours or at least understands Brand's action. But later, after the 'terrorism' speech, he exposes the MP to the local Party's full fury. An MP must remain close to and accountable to the people. 'They *are* the Party, Bill. You'd do well not to forget it.'

Despite his disapproval of Brand's personal life, Jowett is

The local party machine: Albert Stead (John Barrett), Brand (Jack Shepherd), Frank Hilton (Clifford Kershaw) and Alf Jowett (Allan Surtees).

sympathetic and protective, especially when the press chase him about his involvement in the abortion issue. But he demands in return a full allegiance to the constituency, particularly during a summer recess dominated by rumours of an autumn election. In episode five, Jowett briefs Brand on engagements to judge a beauty contest, to attend a Masonic Lodge banquet, and to award a Young Executive of the Year prize 'What is this *shit*?' an incredulous Brand asks. 'I'll tell you what this *shit* is,' Alf Jowett says. 'It's your bread and butter, iron rations for the duration. I don't give a monkey's tosser what your personal views on masons or beauty contests are, because the object of the exercise is not to set you at ease with your sodding conscience but to get you a platform and win a few votes if there's an election this autumn.'

In the next episode, both MP and agent attend the Annual Conference. On the first evening, a drunken, maudlin Jowett remembers attending his first Conference twenty years before. Twenty years of sacrifice to the Party, twenty years of not seeing his kids, of a growing distance from his wife. 'So what have we achieved?' he asks, to himself as much as to Brand. 'Twenty years of struggling and arguing and wheedling and bullying and hustling and chiselling and welching and offering and not delivering. Jesus Christ.' Later in the week, Brand gets his motion on the textile industry passed, and both he and Jowett are exuberant. But the perennial Griffiths concern remains: the clash between a – perhaps ineffective – political commitment and the expression of full personal relationships.

None the less, Alf Jowett's faith in the people and in socialism remains unshakeable. Albert Stead expresses the former most effectively with a story about Gorky. Brand states his scepticism about looking over his shoulder 'to see what the people are going to say'. Stead reminds him that Gorky once went to lecture the Russian peasants. Arriving in the back of beyond, he looked about him and asked, 'Is this the rabble on which we are to build a revolution?' 'And the answer is yes, Mr Gorky,' Albert Stead says, 'and yes, Mr Brand. Because without them there is no revolution. We're all you've got, comrade.' Jowett himself affirms his socialism in the final episode. 'Capitalism is the structure, the reality,' he says. 'And it splits us up, sets us against each other in classes, in thought, in life-style, in aspirations and all the rest of it. But it breeds resistance – in every worker who goes down the road, in every tenant who's evicted, in every man and woman who's denied the chance to be human.'

Much of Brand's dealings with his constituency are focused on Alf Jowett. But two particular issues, both with local and national dimensions, are highlighted separately: abortion, and the economics of the textile industry. In episode four, a local woman with three children visits Brand's constituency surgery. Her husband has left her, she is pregnant again, but she has been refused an abortion. Brand promises to help if he can. He visits her gynaecologist and finds a right-wing Catholic and a fanatical anti-abortionist. Griffiths wrote the episode as the regressive and ultimately unsuccessful James White Abortion Act Amendment Bill was being put before Parliament, but he develops the wider resonances of the issue and pinpoints a fundamental contradiction in Labour Party philosophy. For in episode five, Brand has obtained – perhaps even paid for – a private abortion for the woman. Alf Jowett shields him from a rapacious local and national press, which has heard rumours of the story, but privately the agent is furious. There are 23,000 Catholics in Leighley, he points out, and most of them vote Labour. So, facing the possibility of an autumn election, Brand is forced to compromise his public statements. Concurrently, Winnie Scoular tells him that she also has had an abortion, and that the child had not been her husband's. Again – although the point is only sketched – Griffiths alludes to the interconnections of personal emotions and political involvement; as he does also with the character of Bill and Winnie's colleague Tom Mapson, whose wife dies of cancer and who later suffers a serious heart attack.

84

Brand's fight on behalf of the textile industry runs through most of the episodes, and binds together the depiction of the life of the backbencher and of the Party's industrial base. His first contact with the latter as an MP comes in episode three, when he receives a union deputation from Bryants, a factory threatened with closure in his constituency. Subsequently frustrated at meetings with other MPs from textile constituencies, with the employers' federation and with the responsible government department, Brand collars the Minister outside the House of Commons bar. Ruffled at Brand's directly physical challenge about closures and a three-day week in the industry, the Minister can still only offer platitudes: 'It's a contracting industry, some redundancies are inevitable.' Then the Minister informs Brand that the workers at Bryants have occupied the factory that afternoon.

Brand leaves immediately for the occupation and is joined by Alf Jowett and a local union official, who is angrily sent away at the gates. The organisers explain that they are staging a work-in; Brand offers to speak to the men. In a rousing speech (impressively caught by director Michael Lindsay-Hogg in one long tracking shot through the listening workers), Brand pledges his total support for their action. 'And I will do everything I can to see that the fight is represented in Parliament,' he promises. 'Because I can offer no allegiance to a government of a Party that will allow closures and redundancies to occur when they have pledged themselves repeatedly not to use unemployment as a means of solving the present economic climate. One final word of advice, brothers and sisters, make sure you win.' He had believed that the press had been kept out, but as he closes, a flashbulb pops. Next day the *Daily Express* carries a picture with the headline 'Rebel MP Lashes Government'.

In episode four, Brand takes the Employment Minister David Last to the factory. Already there are signs that the workers are not gathering the support they need. Nor can Last provide more than the government's sympathy, and the promise of a full review. The union fails to back the occupation, and it collapses. Up to this point the main remedy suggested for the industry's problems is the imposition of tighter quotas on textile imports. But there is also a recognition of the effects of these quotas on already appallingly exploited workers overseas. So in episode six Brand takes a motion to Conference which proposes a restructuring of the industry, bringing it in whole or in part into public ownership. Brand has to fight for this at a compositing meeting where he is opposed by the textile union representative, who argues for a reduction in quotas to protect jobs. Brand's more radical motion is eventually accepted by other constituencies, but not by the union, and he has to fight again – this time with a speech criticising the NEC – to get it put before Conference.

The Blackpool Conference also provides the setting for Brand's introduction to transport union leader Willie Moores, whose support is being sought by the government for a critical conference vote. At a dinner hosted by David Last, Brand witnesses Moores' sparring with Prime Minister Watson, with the union leader looking for confirmation that there will not be an early election. He and the PM hammer out a deal, but Last later points out that Watson had started the election rumours himself so as to be able to quash them to gain the support of Moores and others. Moores duly makes a critical speech but expresses his underlying confidence in the government. Much to Brand's surprise, Moores also casts his union's votes for Brand's textile resolution, ensuring its success. Puzzled, Brand asks Last why he received such unexpected backing. 'I don't know,' Last muses, 'perhaps he wanted to record one principled action in an otherwise thoroughly nasty week's dealing.'

Moores appears again in episode ten, when Brand and Albert Stead go in a deputation with the Fight for Work campaign organiser to see the TUC General Secretary. He and Moores receive them reluctantly and, like the government earlier, the TUC offers only 'sympathy'. The organiser states how he will convey this to the march outside: 'The TUC will continue to turn a blind eye on the situation for as long as this reactionary Labour government tells it to.' Despite the recent victory of the revisionists, Moores says he feels the government should be supported for some months more. Then he rounds on Brand for suggesting that he is not representing the interests of his workers. In a passionate outburst, he recalls how he and his late father fought against Franco's fascists. 'Now I didn't fight, and he didn't die, so that I could come back and betray my own class, O.K.?'

As the critic Edward Braun points out in his analysis of *Bill Brand*: 'His words are moving, unanswerable – but Bill replies by asking disingenuously if the plans for dock nationalisation still stand: it is Moores who is silenced, and he leaves glowering, without a word. The point is underscored as the camera pans from him to rest briefly on a portrait of Lord Citrine in peer's robes. Moores is discredited yet the memory of his passionate and sincere outburst persists: another contradiction that has to be faced.'[15]

'QUITE A LITTLE SHIT': OPPOSING FROM THE BACK-BENCHES

Despite the detail with which it is treated, industry is only one element in the portrait of Brand's work as a back-bencher. On his

'You won't see it, Bill, but we've changed this country': Chief Whip Cedric Maddocks (Peter Copley) with Bill Brand (Jack Shepherd).

arrival at the House, he is contacted by the Whips' office and his stormy relationship with them is a constant theme in subsequent episodes. Brand determines to vote according to his principles and not to be treated as 'lobby fodder'. The Whips see it differently. As one of them stresses at his first meeting with Brand: 'The Government has a right to your loyalty, total, unquestioning if necessary . . . I don't suppose I need to spell out the powers of this office, do I?' 'No, no,' Brand replies sharply, 'I used to teach the history of our constitution, charting the growth of our freedoms . . .' Brand quickly recognises the need for the co-operation of the Whips, even to get matters raised with a Minister. He also soon experiences their wrath, after he is the only MP to ignore a three-line whip on a Government public spending cuts bill. Summoned like a naughty schoolboy to the prefects' study, Brand is treated with contempt by the senior Whip, Cedric Maddocks. 'Well – you're quite a little shit, aren't you, Brand,' Maddocks greets him, as director Roland Joffé underwrites the formal qualities of the disciplinary ritual with a high-angle, almost overhead shot.

Continuing tension with the Whips comes to a head in episode seven. By voting with the Government at the second reading of a 'Further Prevention of Terrorism Bill', with which he fundamentally disagrees, Brand has secured a place on the committee to consider suggested detailed amendments. Brand himself has put forward an amendment which the pushy young Whip Jeremy Sandiford asks him to withdraw. He refuses and settles to watch the preliminary skirmishes between the Home Secretary and the Tory opposition, who supported the bill at its second reading.

The political background is of Irish bomb attacks in England, which are referred to as a 'wave of terror' organised by 'men of blood'. Brand personally is feeling particularly powerless. As he tells Alex, 'I'm left doing these hundreds of little things, some marginally valuable, some silly, some ugly but necessary, some hugely idiotic.' The specific 'little thing' with the bill is an amendment to reduce the period during which suspects can be detained without trial from the specified ten days to just three days. The Tories are asking for it to be raised to fourteen; and the Home Secretary suggests Brand's amendment is contrary to the whole spirit of the bill. None the less it is called, and Brand takes the opportunity to deliver a wide-ranging rhetorical attack on the government (and on capitalism).

He begins with a preliminary snipe at the Whips' system: 'the polite fiction that a member is responsible for his vote is a piece of cant that even Ministers should be able to recognise.' More pertinently, he points out the erosion of democratic freedoms, the growing strength of the police, and the use of powers of arrest and deportation to silence trades unionists and political militants. He stresses that 'the politics of terror, of bombing, is a bankrupt politics', but shifts the ground of the debate: 'The problem of Ireland will not be solved by passing anti-democratic laws in Britain. The problem of Ireland will be solved by the Irish when the British government acting on behalf of the people relinquishes the imperialist role it has exercised these last three centuries.'

Against increasing vocal opposition, his controlled oratorical fervour continues (in a tone and line of argument that recall Adam Smith's passionate sermon in episode twelve of that series). 'When honourable gentlemen on both sides of the aisle talk about these "men of blood", let them consider *all* the men of blood, not just those who murder with bombs and guns. Let them reflect for a moment on others in our society who might equally bear the soubriquet – currency speculators for example who murder by telephone, who bring the pound down until a Labour government sees sense and gives cast-iron guarantees that it will carry out their policies which inevitably include extended wage standstills, vicious cuts in social spending and a huge increase in the reservoir of the unemployed. Old people will die this winter – thousands of them, of hypothermia – as a direct result of these telephone calls.'

88

His peroration is delivered against uproar throughout the committee room. 'Let us have laws against the capitalists and the employers who have engineered the largest investment strike over the past few years as a means of clubbing a socialist government into accepting capitalist policies. These men kill facelessly, with pen and ink, with telephones and telex machines, but they are men of blood none the less. I beg to move amendment number 84 and I call for it to be put.' Most of the other members are on their feet, some shouting, many waving their order papers. Brand gathers his notes, makes to leave the room but is blocked by a Tory. A quick punch floors the honourable gentleman, and Brand walks out.

This speech prompts threats from a neo-fascist group and an attack on the house where Miriam and the children live. The national press rounds on Brand, particularly as there are further bombs in Manchester, close to his constituency. The local Party is equally outraged, and Brand retreats to the country with Alex to consider whether he should resign. Both the need for and the total inadequacy of the speech are never in doubt.

LAST CHANCE: PARLIAMENTARY PRIVATE SECRETARY

Brand is dragged back from the country, and out of his depression, when Last repeats an earlier offer to him to become his Parliamentary Private Secretary. Last knows Watson is about to resign, and he needs Brand, because he admires him (seeing in him a reflection of his younger self) and because he will help to deliver the support of the Journal group.

After an initial wariness, Brand has become a significant member of the group. Several colleagues urge him to join as soon as he enters the House, but he clings to his individuality. He is unimpressed by the records of those from the group who are in office. 'There is a million and a half unemployed out there,' he tells Winnie Scoular when she asks him to join, 'that's not an act of God, that's an act of *government*. People's lives are being sliced into ribbons in this pathetic attempt to shore up this crumbling edifice of British capitalism, which is of course the historic function of this great Party of ours, and comrades, Journal people, preside over it all, locked away behind their collective Cabinet responsibilities, out of reach, on the other side.' Then, after indicating they would vote against the Government spending cuts, the group's MPs negotiate a change of wording and support the slightly altered measure. Brand is left to vote against on his own, for which the group's chairman Reg Starr later apologises. 'That's how it is with loners,' he points out, and again urges Brand to join the group.

'You're all we have': Brand offers his support to David Last (Alan Badel).

He does so, having already moved into a house with three other Journal group MPs. With one, Winnie Scoular, he establishes a close friendship which has to bear a considerable strain during the leadership contest.

David Last, as Employment Secretary, is one of the group's supporters of whom Brand is most critical. 'How's life in the Cabinet?' he asks Last when they are first introduced. 'Bitter,' says Last. 'Good,' replies Brand. After their visit to Bryants, they drink heavily together in Last's hotel room. Brand's scepticism about Last's role prompts justification of his actions. His acceptance of a Cabinet post was a recent decision, after 'thirty-two years of principled refusal.' Why? 'I want to build socialism,' Last stresses, 'but *this* way, because here, now, for us, there is no other.'

Brand remembers what Last has meant to him: 'I read your book on Morris when I was seventeen, your book on Tom Mann a bit later. I've always seen you in a tradition, a fixity, part of an earlier great refusal. Now there's nobody where you were – and there's nobody where you are.' Last explains further: 'I thought if Parliament is the real power in our society, why when we're in office do we slide and squelch about like shysters and milksops when it comes to translating our programmes into reality? A month later Arthur invited me to join the Government and I just felt that I no longer had the right to say no. It doesn't ever just happen. It has to be made, and it has to be led.' Last leaves the room, and Brand switches on the television, to see a flea sucking on human skin. The slightly clumsy symbol refers back to Alex's memory of Brand's earlier characterisation of Parliament: 'a club for fleas, a place where the fleas on the body politic could swap leaps and pirouettes, before returning to their pelts for the serious business of sucking our democratic life-blood.' Brand's justification, then, for his change of mind – 'I've got to do something. Something has to be done' – has been echoed by Last. Together they quote a lengthy passage of T. S. Eliot and, an intimacy established, Brand struggles off into the night.

At Conference, Brand is surprised, and pleased, to be invited to a private supper given by Last. 'Do you think I'm being groomed for office?' he asks Alf Jowett. 'Groomed or gelded,' is the reply. Last does indeed offer him the post of his PPS, and Brand asks for time to consider. After a sticky exchange over dinner, where Brand is repelled by the political horse-trading he witnesses, Arthur Watson gives his approval to the appointment, but Brand does finally reject the offer.

Later in the autumn, with Watson about to resign, Last repeats his request, despite the clamour after Brand's 'terrorism' speech. He confirms that he is going to seek nomination in the inevitable battle for the leadership, and he wants Brand's support: 'There are thousands like you, tens of thousands, full of energy, committed, just beyond the rim. The Party needs you. And if I can't take you there with me, where the hell do I think I'm going anyway?' Again Brand delays before replying, then goes to see Last at Westminster, and agrees. 'It started out no,' he admits. 'I re-read your Tom Mann on the train. A man who hates capitalism as much as you do can't be all bad.' Also the leadership contest is beginning: 'You're all we have. And it's now, isn't it? So it's you.'

Episodes eight and nine, dealing with Watson's resignation and the succession, were apparently scripted well before Harold Wilson announced his decision to step down on 16 March 1976. But when the programmes went out just four months later, they did still appear strangely prescient, indicating the depth and seriousness of Griffiths' detailed preliminary research and discussion within the Party. At that moment Wilson was facing precisely the problems which form the backdrop to *Bill Brand*'s leadership contest. As one history puts it: 'Wilson's critics were ready to argue that the Prime Minister had quit with three major crises looming along the horizon – the economic crisis, including the steady slide of sterling on the foreign exchanges, a deep Left-Right split in the Party and an ever decreasing parliamentary majority which might force an election on the country.'[16]

This too is very much the situation which Griffiths presents, with a choice between the right-wing Venables, the centrist Kersley, and Last. Kersley is at first seen as unstoppable, but Last intends to split the Centre so that he will face Venables in a final ballot. Brand sees the danger: if the gamble is lost, Venables will turn the Party's back on socialism. Last maintains that the risk is worth it: 'All my political life I worked to move this party to the Left. In two days we have the chance to move it further than it's moved in the last fifty years or more. Is that a chance we have the right to pass up?' The economic crisis is compounded by constitutional fears: as the government is a minority one, there is the possibility that the Queen will call on the Tories to form a government. Quick, decisive action is regarded as vital. Last's Machiavellian manoeuvrings ensure that Jim Wilks, another centrist candidate, also allows himself to be put forward. Then Last has to tie up the backing of the Journal group.

The group meets to consider its voting. Winnie Scoular is disappointed that Brand has agreed to be Last's PPS; she sees Last's invitation as a cynical calculation to impress the Left. She also suggests in a speech that Last is not the Left's automatic candidate. If the Left cannot win, she argues, they should at least put forward a truly socialist candidate, perhaps Trevor Brent. Tom Mapson disagrees: 'We should fight as if we mean to win, and that means we should put up our most politically and electorally credible candidate.' Last is delayed, and in his absence Brand is called on to speak. He too argues that a victory is possible. But he poses the question, a win to do what? Last enters the room and stands listening attentively. Brand says that they must seek a commitment to radical policies from whoever they decide to back. Now Last receives a round of applause as he steps forward to address the meeting. The camera executes a dramatic pan through a full circle as Last says simply, 'I've very little to say. Except perhaps, good to be home.' The group acclaims him on their feet.

In the first ballot Wilks is eliminated. As the results are announced, Kersley shouts angrily across to him that he has been used. Last and Brand go to see the Chief Whip, Cedric Maddocks, who has been acting as campaign manager for Wilks. Having deliberately kept them waiting, he rapidly reaches a deal, ensuring Wilks a place as Deputy PM in exchange for his support of Last. Round two sees Kersley narrowly eliminated, and he reacts bitterly to Last's attempt to woo his votes. Last points out that Venables will destroy the Party. Kersley is obdurate: a government led by Last would lead to economic chaos, he claims; in addition, only Venables has the charisma to beat the Tories at the next election; and in any case Venables has offered him the posts of Deputy PM and Foreign Secretary – 'The interests of my section of the Party will be fully represented.'

Kersley adds one final reason: 'If you are returned as the leader of the Party with no overall majority in the House, I don't believe for one moment that the Queen will be advised to send for you.' Brand and Last recognise that they have lost. Cut to a brief post-mortem, as Last confirms to Brand that he will stay on for the moment in Venables' government. He reflects that he could not top Venables' offer to Kersley, since he had already offered the posts to others. But he is more concerned that Kersley actually believed that the Queen would not have sent for Last. 'And yet objectively,' Brand reflects, 'she sat there and never moved a finger.' 'Power indeed,' Last replies. End credits.

The next, penultimate episode illustrates the reactions of the various sections of the Party to Venables' triumph. The Journal group is completely disheartened, and despite Brand's belief that Venables will try to rewrite the Party's programme in the imminent Queen's Speech, they agree to do no more than wait and see. Then the series shifts – for the only significant occasion – away from Brand's immediate experience and on to the Cabinet. There Venables smoothly lays out his plans: public spending cuts, reversal of reflationary measures, open acceptance of a seven per cent level of unemployment as a weapon against inflation, and so forth. Last and one or two others are horrified, and the Chief Whip points out that he could not guarantee the PLP's backing for such measures. Venables accepts this and speaks of looking for support in other parts of the House. As the meeting breaks for tea, David Last shakes his head sadly. 'What are we doing here?' he wonders aloud. Within days he and Trevor Brent have resigned.

In episode eleven the Chief Whip, Cedric Maddocks, is being moved on to the Lords. He and Brand have a last drink together, each acknowledging his respect for the other, and recognising that the Party is now as neither would want it to be. Maddocks defends its achievements: 'You won't see it, Bill, but we've changed this country. *We* have changed this country.' But he is aware of Brand's ambivalence: 'You've got to love this Party. You're in it, of it, but you don't love it. Not family.' Maddocks' deputy, who welcomes the new order, is about to take over, and he breaks their reverie by entering the room to say that the Tories intend to abstain on the Queen's Speech vote. Later Brand watches Venables on TV. He promises a New Deal, and says that his programme has one aim, 'to make this country once again a place of freedom and enterprise and justice . . .'

The final analysis of parliamentary struggle is, then, that at this historical moment it is inadequate as a means of achieving a more equitable, socialist society. Not irrelevant, however, for Brand stays on to fight, preparing to vote against the government in a vote of confidence. But as Griffiths has confirmed, 'What I was trying to say throughout the series was that the traditions of the labour movement were inadequate to take the struggle further, and that we had to discover new traditions or revive even older ones. And that we had to seek connective tissue between electoral party politics, which still has a mystifying mass appeal, and extra-parliamentary socialist activity.'

'POPULAR BUT IMPOTENT': LABOUR'S FAILURE

Throughout the series, a major focus for a discussion of this extra-parliamentary activity is the character of Alex, a worker in the Department of Health and Social Security, a feminist activist and theorist, and Bill's lover. She is also the focus for the series' central metaphor of the inadequacy of parliamentary struggle – Bill's sexual impotence.

Impotence, both sexual and political, is inscribed throughout the text. In the first episode, Brand justifies his decision to enter Parliament saying, 'The illusion that has to be got rid of is the one that says we're all impotent in the face of the juggernaut, the system.' In the next programme, the junior Whip quotes what he says is Nye Bevan: 'Purity is the worst sort of impotence.' Brand replies that it sounds more like Mussolini. In part four, Brand describes the reception given to Last and himself at Bryants: 'Last took a hammering; I remained popular but impotent.'

As the Party and Parliament force tactical compromises on him, Brand's political impotence is translated into a sexual one in his relationship with Alex. He is preparing his speech on Ireland when Alex comes down to London and stays the night. Their love-making is a failure, and afterwards Brand characterises his intellectual conflict: 'I have these two voices in here, I say two, it's never less than two, sometimes it's in the upper thirties . . . might, right – power, principle – pragmatism, precept.' Alex echoes the dialectic: 'Parliament, people.' 'Quick, slow.' 'Consensus, struggle.' 'One day, now. I've stopped feeling real.' 'The logic of being in Parliament is to struggle for power,' he continues. 'It has to be, yet I don't, won't, because I can't. Partly because I suspect that struggle very deeply . . . And partly because I think the parliamentary struggle is illusory, a chimera, mystificatory, circular, perfectly self-contained.'

94

The sexual failure is repeated in the subsequent episode, after Brand and Alex have retreated to the country. Together in the cottage, Alex admits she has been sleeping with other men throughout the summer. Brand is angry, and sad, but recognises that, as she says, she probably has 'moved on'. She accuses Bill of making her feel married, and says she does not want that sort of dependence; she also wants a child. Their conversation degenerates into a bitter argument before they make up, and do finally make love, just 'as friends'. Alex then remains just a memory in the final three episodes.

Alex's feminism until this point has been an important influence on Brand, and has provided both a critique of the traditional Left and a suggestion of one of the important elements in 'taking the struggle further'. Brand himself delivers this critique at the Ruskin summer school on 'Women and Politics'. In a seminar he refers to Lenin's reactionary thoughts on sexuality. 'When it comes down to it, for Lenin as for any normal patriarch, communist or capitalist, things ultimately turn around what is good for the normal *man*.' Later, in a discussion with Venables, he challenges the Home Secretary's complacent description of the Party, pointing out that the domination of women by men 'is as characteristic of parties of the Left as it is of parties of the Right'.

'I've stopped feeling real': Brand's political impotence is paralleled in his relationship with Alex (Cheric Lunghi).

In the previous episode, Brand meets Alex after a discussion, at which she is speaking against a separatist politics for gay liberation. Sexual oppression, she argues, cannot be divorced from political inequalities, from questions of housing and unemployment. As she speaks, the picture mixes to Bill and her making love, providing a graphic visual parallel to the interconnections she is asserting. Afterwards they talk about whether the working class will accept those engaged in sexual liberation struggles as allies in a general fight against oppression. She is optimistic.

In a similar vein, Brand points out at Ruskin that the inadequate, but not unimportant, Sexual Discrimination Act was forced on the Party by a largely autonomous group of women. Here is the kind of extra-parliamentary socialist activity which Griffiths is advocating. But as noted above, and as the writer himself recognises, this strand – together with the complexities of the relationship between Bill and Alex – is not adequately worked through in the final episodes.

The last programme does, however, recognise other forms of this struggle: cultural politics, the Fight for Work campaign, international revolutionary and anti-imperialist movements (signalled by the overheard discussion of two black Africans in the television reception area, and by the references to Chile). Yet the final expression of solidarity, joining the support of Bill's neighbour to the theatre group's singing of 'Venceremos' and a shot of a message from the Fight for Work campaign, remains unconvincing.

THE LIMITS OF NATURALISM

One of the most impressive features of *Bill Brand* is its capacity for dramatising ideological conflict. The final three episodes, in which the leadership contest is used to map out Labour's shifting political terrain, brilliantly anticipate the rise of the SDP out of the Party's revisionist wing. The complex provenance and significance of John Venables' apparently successful attempt to capture Labour for social democracy are dramatised almost exclusively through the shorthand of the parliamentary head-count. Thus, the willingness of the Party to go back down the Gaitskellite road by electing Venables is conveyed largely in terms of the arithmetic of the factional finesse and the trade-off. Venables' own confidence in his ability to drive a coach and horses through any residual commitment to socialism is presented in terms of his appeal to Parliament, to 'countervailing support from the rest of the House' over the heads of the Party. But neatly symbolic as this is of the kind of consensual politics on which the appeal of social democracy depends, it is too straitjacketed by its chosen perspective of parliamentarianism to be able to offer any *analytic* framework. *Bill Brand* conveys very little sense of the social, historical and class forces – as opposed to the political forces – that laid the conditions for an SDP-style split. This limiting focus is part of, and raises questions about, the wider limitations associated with the series' realist form. It is not just that scenes, say, of the Venables Cabinet discussing public spending cuts against the background clamour of a Fight to Work march filing past Downing Street are crude. They display an embarrassingly mechanistic, almost nineteenth-century conception of mass politics and mass struggle: the product of television realism's inability to step outside the demands of studio-manageable verisimilitude.

What we are dealing with in *Bill Brand* is, more accurately, a form of *naturalism*. And its operation is never more apparent than in the key parliamentary sequences. The Palace of Westminster, its rooms and corridors, practices and conventions, emerges as a determining 'environment' in the classical Zolaesque sense. Brand enters a world in which the political, at least as he understands it, has been reconstituted and redefined by the consensual framework of parliamentary procedure. Even the Journal group seems to function in a vacuum, cut off from the wider political forces that ought to be shaping its policy and every bit as much at the whim of the Whips as Labour MPs generally. This is not just the environment of the party hack, the fixer and the smoke-filled room. It is a sophisticated closed system which works to short-circuit Labour MPs from their constituencies – both parliamentary and political – in the name of 'party unity' or 'national interest'.

Partly by accident – studios are cramped spaces – and partly by design – we must assume Griffiths intended this kind of environment to have a thematic function – *Bill Brand*'s naturalistic format can therefore be said to contribute to the kind of overall political understanding offered by the series as a whole. Yet in a crucial sense the series remains limited by its format. For while it is possible to read a critique *into* its naturalistic representation of parliamentary democracy at work, the series itself cannot be said *textually* to produce such a critique. Caught up in the naturalistic minutiae of its subject – the wheeling and dealing, the brinkmanship and finessing of opponents, the whole elaborate political game – *Bill Brand* inhabits its fictional world too convincingly to be able to gain (or offer) any distance on it. In trying 'to occupy the space of all the people I'm talking about', as he told *The Leveller*,[17] Griffiths inevitably falls into the trap of simply 'naturalising' them. For all narrative purposes, and hence most primetime perceptions of the series, Brand's manoeuvrings on behalf of Last and the Left are not differentiated from those of his right-wing opponents. Similarly, within the psychology propounded by the series as a whole, which is to say very much the standard psychology of the popular drama series, it is perfectly possible – and in terms of narrative pleasure perhaps even desirable – to interpret Brand simply as a kind of deviant, a stroppy individual who fits in nowhere. And it becomes easier then to accept, say, the studiously commonsensical discourse of a Venables at face value, as *reasonable* in a way that Brand's is not. Even the sexual narrative, fashionably inflected with feminist elements as it is, ends up in many ways inscribing Brand as a familiar kind of macho hero: the man with a remote wife and a 'demanding' mistress.

It was this kind of worry about the way *Bill Brand*'s conventional form allowed its radical politics to be so easily recuperated that prompted David Edgar's famous attack on the series in *Socialist Review*. Part of a wider survey of socialist theatre, it argued *in principle* against the strategy of attempting 'to inject socialist content into mass-populist forms'. For Edgar television is simply not for turning. It addresses a subject permanently unavailable for mass struggle: the atomised individual in the domestic environment, 'the place where people are at their least critical, their most conservative and reactionary'. Consequently, the notion on which 'entryist' strategies are based – that the medium is inherently 'leaky' and open to, in Griffiths' own phrase, 'demystifying . . . counter-descriptions of political processes and social reality' – is a false one. For Edgar, the television audience 'approached in the midst of their private and personal experience' is always likely to 'take an individual, personalised (and therefore psychological rather than social) view' of what is presented to it.

Edgar's specific objections to *Bill Brand* centre on the series' empathic, psychologistic structure:

> The danger of a project like *Brand* is that, by the end of eleven episodes, the audience is identifying with Brand exclusively as the pivot of the story (my hero right or wrong), and sympathising with his views and actions only in so far as is necessary to a satisfactory dramatic experience . . . the audience is prepared to share Brand's socialism for the duration of the play, but no longer. Moreover, as has been pointed out, the countless other drama serials, series, and plays that are part of the television audience's experiential baggage will lead them to take an individual-psychological view of events if given any opportunity. (Griffiths in fact gave the audience ample opportunity to judge his central character's actions

psychologically, by giving him a broken marriage and a feminist mistress.)[18]

Edgar also identifies a problem with what he calls Griffiths' 'realist dynamic', the interplay between 'the surface naturalism of his characters' represented behaviour and the political essence of their activities'. According to Edgar, 'audiences will react only to the surface unless powerfully prevented from doing so', and Griffiths' attempts to counter this are simply not powerful enough. And he cites the lack of weight in the use in episode ten of a barely recognisable portrait of Lord Citrine – a symbol of class collaboration – to offset the impassioned socialist rhetoric of his contemporary equivalent, Willie Moores.

A COMIC SOLUTION?

Griffiths' response to this kind of criticism has always been to argue that these are problems he is willing to risk in order to reach a mass audience. Edgar's piece itself quotes Griffiths as saying that he 'chose to work in these modes because I have to work now. I have to work with the popular imagination which has been shaped by naturalism.' Interestingly, though, the final episode of *Bill Brand* displays elements which do run counter to the naturalism of the rest of the series. Moreover, these elements seem to have been deployed expressly to comment on what has gone before. In the final episode, Brand meets up with an old actor friend from university days (played by Jonathan Pryce), who is now involved in an alternative theatre group. The group, whose other members are all women, have travelled north to put on a series of shows at community and workplace venues. When the Pryce character tells Brand that the show, a kind of Brechtian burlesque, is 'about sexual politics', an ironical look can be detected on Jack Shepherd's face: *Bill Brand*, too, has in many ways been 'about' much the same thing. And when we get an extended glimpse of the group in rehearsal, the very different, non-naturalistic methods of representation they employ inevitably have the effect of drawing attention to, and eliciting comparisons with, the surrounding naturalism of the rest of the series.

One reading of this surprising intrusion from the anti-naturalist fringe would be that it registers the inadequacy of Griffiths' chosen form as a vehicle for the kind of politics with which *Bill Brand* attempted to deal. After buckling under the cumulative pressure of this inadequacy, the series finally *had* to break open and admit alternative forms of representation. Such a reading seems especially feasible given that Jonathan Pryce's cabaret act in the scene-within-the-show is very much a reprise of his role in *Comedians*, the one work in which Griffiths did make a significant break with naturalism. More likely, though, and far less pat an explanation, is that Griffiths was actually using Pryce and the company to make a point at the *expense* of his critics. It is very noticeable that on several occasions both the Pryce figure and his women colleagues express doubts about how their act will go down with working-class audiences, whether it will be accessible enough and whether they themselves will be booed off. As one of the group reflects, 'If you're going to make connections, raise consciousness, you've got to start where people are actually at. Not at some notional point in the middle of your own middle-class, guilt-ridden hang-ups.' In one of the final exchanges of the series we learn that their fears were justified and that they are rethinking the whole show in the light of their experiences in the various venues. Griffiths would seem to be saying that, whatever its flaws, *Bill Brand* at least did not fall into the trap of alienating its working-class audience. Consistently good viewing figures, if nothing else, tended to bear this out.

5 'Taking the struggle further': *Comedians*

Griffiths has described *Bill Brand* as an attempt to demonstrate 'that the traditions of the labour movement were inadequate to take the struggle further'.[1] This sense that the forms assumed by mainstream socialist politics in the mid-1970s were outmoded begs the obvious question about the extent to which the *dramatic* forms employed by Griffiths were equally in need of renovation. On the face of it, a stage play about an evening-class for would-be comics could hardly have seemed the most promising of vehicles for such a formal revaluation. But under the pressure of a new kind of politics, developed on the fringes of the traditional Left and centred round the Women's Movement, anti-racist struggles and youth cultures of resistance, Griffiths produced in *Comedians* a text that, unlike *Bill Brand* and his earlier work, went a long way towards realising its political concerns at a formal level.

Although it begins conventionally enough in broadly naturalist fashion, with a fly-on-the-wall view of Eddie Waters' teaching technique, *Comedians* reaches its dramatic climax in play-within-a-play scenes at a nearby working-men's club. Gethin Price's act erupts with a sub-cultural violence that radically calls into question both the notion of a unified working class and the realist aesthetic through which Griffiths had always previously sought to express it. Price and his angry, ugly mime-cum-harangue thus has a double presence in the text: as both signifier and signified of the new politics Griffiths was grappling with. Dressed like a skinhead (a motif that would recur in *Oi for England*), he embodies a notion of politics as resistance that cuts across Waters' more traditional liberal humanist belief in solidarity. This core contrast provided Griffiths with a characteristically dialectical structure for the piece. But before considering *Comedians* – and its 1979 television version – in detail, it is worth pausing to look at some of the wider aesthetic, critical and political contexts out of which this major departure for Griffiths developed.

Comedians, originally directed by Richard Eyre at Nottingham Playhouse in February 1975, transferred to the Old Vic in September of the same year, opening to London audiences at the same time as *Days of Hope* was flagshipping the BBC's new autumn season. The Jim Allen-scripted *Days of Hope*, and its portrait of working-class politics during the crucial decade 1916–26, represented the culmination – and, arguably, the finest achievement – of the social realist school of television drama, associated with its producer-director team of Tony Garnett and Ken Loach since their ground-breaking work together on *Cathy Come Home* some ten years earlier.

Although *Days of Hope* employed a variety of *vérité* effects, particularly unsynchronised sound, to produce its strong 'documentary' feel, it also drew on some of the visual rhetoric of period drama for its 'historical' look. The sometimes prettified images that resulted, together with the concentration of all four films on the experience of a single working-class family, led some commentators, notably those associated with *Screen* magazine, to question what was taken as read by almost everyone else: namely that *Days of Hope* was a politically 'progressive' text. A writer to the *Daily Telegraph*, for instance, had described the series as 'politically biased' to the Left;[2] and a lively correspondence in the letters pages of the *Radio Times* and the national press helped fuel an often angry debate about the ethics of drama-documentary, especially its use in presenting relatively recent history. The *Screen* debate, too, which spilled over into the spring of 1976, centred on the relative merits of a realist aesthetic applied to a historical subject. The terms, of course, were very different. Colin McArthur found *Days of Hope*'s realism 'problematic':

> *Days of Hope*'s realism involves the shedding of certain classical (primarily Hollywoodian) mechanisms and strategies, most notably the star and the dramaturgical device (most evident in the melodrama) of the climax. In almost every other respect *Days of Hope* retains the mechanisms and strategies of classical Hollywoodian narrative: e.g., linear construction; positioning of actors (in relation to the camera) to reveal mood and motivation; 'sculptural' lighting; heavy reliance on set decoration and costume. It is this massive retention of classical features which render it accessible and open it up to the charges of 'recuperation' (meaning something like 'absorption' or 'nullification', usually in a political context) which, I am sure, some of the writers in *Screen* would use to dismiss *Days of Hope* out of hand.[3]

But he also went on to add:

> However, the fact is that *Days of Hope* (and previous Loach/
> Garnett work) does, by its shedding of certain features of classical
> realist narrative, set itself markedly apart from most other British
> film and television fiction, which arguably renders it *in some respects*
> progressive not only at the level of subject-matter but at the formal
> level too.[4]

The other *Screen* writers referred to by McArthur were those
associated with Colin MacCabe and his theorising of the workings of
the 'classic realist text'.

In what for a number of years proved to be a highly influential
study,[5] MacCabe had argued that realist narrative in the cinema
works in analogous ways to the realist literary text. Both organise a
hierarchy of discourses around a dominant point of view – the
narrator in the novel, the narration of events in film – which then
offers privileged access to 'knowledge' of or the 'truth' about the
'reality' being dealt with. MacCabe was thus able to make Brecht's
point in a new way: realist texts were texts that offered no point of
entry for the reader or spectator; they proffered rather than *produced*
their version of 'reality' and were therefore, by definition, un-
dialectical, unable to handle contradiction – the key Brechtian test of
the truly revolutionary work. This updated Brechtianism (its literary
component a curious anomaly given the aggressively non-literary
stance of *Screen*'s overall project) enabled MacCabe to dismiss any
number of seemingly radical works as ultimately compromised
politically by their chosen realist form.

Days of Hope was clearly a case in point, but despite his own
reservations about the Loach-Garnett films, McArthur felt it
necessary to challenge the idea that they could not deal with
contradiction, citing as evidence the scene in which a coal-owner
lectures his miners on the need for peaceful, constitutional change
while, in the background, troops brought in to strike-break practise
bayonet charges. This drew a response from MacCabe, who argued
that, on the contrary, this scene proved his general point:

> What McArthur here confuses is the narrative's ability to state a
> contradiction which it has already resolved, and the narrative's
> ability to produce a contradiction which remains unresolved and is
> thus left for the reader to resolve and act out. In other words while
> McArthur looks simply for contradiction in the text, we must look
> at how contradiction is produced in the audience. In the example

McArthur cites there is a contradiction between what the mine-owner says and what the picture shows. But this is exactly the classic realist form which privileges the image against the word to reveal that what the mine-owner says is false. In this manner our position of knowledge is guaranteed – we may choose to disagree with what the narrative tells us but if it has already placed us in the position where we are sure we are right, it has not questioned the very construction of that position.[6]

Writing in a similar vein in *Screen* a year later, Keith Tribe pushed the case against *Days of Hope* to its political extreme:

The objection is that it endows its Trotskyist conception of revolution and reform with a truth which is underwritten by a constructed history. The truth of the argument is thus conditional, not on the actual viability of the politics that set this history to work, but rather on the apparent truth of this history as an autonomous object. The work of memory is thus duped into a particular political position, not through a historical discourse with its own principles of truth, but rather through the organisation of an image of the past which, through its 'verity', bestows its own truth.[7]

Now, when a Left-oriented journal like *Screen* devotes this amount of space to attacking what was probably the most radical and certainly the most sympathetic portrait of working-class politics ever to appear on British television, something is clearly afoot. For all that it chose to elaborate it at a rarefied theoretical level, *Screen* had actually put its collective finger on some highly concrete *political* shifts in Britain in the mid-70s. The crisis in representation which its writers had identified had a complex provenance in a crisis in politics. There was a widespread sense of defeat and indirection on the Left after the militancy of the early 70s and the radicalism of Labour's *Programme 73* had petered out into the Social Contract and IMF-wrapped austerity packages. In this climate Labour governments and films about working-class history were likely to seem all of a piece: political dead-ends. Was not *Days of Hope* itself about a massive defeat? In any case, as Althusserianism, then significantly enjoying its fashionable vogue in Britain, insisted: everything was, one way or another, 'ideological', including, and perhaps especially, labour history. In short, there could be no return to some golden age of working-class consciousness as envisaged by *Days of Hope*.

Much of the crisis on the Left had in fact been generated precisely by the growing realisation that it was no longer possible to think in terms even of a unified working class. As structural unemployment began to bite, creating a new labour aristocracy out of those in work and turning those without a job into a new underclass; as anti-racist campaigns began to reveal the scope of the problem within the working class itself; and as women struggling against sexism in the workplace increasingly ran up against opposition from their own male trade union colleagues, it became clear that the working class in the mid-1970s was not just divided but divided against itself. Anyone who doubted this only had to wait until the spring of 1979 when a Labour government was defeated by a revolt of skilled working-class voters who turned Tory at an election the overall outcome of which, to a considerable extent, had itself been determined by another revolt: that of low-paid public sector workers in the so-called 'winter of discontent'.

Significantly, from Griffiths' point of view, Leninist politics seemed as ill-equipped to deal with this new conjuncture as their Labourist counterpart. This was how Sheila Rowbotham described the situation in an influential article in *Red Rag*:

> . . . the old controversy of means versus ends needs rephrasing, because the struggle against advanced capitalist society is of such complexity and we are so tenaciously held down, that subjective forms of struggle have become vital. . . .
>
> Within Leninism there is no conscious commitment to struggling against the forms of relationship, which are created by the division of labour under capitalism, as part of the effort to make socialism. It is assumed that the existence of the revolutionary party itself can transcend the particular interests of sections within the working class. The actual conflicts between skilled and unskilled workers, between white and immigrant workers and between men and women for example, are thus obscured by sleight of hand.[8]

Now, whether or not one chooses to call playwriting a 'subjective form of struggle', it is clear that *Comedians* was written within an understanding of the need for the kind of political reorientation called for by Rowbotham. It uses comedy to take the temperature of a working-class culture that emerges as more and more debased under late capitalism the deeper Griffiths digs into its experiential texture. Unlike his earlier work, *Comedians* is emphatically not posited on the notion of a unified working class. Nor is this just a warts-and-all syndrome – though comedy, being the repository of prejudice, does offer a pretty telling index of the extent of working-class racism and sexism. Rather, perhaps, it is a case of an implicit rethinking of the classic Marxist understanding of the proletariat as the subject of history – and its valorising of every social movement, political strategy or individual trajectory solely in terms of its closeness to some 'authentic' working-class consciousness. In any event, in both theme and form *Comedians* can, with hindsight, be seen to have registered the beginnings of a major revaluation, crisis even, in Left politics and culture, the outcome of which is, at the time of writing, still unclear. What is particularly interesting from a textual point of view is the way this wider conjuncture in turn registers itself in the play in a major disruption of Griffiths' habitual realist technique. This is not the place to explore the broader implications of what seems to be a structural homology between the break-up of a dominant form of politics and the break-up of a dominant form of representation, but it is the indispensable context in which *Comedians* needs to be seen.

THE POLITICS OF RESISTANCE

One further aspect of *Comedians'* divergence from Griffiths' other work merits consideration here. The politics of recovery, of retrieving a 'usable' past, which are central to everything he had previously written, is replaced in *Comedians* by a politics of resistance based on a much more uneasy attempt to grapple with the present in all its ambivalence. This is reflected in the structure of *Comedians* which moves from a Frankfurt School-type critique of the consumerist debasement of working-class culture – as represented by the decline of stand-up comedy – to the semiotic sociology of Price's iconoclastic act seen as, in Stuart Hall's phrase, a 'ritual of resistance'.

The initial stimulus for the play was a conversation with a group of comics who worked on the Granada television series *The Comedians*. They talked of a highly respected club comedian who ran a class for comics above a pub. 'There seemed to be this split,' Griffiths has said, 'between what they thought of *him* – he was marvellous and he was principled and all the rest of it – and what *they* actually did in their lives to earn their money, which I thought to some extent was nauseating and reinforcive of all sorts of prejudices.'[9] Griffiths himself had long been fascinated by comedians and had often been to see them in the late 40s and early 50s. He recognised in the subject a potential stage play which could be as accessible as his television work. Moreover it offered the opportunity for an exploration of the politics of popular culture: 'When I come to write I want to find that

106

amount of pleasure in plays that I find in popular pursuits and pastimes. I don't believe they're moribund, bland, banal and finished . . . Many popular activities are genuine sites of resistance to other forms of activity and one of the great battles to be fought popularly at the moment is to seek to find those activities which genuinely summate a working-class life, as against those which are commercially imposed and clearly manipulative.'[10]

Griffiths began the drama intending that its central conflict should be between the pressures to conform and the need to remain principled. But as the writing progressed, he found a third element – the position of Gethin Price – forced its way into the text. Drawing on an environment he knew well from his teaching days in further education, the writer set the first and last acts in a post-war school in Manchester used for evening-classes. It is here that Eddie Waters, a former professional stand-up comic, runs his weekly class for would-be comedians (as with all Griffiths' titles, there is an ironic play of meaning on the word), sandwiched between Adult Literacy and Karate. The six hopefuls availing themselves of local authority largesse in order to get a first gig on the local club circuit are all from working-class backgrounds, as is Waters himself. Phil and Ged are brothers, the one a salesman type, the other a happy-go-lucky milkman; there are two Irishmen, George a Protestant docker from the North, and Mick, a building worker from the Republic; Sammy, spivvy and from a Manchester Jewish family; and the ambivalent Gethin, a British Rail van driver of threatening appearance.

Occupying an evening of real time, the play hammocks the club performances between two classroom scenes. The first act opens with the men arriving and swapping banter in an atmosphere underlain with tension, nervousness and rivalry. Their joking runs over a familiar gamut of Jews, Irishmen and 'the wife'. Price is immediately set apart from the others, quietly contemptuous of them and confident in a new, unseen act which he has put together during the preceding week. Waters drily explains that their acts will be seen tonight by a talent-spotter, also a former comic, Bert Challenor. He admits that there is little love lost between them, that neither has ever really respected the other, and that he, Eddie, has always refused to join Challenor's Comedy Artists and Managers Federation: 'I didn't like what they stood for. I've been a union man all my life . . . it wasn't that . . . They wanted the market . . . They wanted to control entry into the game. I told 'em no comedian worth his salt could ever "federate" with a manager. And as far as I'm concerned no comedian ever did.'

As a sympathetic and inspired teacher, Waters is clearly a

107

reflection of Griffiths' involvement with pedagogical concerns. Before Challenor arrives, he drills the class with some exercises. One is to prepare them to deal with a cough in the audience, to which Price responds with an obscene limerick. Another is built on the tongue-twister 'The traitor distrusts truth'. In a matter-of-fact tone Waters then lays out a vicious catalogue of attributes of the Irish ('the niggers of Europe') and Jews ('the effluent of history') and widens his attack to include 'Negroes. Cripples. Defectives. The mad. Women. *Workers'*. The class are puzzled, amused, embarrassed, uncertain how to react. Finally Waters explains: 'It's not the jokes. It's what lies behind them. It's the attitude . . . A true joke, a comedian's joke, has to do more than release tension, it has to *liberate* the will and the desire, has to *change the situation*. There's very little won't take a joke. But when a joke bases itself upon a distortion – a "stereotype" perhaps – and gives the lie to the truth so as to win a laugh and stay in favour, we've moved away from a comic art and into the world of "entertainment" and slick success.' Drawing out the consequences of this understanding, Waters illustrates how Price's limerick is a joke that hates women. 'Most comics *feed* prejudice and fear and blinkered vision, but the best ones, the best ones . . . illuminate them, make them clearer to see, easier to deal with.' Casual clowning and the exercises continue, revealing the backgrounds and the aspirations of each member of the class. Waters encourages them to go deep into themselves, to find an intimate, important moment and then try to tell it and make it funny. Challenor arrives, with 'a couple of . . . hints. Don't try to be deep. Keep it simple. I'm not looking for philosophers, I'm looking for comics . . . Any good comedian can lead an audience by the nose. But only in the direction they're going. And that direction is, quite simply . . . escape. We're not missionaries, we're suppliers of laughter.' His words panic the comics, who recognise a man with a quite different conception of comedy from Waters' responsible, revelatory art. And through the clash of these views, laughter is revealed as a choice between 'entertainment' and truth, a moral choice, and a political one.

ON THE LINE

In the theatre, the second act forces this choice on the audience, since they are translated into the customers of the club where the aspirants perform. Each of the class offers his act, reacting in different ways to the presence of Challenor. Mick Connor tries to ignore him completely and stumbles to put across his confessional account of what it means to be an Irishman in England. This is his own form of

108

'A true joke . . . has to change the situation': Bill Fraser as Eddie Waters in the TV
version of *Comedians*.

Waters' truth; Challenor is unappreciative. Following him on stage,
Sammy Samuels begins a similar act, although rooted in his Jewish
childhood. Then halfway through he abandons his rehearsed spot
and ad libs a succession of sexist and racist one-liners. Phil and Ged's
double act is similarly interrupted when Phil diverges from their
agreed patter; unlike Samuels, they do not recover their confidence

109

and appear merely inept. Only George McBrain, fourth on the bill, manages to rework his act smoothly so as to suit what he believes Challenor wants to hear. Again it is a catalogue of anti-women and anti-Irish 'jokes'. And with him, as with the others, the audience is made to recognise in the most direct way possible the implications and consequences of unthinking laughter. The compromises of the comedians are pointed up when Challenor reports on each of them back at the school. On Mick Connor: 'You might find being an Irishman in England fascinating, there's no reason why we should. Had a sort of earnestness about it I didn't much take to.' On Samuels: 'Same mistake as the Irishman. Fortunately you pulled out of it and got very good. It was a different act, the wife, blacks, Irish, women, you spread it around . . .' Challenor simply dismisses Phil and Ged Murray, but is complimentary to McBrain. After reacting to Price's performance, which followed McBrain, he holds out the prospect of work to just the two comics he liked. Waters is sad and angry. 'You wouldn't know a comedian from a barrowload of crap,' he tells Challenor.

As indicated above, Griffiths had initially developed the play around this conflict: 'a play about the man who was uncorrupted and the man who was deeply corrupted.' But, as he speaks of it, there *emerged* in the text a third element (*Comedians* is his only play with three acts) which explodes in the drama with Gethin Price's compelling act. Developed from the work of the Swiss clown Grock, this performance is a terrifying part-mime, part-monologue, the latter delivered to two dummies in evening dress. Price himself is 'half clown, half this year's version of bovver boy'. Drawing on elements of working-class life, his actions and words are threatening, violent, aggressive, *hard*. Towards the end of what in the theatre must be a sustained *tour de force*, he pins a flower on the front of the female dummy. Blood seeps out.

> I wonder what happened. P'raps it pierced a vein . . . I made them laugh, though. (Depressed.) Who needs them? Hunh. Who needs them? We manage. (Chanting.) U-n-i-t-e-d. Uni-ted. You won't keep us down there for long, don't worry. We're coming up *there* where we can gerrat yer.

Challenor's later reaction is just as uncompromising: 'Personally, I found the content of your act . . . how shall I put it? . . . repulsive. And aggressively unfunny. If you want to get on, lad, you'd better sort out a few problems first. Get some distance, see what I mean. Don't give us your hang-ups straight. Too hot to handle.' But it is Waters'

110

reaction that Price wants, and has to drag from him. Waters admits the act was brilliant but says that he too found it repulsive. And it is in their final extended exchange that the play works out its central dialectic.

THE NECESSITY OF HATE

Waters argues that Price's act was pure hate: 'You can't change today into tomorrow on that basis. You forget a thing called . . . truth.' Price replies that his truth *is* hate, that the working class *has* to respond to its continuing exploitation with hate, and that maybe Waters has forgotten how to hate. Stung, compelled to delve into himself as he has taught the others earlier, Waters tells his pupil about going round a concentration camp after the war, and then hearing a comic tell a joke about Jews, at which people laughed. 'I discovered there were no jokes left. Every joke was a little pellet, a . . . final solution.' Yet he was also stimulated by the camp, for he got an erection there. This brought him to recognise that hate was too simple, too inadequate an emotion with which to react to the complexities of the holocaust: 'We've got to go deeper than hate. Hate's no help.'

Price is unrepentant. Grock's hardness, Grock's *truth* contain a vital quality. 'I found this in another book,' he says, 'I brought it to show you. "Some say the world will end in fire. Some in ice. From what I've tasted of desire I hold with those who favour fire, but if I had to perish twice, I think I know enough of hate to say that for destruction ice is also great and would suffice . . ." It was all ice out there tonight. I loved it. I felt . . .' The play offers no resolution here, only forceful and striking statements of two positions. As Griffiths has explained: 'It's basically about two traditions – the social-democratic and the revolutionary tradition. It's about a tradition in culture that, say, Richard Hoggart represents, which is the persuasive, the rational, the humane tradition – arguing, educating for good, trying to change through education, through example. Set against that there is a younger tradition, very violent, very angry, very disturbed, that says, "No, that isn't the way." That way we can look back down through history and see the objective compromises that emerge, stem necessarily from that tradition. We've got to restate in our terms what the world is like, what the world can be like.'[11]

Yet the play's portrayal of 'the revolutionary tradition' is quite different from, and in some ways more complex than, Griffiths' previous representations. For his earlier plays dealt with revolutionary *leadership*. They asked how the working class could best be stimulated in revolutionary struggle. In *Comedians*, that impulse is

111

'The necessity of hate': Jonathan Pryce as Gethin.

self-generated; Price knows that *he* will have to demand change, just as he demands recognition of his presence from the two dummies. Hence Griffiths' comment that the character represents 'the most daring and the most potential aspects of the working class. There is danger and ugliness there but there is too an enormous grace and intelligence and an enormous capacity to solve problems and a desire to repossess themselves'.[12] So the potential for self-liberation is affirmed, but alongside a clear-headed recognition of the politics of a fractured working class, many of whose members will never glimpse this potential. Either they have been bought off, like Samuels and McBrain. Or they are otherwise rendered impotent, perhaps by their work, like the other would-be comedians. Even Waters himself has been made ultimately ineffectual, which Griffiths deeply regrets: 'I think that it is a long time before that is realised because [his position] has inside it some extraordinarily fine and remarkable things, and great qualities and great virtues. It is an extremely lonely position but it seems to me also an increasingly irrelevant position.'[13]

Gethin Price is different: 'Price *smashes* the categories and says NO – I stand in no line, I refuse my consent. He is unremittingly hard and decisive, discovers himself and takes the first steps towards repossessing himself.'[14] While Griffiths welcomes this potential, and indeed uses the play to celebrate it, he is also uncertain about it. Partly this is reflected in the resonant, but undoubtedly ambivalent 'bovver boy'

112

persona of Price. Moreover, the potential is 'frightening', Griffiths has said, 'because it's full of passion and it's full of a sense of injustice and because it will not be, I suppose, when it finds itself, enormously selective in its targets. And a great many people, liberal humanists like Eddie Waters, will be discovered to be objective enemies of that energy and that potential and will not be treated kindly . . . And who knows, *I* might be one of those people whom "truth hits like a fist" to quote the play.'[15] Nor is the writer arrogant enough to suggest how this potential could or should be exploited: 'It would be extraordinary dishonesty to say that a programme of behaviour can be laid down for that man either by himself or by me at this moment in time. I mean the play says here we are, what do we do?'[16]

Importantly, this refusal of a programme is of a quite different order from the stasis evident at the end of *Sam, Sam* or *The Party*. Indeed the shift to an affirmation of the potential for self-liberation seems to be a sea change of foremost importance in Griffiths' writing. It can be seen to reflect the beginnings of fundamental changes in political understanding by certain sections of the Left – particularly the advent of 'autonomous' struggles. Yet it is a shift of emphasis and focus that, at least to date, remains disappointingly unexplored in all of his later work. The *Oi for England* project attempts, but largely fails, to take this politics further. Nor is the potential identified in *Comedians* developed in the television work which followed. *Bill Brand* states the need to link the Labour Party with external expressions of this change, but the series falters at precisely the point of suggesting how those links could be made. And they are not forged in any of the other texts – just as the connections have not been made in the world of 'real' politics.

ENCOUNTERING 'NANNY BEEB'S CULTURAL BOUNCERS'

The stage premiere of *Comedians* was directed at the Nottingham Playhouse by the theatre's Artistic Director, Richard Eyre. From there it transferred successfully to the National Theatre at the Old Vic and then to a short commercial run at Wyndham's Theatre in January 1976. Two years later Eyre left Nottingham to become the main producer on BBC1's 'Play for Today' series. There he learned the techniques of directing for television and the following year he mounted a further production of the play, this time for the small screen. The drama was transposed far more brilliantly than *Occupations* had been, although since the theatre was so integral to its original conception, its impact was inevitably somewhat diminished. Jimmy Jewel, a former comic himself, had played Eddie Waters in the

113

original production; but because of availability problems, Bill Fraser was cast for television. His performance is totally convincing, powerful and deeply affecting. Jonathan Pryce reprised his devastating Gethin, and Ralph Nossek similarly reworked his creation of Bert Challenor. An audience was added to the club scene, but otherwise the studio production faithfully reflects a theatrical staging. Of course, the audience is not put 'on the line' in the way it is in the theatre; none the less, the presence of conflicting portrayals of comedy does necessarily resonate productively with the dominant forms of television light entertainment.

The text was tightened, with most of the cuts coming from the central club acts, though not from Price's. These trimmings eliminated certain of the original's expletives, but sufficient remained for the completed drama to be directly censored. It was scheduled in the usual 'Play for Today' slot, at 9.25 p.m., but at the last moment it was switched to 10.10 p.m. Griffiths wrote an angry letter to the *Guardian*: 'True to form, therefore, Nanny Beeb's cultural bouncers, [Bill] Cotton and [Alasdair] Milne, have shunted the play towards the witching hour, without consulting writer, director or anyone else creatively involved in making the play. At its new transmission time, the programme will now lose several million potential viewers (about which, I should add, writer, director, actors and technicians care passionately).'[17] Later he explained further: 'I even said I'd have it edited as long as they put a whistle where the word "fuck" should be, so that people watching would know that the BBC had taken that decision and not me. But of course they don't like censoring in the way that you insist on them censoring.'[18]

In the four and a half years between the stage and television versions of *Comedians*, much of Griffiths' time was devoted to his two monumental projects: first *Bill Brand*, and then the *Comrades* script which was to become *Reds*. He also executed his two labours of literary recovery, with adaptations of Chekhov's *The Cherry Orchard* and Lawrence's *Sons and Lovers*. In addition, there was another television play, like *Comedians* written in 1974, and two co-scripted works. One of these latter is an oddball undertaking which defies all categorisation in Griffiths' output; the other, and the earlier play for television, explore variants of the 'subjective' politics first examined in *Comedians*. Even so, neither is nearly as powerful or as rewarding as that key stage-work. Both later scripts do also extend the sociological impulse of *Comedians*, a direction and emphasis in his work which Griffiths himself has on occasion contrasted with a complementary historical impulse, which was to gain precedence towards the end of the 70s.

114

Of the three plays which followed *Comedians*, *Through the Night* is the most substantial and it remains one of the writer's best-known scripts. After *Occupations*, Griffiths was commissioned by Granada to do a play about a Sheffield prison, but before he began serious work on that his wife Jan was taken into hospital. From the moment she was admitted for a biopsy on a lump in her breast, she kept a diary and these detailed observations subsequently became the basis for a play which follows her experience closely. Composed rapidly by Griffiths himself, it was written 'out of anger and fear', and then submitted immediately to Granada. The company rejected it, and so he sent it to Ann Scott, who had been script editor on *All Good Men* earlier in the year. Moved and disturbed by the writing, she found the resources to produce it at the BBC, and engaged Michael Lindsay-Hogg – who had also worked on *All Good Men* – to direct it. The text was then revised considerably, to accommodate medical advice; as one critic has written, basing his comment on an interview with the writer, Griffiths 'was confronted with the moral obligation to ensure that the play did not deter women from referring lumps in their breasts to their doctors'.[19] The drama's central character, Christine Potts, is discovered to have a malignant tumour and, without any consultation, her breast is removed.

The patient's exclusion from all the medical discussions about her case is established in the opening scene. The pattern of this preliminary examination is repeated several times later, with a camera taking Christine's point-of-view and seeing only distant, murmured conversations and uneasy glances over shoulders. When she is spoken to directly, she is patronised, or treated as an idiot child, no one talks to her as an adult. After the operation – the shocking impersonality of which is underlined by her breast tissue being sent to a laboratory for tests with mice – this sense of isolation exacerbates her expected depression. One night she locks herself in a lavatory and has to be coaxed out by the most caring and unconventional of the doctors she has encountered. The subsequent conversation over a mug of cocoa with this Dr Pearce, who is slightly drunk and extremely sympathetic (and played by Jack Shepherd), erects a rather self-conscious framework of ideas for the play.

Christine learns first about her tumour. Pearce endeavours to explain why she has not been told before: 'Mainly, I think, because we have lost all idea of you as a whole human being, with a past, a personality, dependants, needs, hopes, wishes. Our power is strongest when you are dependent upon it.' The system has faults, he admits, but on the whole those running it are honourable. 'Two

115

Excluded, patronised and isolated: Christine Potts (Alison Steadman), with her husband Joe (Dave Hill) in *Through the Night*.

thousand years ago Hippocrates said, "For whoever does not reach the capacity of the common people and fails to make them listen to him, misses his mark".' Pearce continues: 'Well, we're all missing the mark, Mrs Potts, and we need to be told.' Finally he broadens this remark to point up the underlying politics of the play: 'Not just doctors and nurses, but administrators and office men and boards of management and civil servants and politicians and the whole dank crew that sail this miserable craft through the night.' She is grateful for his attention, and even though he offers her only partial comfort, it allows her to come to terms with her mastectomy and, in the following scene, to look for the first time at the scar which she had previously avoided. He refuses her gratitude, however, with the gentle instruction, 'Don't thank. Demand.' And as he says this the camera tightens on his face, adding one further emphasis to this central statement. For the disguised demand in Christine's actions has brought her strength. Consequently it is not surprising that Michael Lindsay-Hogg apparently adopted as an epigraph for the play a line spoken by Gramsci in *Occupations*: 'Find your courage where it is.'

Christine's personal struggles are presented against a finely textured picture of the life of the ward, but it is only the patients who are developed as characters. In particular, there is the elderly Mrs

116

Scully, who has had much of her stomach removed but who continues to fight against her illness and the instructions of the staff, often expressing her resistance with a string of expletives. And it is with Mrs Scully that Christine celebrates in the final, sentimental scene. Their communal toast is drunk with illicit gin: 'Sod it.'

Although almost ignored by critics, *Through the Night* generated a sizeable public response and in the preface to the published version Griffiths writes of the numerous phone-calls and letters which it provoked. Yet seen now against the range of his work, it appears as less rich and provocative than much of his other writing. Immediate observation has been structured more as journalism or as an explicit 'issue' play than as fully satisfying drama, and the piece remains in many ways almost stubbornly one-dimensional. Griffiths clearly intended, as Pearce's set-piece address indicates, that the resonance should extend to an audience's understanding of all institutions. His attack was directed at the treatment of 'people as the sum of their parts rather than as a whole human being. That's not just true of medicine, it's true of every sort of bureaucracy – industrial bureaucracies, commercial bureaucracies. People are what can be done to them rather than what they can do. It's basically a problem of democracy.'[20] In another interview Griffiths has spoken in even more general terms: 'What I was trying to say there was, "We have lost sight of human possibility, of the possibility of being human, in the way in which society is now organising itself, through institutions and systems and structures." That was the broad thing I wanted to say, and I thought the best way to say it was to be very, very particular indeed, about one process, one set of experiences.'[21] As impressively revealed in Alison Steadman's powerful performance, Christine's growth is undeniably moving, but this individual focus is ultimately limiting and the broader ideas emerge in a partly schematic and unsatisfactory form.

Perhaps this criticism is unfair, for the play's presentation of a hitherto almost taboo subject for television – breast cancer – was cathartic and singularly meaningful for many viewers. In 1975, women's health issues were far less frequently discussed on television or in the newspapers than they are today, and *Through the Night* was certainly a significant pioneer as a popular dramatic exposition. But to those to whom it does not speak directly now, its most interesting aspect is an attempt to work within, and against, the genre of hospital serials on television, such as *Emergency Ward Ten* and *General Hospital*. As Griffiths has pointed out, 'It's really a demand for the audience to see the hospital as a site of so much more than romance between doctors and nurses . . . to ask questions about hospitalisation, the

National Health Service, relationships between experts and non-experts.'[22] The difference between the substance of *Through the Night* and of, say, *General Hospital*, is illustrated the more effectively by the former's use of much of the visual style of the latter. For instead of opting for a strictly 'realistic' use of locations and film (which would probably have been excluded in any case by the additional costs), Ann Scott and Michael Lindsay-Hogg mounted the play in a studio, exploiting the look and feel of hospital serials. This self-consciousness, together with a limited use of Christine's point-of-view shots, imparts an edge of non-naturalism to the rigidly naturalistic writing, and thereby certainly increases the work's impact.

PORTRAIT OF A NATION: 'DON'T MAKE WAVES'

Despite its touches of non-naturalism, *Through the Night* remains firmly embedded in a predominant style of detailed naturalism. But in his two other contemporary scripts from the mid-70s, Griffiths embraced the challenge of non-naturalism far more fully and explored its techniques in collaborative writing with Snoo Wilson, Howard Brenton and others.

Judging from the script alone, *Don't Make Waves*, the half-hour television play which Griffiths co-scripted with Snoo Wilson, was truly bizarre. Such an appraisal has to be made from the text alone because the production itself, the seventh in the series 'Eleventh Hour', does not exist in any other form. A feature of the BBC schedules in the summer of 1975, 'Eleventh Hour' was transmitted live, supposedly to increase its immediacy and topicality, and in fact only one of the individual plays was committed to videotape. This was despite the presence of the names of Tom Stoppard, David Edgar, Fay Weldon and other major writers in the credits. The attraction and challenge to all of them was the series' peculiar schedule, which began on a Monday morning with a meeting of production staff and two or three writers. A topic was chosen from the week's news and the writers then scripted a drama which could be cast, rehearsed and mounted, *live*, on the following Saturday night. Inevitably this posed almost insuperable problems, and Griffiths and Wilson's contribution is likely to have been no less uneasy than most of the plays in the series.

The setting of *Don't Make Waves* is a bar in the immediate aftermath of a nearby explosion. This allusion to a recent IRA bombing campaign in mainland Britain is one of the script's closest approaches to contemporary reality, for the bar is hosting a fancy dress party with characters attired as Queen Elizabeth, Henry VIII and a Chief

118

Scout. Their reactions to the smoke and confusion are written as odd, almost unconnected flights of fancy, jumbled up with musings on time, sex and history. Trapped together for the duration of the play, they talk at each other, all the while watching the spread of a substantial pool of water in the centre of the room. Potatoes and a gumboot fall through the roof just before a fireman bursts in to reassure the guests that the explosion was in a gas main. A parody of a Churchillian speech about winning through precedes the appearance, from under the water, of a 'Potato Man' searching for the party. He joins the others in a drink, and leaves.

Conceived as a farcical portrait of a threatened nation obsessed with myths of a glorious and powerful past, *Don't Make Waves* forces elements of Griffiths' continuing examination of history into the frame of one of Snoo Wilson's surreal fantasies. An important unifying spine would seem, from gaps in the script, to have been several songs by Kevin Coyne, but these too are lost. The dialogue has an engaging absurdity, which might have been heightened by a stylish production. But it is difficult to see the play as little more than a footnote in Griffiths' career.

'ONE QUESTION AND ONE PLACE TO ASK IT': 'DEEDS'

A second collaboration involving Griffiths, three years later, was *Deeds*, billed by the Nottingham Playhouse as a play 'by Howard Brenton and Trevor Griffiths with Ken Campbell and David Hare'. Such unconventional credits reflected the relative contributions of the four authors, since Brenton and Griffiths undertook the bulk of the work; Hare contributed to several sections and Campbell sent in just one scene – an extended paranoia joke about plastic conquering the world. The project began with the idea of several writers associated with Richard Eyre's time at the Nottingham Playhouse composing a satirical revue to mark the director's departure from that theatre. But it evolved into a more ambitious picaresque tragedy which embraces many of the worlds within contemporary Britain: a hospital, a prison, Parliament and a multi-national company.

To enter and pass rapidly through these separate worlds the drama adopts the structure of *Candide*, and follows the adventures of an innocent abroad today, one Ken Deed. Coming home from work, Ken finds that his wife has disappeared and that his baby has died. Mystified by the subsequent explanations from a doctor and a coroner, he rejects the equally unilluminating platitudes of a Catholic priest. Instead of condolences he takes money from the priest and sets out to find why his baby died: 'There's got to be one question and there's got to be one place to ask it.' He soon discovers that the cause was milk powder, and his anger leads to his arrest and imprisonment for causing a disturbance. In jail he resolves 'to learn to climb walls, buildings, tower blocks, monuments'. When he is released, he starts climbing.

The second act opens with a board meeting of 'Nuzzles (English Division)'. As the managers discuss the marketing strategy for powdered milk in the Third World, Ken appears in climbing gear on the window-ledge outside. Having identified the culprit, he then goes off to see his MP and demand action. The MP can also offer him only platitudes, so Ken continues his individual crusade by button-holing the Minister for Consumer Affairs in a lift. Effectively as powerless as the MP, she suggests inquiries and investigations. Ken is not satisfied, and he continues his climb up society by scaling the Savoy hotel and breaking into the bathroom of a Nuzzles director. In a passionate confrontation, he forces the director to alter the baby's death certificate so that it reads, instead of mystery, murder. Then he leaves behind him a parcel which he has been carefully looking after – the corpse of the baby.

Before the final scene, the play builds in Ken Campbell's Speakers' Corner set-piece where a Mr Wills argues that plastic, and its progenitor oil, are taking over the planet. Fleeing from this further madness, Ken meets his wife Mary in a railway siding. She too has been waging a campaign, but Ken is now desperate: 'I've been trying to get these buggers. Somebody anyway. Only the further you go, the more there are of 'em.' His plan is to drown in a wagon of powdered milk, to show up the cynicism of Nuzzles' operations. Mary, who is pregnant again, is more sanguine: 'I tried all this stuff. I got one of 'em in a car, smashed his hand in the door. Hurt him a lot. I got at one of their wives. Made no difference.' She is also clear about the appropriate response: 'Those buggers aren't going to get this one. He's going to get them. Because this one (taps stomach) is going to be *armed*. I'll give him whatever he needs. If he needs hate, I'll give it him by the gallon. If he needs to kill, I'll give him a gun.' Ken is won over and immediately builds the baby a cot of bricks, at the same time arguing with a railway worker about the importance of armed struggle. Anticipating the revolution, he says that the new baby will be called Boadicea or Geronimo; the railway worker is a rapid convert.

Richard Eyre, who directed the play, acknowledges that 'the whole exercise was a piece of wish fulfilment, to think that we could have produced a wonderful play in that spontaneous way'.[23] Yet he feels that the production was a powerful and convincing one. In an extended review, Ned Chaillet wrote of it, 'Time and again [Eyre's] production captured flawlessly the power of individual images,' and commented especially on the achievement of a naturalistic playing for even the most absurd scenes.[24] He was troubled by the ending, however, and certainly what reads as an invitation to armed struggle sits oddly with much of what precedes it. As an analysis of power – and the lack of it – in our society the play is pessimistic, even defeatist. The sudden idea of salvation through insurrection, within the context of the late 70s, appears naive fantasy. Eyre too recognises the problem: 'I suppose it came down to the fact that to provide a fatalistic conclusion, a pessimistic conclusion, just felt like an act of bad faith towards the character – although the truthful conclusion is that this bloke gets absolutely fucked . . . it was the compulsion to deliver an optimistic conclusion. And I think because the responsibility was split, and because it was being written as we were rehearsing, so we were never looking at a finished script, you weren't able to look at it as a whole.'[25]

In addition to its unsatisfactory conclusion, the play also lacks the political rigour and dialectic which might have been expected from Griffiths. In this it shares common ground with *Through the Night*. Other comparisons are also clear: Ken is the projection of Christine into a wider world, refusing his co-operation, rejecting society's placebos. Yet for all the play's validation of the resistance of the individual, the final sense remains one of impotence and failure. Ken's dogged and honourable questioning of the system stays pertinent, but is subsumed by the inevitable 'What is to be done?' Or, as Mary says, 'What you gonna do then?' The play has no plausible response to offer.

6 'Mucking about with love and revolution': *Comrades* and *Reds*

The story of Trevor Griffiths' relationship with *Reds* began with the writer's removal from his own culture. In early 1976 he flew to America, for the first time, to New York where *Comedians* was to be presented on Broadway in a production by Mike Nichols.[1] There he met Warren Beatty and spent a day with him and others talking about American politics. Then, as he recalls: 'A couple of weeks later I got a phone call from Warren asking me what I knew about John Reed. I thought this was just a casual request so I said, "I know a bit, what do you want to know?" He said, "I don't want to know anything, I've been researching him for six or seven years. I want to do a movie, are you interested?"'[2]

Griffiths apparently took almost six months to decide whether the project could have any useful 'yield', but after that work on the script occupied him almost exclusively for the next two years. Even though he wrote much of it back in England, the sense of distance from his previous creative experience and from his own background continued to mark the project. He flew back and forth to America, he participated in lengthy transatlantic script conferences by phone, and he and Beatty locked themselves away in a London luxury hotel to hammer out a second draft. He was dealing with Hollywood, a nexus of attitudes, understandings and working practices utterly distinct from anything he had encountered before, but to which he was drawn by a desire to reach in significant ways the widest popular audience.

From *Adam Smith* onwards, as we have seen, Griffiths had always insisted on and fought vigorously for the right of control over his own texts. Not, he has frequently explained, as a matter of ego, but to preserve meanings and values. This struggle had been almost continuous and had involved numerous compromises and defeats, as well as some significant victories. Now the battle was absurdly unequal, since the writer within the Hollywood system has traditionally been treated as little more than a technician, a wordsmith. And Griffiths recognised that any attempt to contest the different meanings being inscribed in his text would merely contribute to his being marginalised as a half-cracked artist.

Of course, one of the strangest of the many ironies about *Reds* is John Reed's constant repetition of the phrase 'No one changes a word of what I write'. In the finished film it is a key signifier of Reed the lover, the artist, constantly asserting his individuality against the collective repressiveness of both pre-First World War America and post-Revolution Russia. Only in his mature collaboration with Louise Bryant does he abandon the principle.

Griffiths delivered his first draft in the spring of 1978, and he later collaborated with Beatty on a second, but by the time production began in August 1979 the words had been changed many, many times and he had withdrawn completely from the project. To save money, the unit shot in English studios and locations, and apart from trips to Finland and Spain, they continued to work in Britain for a full year. Yet despite a predominantly local crew, the sense of isolation from Britain remained, as Beatty decreed that all filming take place in total secrecy, with none of the usual press junkets or interviews.

The involvement before and during filming of at least two other writers has been generally recognised: Elaine May, the comic actress, author and director with whom Beatty had co-written *Heaven Can Wait* and who was the former partner of Mike Nichols; and Robert Towne, who had scripted *Chinatown* and worked on two of Beatty's earlier movies, *Bonnie and Clyde* and *Shampoo*. The script, however, seems to have remained almost chimerical throughout shooting. *Variety* reported: 'What there is of a drastically revised script seems to be classified or at least in strictly limited circulation around the unit, with unsuspecting actors frequently asked to improvise dialog. Even assistant directors are without a copy, so it's said.'[3] Edward Herrman, who played *Masses* editor Max Eastman, later confirmed the absence of a script to *Rolling Stone*. At one point he had complained about it to Diane Keaton: '"It doesn't matter," she said. "It's all in Warren's head anyway. He keeps changing it all the time."'[4]

Griffiths himself had little contact with Beatty or the film throughout this period and only re-established a relationship late in the editing, in the middle of 1981. Again he left England, to view the film, expecting to admire its technical achievement but to react against its politics. To his surprise, as he has said, 'It was much more difficult to weigh its positive and negative yields.'[5] There was now an at least equal difficulty about ascribing its authorship; the question was settled in contractual terms with Griffiths and Beatty credited as co-writers, but it remains a thorny critical problem – and one on which this chapter attempts to shed some light. It should be stressed, however, that what follows is in no sense intended as a full reading of the film-text eventually distributed as *Reds*. What it attempts is rather to establish the exact nature of Griffiths' involvement in the project as a contribution to such a reading, which partly for reasons of space lies beyond the scope of this book.

PLAYBOY OF THE REVOLUTION

There is no doubt that the initial conception was Warren Beatty's. A young romantic actor through the 60s, Beatty had scored his first huge success in 1967 with *Bonnie and Clyde*, which he starred in and produced. Throughout the 70s he continued acting but became increasingly involved in making his own movies, producing and co-writing *Shampoo* (1975) and co-writing, co-directing and co-producing *Heaven Can Wait* (1978).

On *Bonnie and Clyde*'s release, Beatty was invited by Russian producers to play the radical journalist, witness to the Revolution and author of *Ten Days That Shook the World*, John Reed, in a forthcoming epic about his life. (The film has since been made, by director Sergei Bondarchuk, but it remains unseen in the West.) Beatty read the Russian screenplay, rejected the approach as propagandist, but became fascinated by the character whom Upton Sinclair had described as 'the Playboy of the Revolution'. After extensive reading, Beatty reportedly wrote a first treatment in 1969 and a step outline in 1971. Next he began to film people who had known John Reed and his colleague and lover Louise Bryant in the early years of the century. Beatty interviewed them on 16mm film, to capture their memories, although none of these preliminary research testimonies was used in the eventual film itself.

At this time Beatty also became increasingly interested in politics. His first contact came through the Kennedys, for whom he worked in 1968, and three years later he was closely involved in the McGovern campaign, for which he organised a string of political concerts. (McGovern, coincidentally, wrote his doctoral thesis on Reed.) Fifty-eight years earlier Reed had organised a pageant in Madison Square Garden to raise money for the IWW labour union, the Wobblies; now Beatty was putting on similar shows.

Further parallels were apparent as the actor's interest in Reed developed into an obsession. Several friends and critics have since

124

commented on how he came to identify intensely with him. Such a correlation of star and character is a frequent technique of journalistic hype in the movies, but in this case it does seem to be based in truth. Jerzy Kosinski, who took the role of Zinoviev in *Reds*, has been quoted as saying: 'Warren does see himself as John Reed. In his movies so far Warren has been as socially insignificant as John Reed before he began writing about the Revolution. Beatty's *Bonnie and Clyde* was like Reed's book about Pancho Villa – gangsters shooting at one another. And Beatty's *Shampoo* was about the morality of the middle class, like John Reed's little articles about the minor failings of America . . . Warren looked for a big subject, just as John Reed also looked for something big to report for the *Masses*. And so one day Warren came across the story of John Reed – and he saw himself as John Reed. The project of making a movie about John Reed became what going to Russia was for Reed.'[6]

Both *Shampoo* and *Heaven Can Wait* were substantial money-earners. Beatty was highly bankable, bankable enough even to sell to Paramount Pictures, a subsidiary of the multi-national conglomerate Gulf + Western, what he later called his 'romance' about the beginnings of American socialism and American communism. The first budget was $20 million, but calculations of this figure at the pre-production stage were insufficiently precise. Then when Beatty began working with actors he was reportedly profligate in the number of takes he forced on them, sometimes going through the same shot over thirty times. This dragged out the shooting and the budget soared, to at least the final accepted figure of $34 million and perhaps as high as an estimated $55 million. One irony, which was commented on at the time, was that it cost American capitalism so much to restage the Russian Revolution. Another is that the financing deal was such that Barclays Bank owned the negative of the film, only leasing it back to Paramount; this meant that Barclays could take advantage of tax laws and so effectively reduce by a substantial amount the sum of money laid out.

But well before this money was spent, Beatty needed a script. Lillian Hellman, Arthur Miller and Paddy Chayevsky were all considered, and rejected. Then someone mentioned a brilliant left-wing British playwright whose only previous experience of commissioned movie-writing had been a screenplay about the life of Strindberg for a freelance Italian producer. (Written between 1972 and 1975 in three versions totalling some 1,000 pages of typescript and called *Marriages*, it was never produced.)

'I set out to write a screenplay which says X, Y & Z and it turns out saying not X, not Y, not Z.'[7] As already indicated, the history of Griffiths' involvement in *Reds* was a fraught affair; and the end product is deeply problematic. It is curious, then, that Griffiths, with his extensive experience of television, should have been surprised by this. All scripts are radically transformed by the very nature of the filmic process, and notions of literary property hold little sway in the film industry, least of all in Hollywood. British television, it is true, still tends to privilege the writer as against the director, but even here things are changing fast. It was undoubtedly a perception of his relative success in finding 'strategic' ways round these difficulties in a television context – together with his overall view of the medium as a 'leaky system' capable of being made to carry radical 'messages' – that contributed to Griffiths' disillusion with *Reds*. For in several interviews, he has made it clear that he genuinely believed that similar interventionist strategies could open up an oppositional space even in Hollywood.

Griffiths' critics tend to put this down to straightforward naiveté on his part. And certainly many of his utterances display a certain lack of sophistication about the kind of processes involved. He told *Screen*, for instance: 'That a major Hollywood producer wanted to do a life of John Reed seemed to me fantastically important *in terms of content*'.[8] The same willingness to separate out content from form in a crude textual dualism was also revealed when he confided to an earlier interviewer that despite his experience on *Reds* he was still 'interested in the movie[s] to communicate certain ideas'.[9] As we have seen, Griffiths has always been highly susceptible to the kind of massification fallacy which translates quantified audience into qualitative 'effects', and he seems to have been genuinely enthused by the prospect of a film about revolutionary politics being seen worldwide. But one need look no further than Warren Beatty's half-ironical, half-serious and wholly contradictory Oscar-acceptance speech to see how the vast capitalisation costs of *Reds*, and hence its dependence on a recoupable market, meant that, inevitably, the logic of capital alone determined that its politics had also to be recuperable:

> I want to say to you gentlemen that no matter how much we might like to have strangled each other from time to time, I think that your decision, taken in the great capitalist tower of Gulf and Western, to finance a 3½ hour romance which attempts to reveal for the first time just something of the beginnings of American socialism and American communism reflects credit not only on

you, I think it reflects credit on Hollywood and the movie business wherever that is, and I think that it reflects more particular credit on the freedom of expression that we have here in our American society and the lack of censorship that we have from the government and the people that put up the money.[10]

The fact that Griffiths adopts a proprietorial rather than collaborative stance on the relationship between his script and the film called *Reds* makes it difficult to assess his claim that '*Reds* is only 35 per cent mine'.[11] This may seem paradoxical, especially since the first draft manuscript lodged in the British Film Institute library can easily be consulted to bear out these contentions. But there is a problem here. Much of *Reds* appears to follow the structure of the manuscript fairly closely. The architecture and overall scope of the narrative *are* Griffiths': the differences are differences of inflection and emphasis, of the varying weight and interpretation given to the material handled within it. In other words, we are dealing as much with the effects of the Hollywood production process in general as with the hotel-closeted 'rewrites' with Beatty to which Griffiths himself has always drawn attention. And while, as we will go on to show, Griffiths is right to feel that *Reds* travestied his script's intentions, there is also a case for saying that even had Beatty kept scrupulously to that script, the industrial-commercial machine that is Hollywood would have ensured that what emerged was still only a mildly radical film.

THE 'WITNESSES'

The first draft manuscript of *Reds* reveals that Griffiths toyed with a number of other working titles for the project: initially the more straightforward *John Reed*, and then the less ambivalent *Comrades*. The manuscript in the BFI, dated April 1977, is headed *Comrades (The John Reed-Louise Bryant Story)*. What is immediately striking is the extent to which the 'witness' element is already well developed at this stage. This suggests that Griffiths was working very much to an overall framework provided by Beatty, who had been filming interviews with surviving members of Reed's generation since the mid-70s with a view to incorporating their testimony into the final structure of his *hommage* to the radical journalist. Like much else about Beatty's involvement in *Reds*, it was hardly an original idea.

The standard biography of Reed, on which much of Griffiths' own research was based, is Robert A. Rosenstone's *Romantic Revolutionary*. Rosenstone is an American academic and as the book's rather uneasy title suggests, he was clearly puzzled by contradictory elements in both Reed's personality and his politics (as was Griffiths). He tried to convey this difficulty in the book by calling the first chapter 'The Legend' and filling it with contrasting historical estimations of Reed from seven of his contemporaries. Yet while *Comrades* obviously draws on the Beatty-Rosenstone use of a 'witness' element, Griffiths also invests the device with a *dramatic* function. The 'old folk' – as Beatty is said to have liked to refer to them – are envisaged as a kind of narrative chorus. They are to comment on and advance the action, as well as providing insights into Reed's character and generally 'validating' the film's claims to historical authenticity. Significantly in this respect, *Comrades* also *fictionalises* them. After a pre-title sequence featuring Reed covering the war in Eastern Europe in 1915, an old IWW member or 'Wobbly' offers a scripted perspective on Reed as the 'playboy of the Social Revolution'. Later, the same character – for that effectively is what he is – describes New York in 1916 in the following terms: 'An election year, the year Wilson ran on the "I kept America out of the war" ticket and other jokes. Bread lines. Picket lines. Roosevelt. And the overworked American ego making sure America stayed free (*shots of swinging billy clubs and split heads*) . . .'[12]

Other 'narrators' or 'recounters' – as they are also variously referred to in the manuscript, anticipating perhaps something of the confusion over their exact role which would afflict the final film-text – include a group of elderly women who discourse in fairly risqué fashion about Reed's sexuality ('Screwed everything that moved'). Like the Wobblies, they were dropped from subsequent drafts. Also written out as a 'witness', though not as a character, was a young *Pravda* journalist assigned to Reed and Bryant when they first arrived in Petrograd and who is used by Griffiths in *Comrades* as a structuring device. It is he, for instance, who wakes up the two Americans with the news that the final insurrectionary moves have been taken in the night while they slept. In *Reds* he is briefly glimpsed meeting Reed and Bryant at the railway station and then disappears.

The 'witnesses', or more appropriately the 'old folk', who eventually appear in *Reds* photographed against austere black backdrops by Beatty's cameraman, Vittorio Storaro, bear virtually no resemblance to the 'narrator' figures in *Comrades*. They are real people. What they say is not scripted. There are more of them. Their memories are loosely tied to stages in the narrative, but they cannot be said to comment on it and in no sense advance it. Wrinkled with age, they offer oral history at its most individualistic: which is to say authentic enough but fragmented into so many points of view as to become hopelessly relativist in its implications, unless rigorously

128

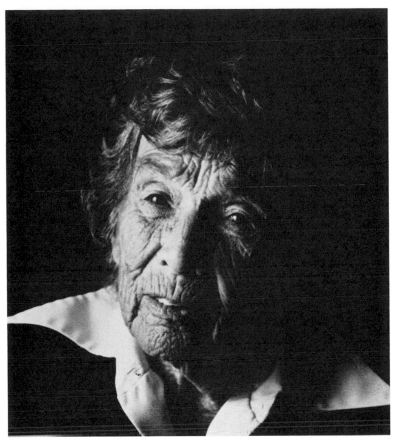

Oral history at its most individualistic: one of the witnesses, Adela Rogers St John.

cross-checked against some larger framework. Something *Reds* never provides. The cracked voices range from the cool intelligence of Henry Miller, through the failing reminiscences of Rebecca West and Dora Russell, to the sheer dottiness of the man who suddenly blurts out, 'I'm a big-head!'. The overall impression, though, is of a discourse bordering on senility and madness, a Babel of competing memories most of which have long since become unhinged from the events they are meant to be living traces of. There is even a hint that this may have something to do with having come into contact with a certain kind of socialism. This is echoed in the closing stages of the narrative itself when the onset of Reed's fatal illness is registered first by the delirium he experiences trying to make his Baku speech – a sales pitch for revolution – against the babble of continuous (mis)translation into a bewildering number of Asiatic languages.

Significantly, most critics responded to the witnesses as an index of the film's historical relativism, of the ultimate unknowability of history. 'Who knows what happened in history?' wrote Alan Brien in the *Sunday Times*, while the *Observer*'s Philip French talked about 'a twilight chorus reminding us of the untrustworthiness of memories, the deceptions of history and our own mortality'. Far from legitimising the fictional narrative, the 'old folk' seemed, on the contrary, to have jeopardised it. Ed Buscombe, however, writing in *Screen*, was prepared to see the witnesses as a modernist device, 'denying [any] fixed point of view' and offering in its place 'a multi-layered discourse in which each view is presented only to be countered by another'.[13] For Buscombe this made *Reds* less 'a sell-out to the bio-pic view of history' than a challenge to the 'classic realist' assumptions underlying dominant Hollywood practice. Yet a step outline, also deposited in the BFI library and dated January 1979, envisages a largely 'realist' function for the witnesses, who were to give us access to 'knowledge' precisely in the manner of the classic realist text: '61a: The narrators describe the declining conditions in Russia and give us the information we want to back up what Emma G[oldman] says in a later scene.' Even so, as Buscombe was quick to point out, *Reds* still 'tread(s) a thin line between presenting history as essentially a construction, something made not found, and history as a confused jumble of conflicting voices in which any attempt to decipher a structure will always be undercut by yet another view.'[14]

'AMERICAN BOLSHEVISM'

So what kind of 'structure' did Griffiths attempt to give Beatty's historical project? *Comrades* has a very precise architecture, closely reflecting Griffiths' conception of what the film was to be about. It falls into four broad sections: pre-1917 America; the Revolutionary 'days' in Petrograd; post-1917 America; post-Revolution Russia. Two historical narratives are thus interwoven: the story of the struggle for socialism in the US and the decisive effect the events of 1917 had on its development; and the story of the Russian Revolution itself and the beginning of its decline into Stalinism. All the pre-publicity for *Reds* stressed the latter rather than the former and, within that, the Revolution itself. Presumably, it was felt that Reed was known to the general public only as the author of *Ten Days That Shook the World*. Yet *Comrades* was really much more concerned with what Griffiths called 'American Bolshevism'.[15]

130

Whereas *Reds* offers little in the way of political background to Reed and Bryant's early development, choosing instead to concentrate on the fashionable bohemia of pre-World War I Greenwich Village, *Comrades* attempts to build up a cumulative set of vignettes which place the couple in the wider context of the brief flowering of American socialism and its violent repression by the State. Reed's address to the Portland Liberal Club – in *Reds* simply an anti-war speech that is very much the public come-on to Bryant – is for instance the occasion for the following reference to the Ludlow Massacre of 1913, one of the ugliest moments in American labour history, when 200 striking miners and their families were shot dead by the National Guard:

> J. D. Rockefeller on whose behalf the State of Colorado and the Colorado Fuel and Iron Company recently butchered two hundred and more striking miners, their wives and the children . . . the same J. D. Rockefeller who then sent a telegram to his company's president: 'Hearty congratulations on the winning of the strike. I sincerely approve of all your actions.' Believe me, friend, nowadays when I hear people talking about 'patriotism', I keep my hand on my watch.

Comrades also has Reed covering the 1918 Chicago mass trial of IWW members which effectively broke the back of the American labour movement (101 Wobblies were found guilty on 10,000 counts and sentenced to prison terms of up to fifteen years and fines totalling almost $2 million). Part of the story he files reads:

> One big union – that is their crime. That is why the IWW is on trial. If there were a way to kill these men, capitalist society would cheerfully do it, as it killed Frank Little, for example, and before him Joe Hill . . .

These and other references – to 'race' riots in St Louis, for example, the Palmer raids and vigilante attacks on Socialist Party head-quarters and 'female-suffrage pickets' – drop from view in *Reds*. Even the suppression and prosecution of the radical magazine, *Masses*, which directly involved Reed, merits only passing recognition.

The effect of this stripping away of Griffiths' historical detail – *Comrades*' political memory, as it were – is to transplant Reed out of the conjuncture that produced him, to make his interest in revolutionary politics seem like that of an adventurer, an artist. Similar problems dog *Reds*' sexual politics and 'modern' dialogue. In one major respect, however, the paring-down process actually helped to clarify Griffiths' original structure. *Reds* defines Reed's radicalism largely in terms of his anti-war stance – Beatty is said to have thought of him as primarily a 'pacifist'[16] – and the war question thus becomes the issue around which the film's politics revolve. That the American socialist and labour movement, which had successfully mobilised round an anti-war position, failed to stop Woodrow Wilson taking the United States into the war in 1917 made that year as critical a one for radicals in America as it had been for revolutionaries in Russia. Everything in a sense leads up to 1917 – in America an opportunity lost, in Russia an opportunity grasped – and then falls away; the American socialist movement is swept away on a nationalistic tide; the Russian Revolution has to start getting its hands very dirty in order to survive. This rhythm, pivoting round 1917, emerges in *Reds* very much as Griffiths envisages it in *Comrades*. It helps to make the end result more than just an account of how an American reporter covered the Russian Revolution. Reed's documented experience is used to embody a sense of America and Russia, later to become world superpowers, both briefly sharing the *same* historical moment.

SEXUAL POLITICS: 'THE JOHN REED-LOUISE BRYANT STORY'

Of course, one of the reasons why *Reds* plays down much of the detail of *Comrades* is to play up the relationship between Reed and Bryant. In magnifying their stormy affair, Beatty as both director and actor succeeds in throwing out of focus much of what in *Comrades* is shown to be going on around them. Their whole relationship is differently inflected, though again Beatty did retain Griffiths' structure. The climactic scenes in which the American couple make love to the sound of revolution being made outside in the streets – one of Griffiths' typically Reichian flourishes – unfolds, minus the sexual explicitness, very much as outlined in *Comrades*. The digest of these scenes contained in the 1979 step outline illustrates the kind of merging of the personal and the political, the public and the private, work and pleasure, that all versions of the project, including the film-text, aim for:

49: Another *Ten Days* incident.
50: Making love in the Petrograd apartment.
51: Another incident, it's probably a climactic incident, Lenin in triumph announcing 'We shall now proceed to construct the Socialist order'.
52: We see Reed and Bryant working furiously in the apartment.

Romantic revolutionary: Warren Beatty as John Reed, with Diane Keaton as Louise Bryant.

Where *Reds* differs from *Comrades* is in its interpretation of the sexual politics of the Reed-Bryant relationship. The point about the (in other ways deeply problematic) link between sexual and political potency is that it is intended as an index of lives genuinely and mutually shared on the basis of equality. A manuscript *aide-mémoire* among research papers for *Comrades* notes that: 'Reed and Louise do *everything together* in Russia – for the first time they have politics to share.' Elsewhere in the manuscript Griffiths toys with the idea of having them file a jointly bylined story as soon as they arrive in Petrograd. In this sense, *Comrades* as a title has at least as much to do with the utopian goal of feminism in the realm of personal relations as with the revolutionary goal of Leninism in the realm of social relations. (Nor is it without significance that Griffiths began work on the Reed project immediately after the death of his wife Jan in 1977.)

Reds refracts its sexual politics through a highly specific feminist culture: that of fashionable late-70s metropolitan America. Louise Bryant's fierce independence is thus allowed to come across largely as a product of the 'Me' generation: initially careerist in orientation and ultimately very much a case of, quite literally, 'what about me?'. This is not helped by the fact that the actress chosen to play the part, Diane

133

Keaton, has a screen persona – particularly as developed in Woody Allen's *Annie Hall* – which connotes precisely this kind of chic apolitical feminism. Nor by the fact that it is so *transparently* 'modern'. The kind of consciousness that produces a phrase like 'I don't want to get into some emotional, possessive thing' is, for instance, exceedingly remote from the kind of historical consciousness that informed the actions of the real Louise Bryant.

MADE IN HOLLYWOOD: BEATTY'S DIRECTION

Beatty's role in the transformation of *Comrades* into *Reds* was only partially that of co-writer on the second draft. We also need to look at his contribution as director, much of which consisted in a canny tailoring of the Reed story to existing Hollywood genres. Romance in both the historical and sexual sense, together with elements from the screwball comedy, were fed into the central relationship to produce a predictably larger-than-life portrait of the protagonists which, despite their radical politics, in no way jars with comparable Hollywood productions. This 'naturalising' effect was achieved in a number of ways. Notably through the use of jokey banter and mock-aggressive repartee as the dominant idiom of the Reed-Bryant relationship, in the classic Bogart-Bacall tradition. But also through a systematic sentimentalising of Griffiths' text.

Comrades makes provision for the extensive use of the songs and ballads of the American labour movement, particularly material – like Joe Hill's – associated with the IWW. *Reds* is dominated by a single musical motif: a schmaltzy version of the popular hit 'I Don't Want to Play in Your Yard'. Far from helping to build a sense of a socialist tradition, an alternative culture, this is resolutely mainstream and used merely, it seems, to tug heartstrings. It is most frequently to be heard making its way on to the film's soundtrack when the excruciatingly cute dog which Beatty contrives for the Reeds is in attendance. This sentimentalising, trivialising approach reaches a peak when, following its use in scenes depicting the storming of the Winter Palace, even the 'Internationale' becomes personalised, turned into a private motif: its strains accompany Reed as he wanders round the now empty Petrograd apartment on his lonely return to Russia. Similarly, a poem he writes for Louise in *Comrades* is in *Reds* transferred on to the back of an IWW handbill which then re-emerges iconically at key emotional moments throughout the narrative. In both cases we are dealing with a discourse of the personal-as-political that has been misunderstood and re-separated out into its component parts. The handbill, like the 'Internationale', is always on the point of

134

becoming quite literally a prop, an empty iconographical addition to the film's period feel. A period feel which is of course already largely picturesque, especially in the central, would-be epic 'insurrectionary' scenes.

Yet it is not just the studio-shot sequences of the Reeds marching on the Winter Palace with the Bolsheviks – something of a cross between *Dr Zhivago* and a Broadway musical – that invite the epithet picturesque. Much of *Reds* is necessarily concerned with political debate, with differences, disagreements and splits within both Russian and American 'Bolshevism'; yet remarkably for a film originally scripted by a writer whose hallmark has been his ability to handle ideas dialectically, it contains hardly any scenes in which the politics it deals with are dramatically argued through. Instead we get scene after scene – an extraordinary number of scenes, in fact – in which *speeches* are made: speeches to meetings, dinners, congresses, committees, caucuses, factions, delegations, working parties, soviets. When characters in *Reds* have a point of view, they are not seen debating it but haranguing others with it. Notwithstanding the role of oratory in mass politics, this tends to produce a damaging soap-box effect in which socialism is, through the *mise en scène*, iconographically associated with an implicitly authoritarian form of rhetoric. At a similar level, when Reed's Left caucus within the Socialist Party attempt to gain the rostrum at the national congress from which they have been excluded, they seem merely to be parodying earlier scenes of the storming of the Winter Palace.

Griffiths envisaged a 'massive filmic event at the heart of the piece',[17] necessary in his view to convey a sense of the 'power and resonance in our lives' of the Russian Revolution. A 20-minute section in *Comrades*, including 'dramatised' scenes and incidents from *Ten Days*, was to provide the basis for this. In the event, Beatty opted for *Zhivago*-esque epic, embarrassingly foregrounding Reed's 'role' as an individual. Thus a scene in *Comrades*, in which the Reeds visit a munitions factory where there has been an anti-war stoppage and are asked by a mass meeting to 'convey fraternal greetings to the workers of America', becomes a dockside meeting addressed by Reed who is then promptly mobbed as a comrade and whose speech (in English, note) apparently becomes instrumental in the dockers' decision to join in the march on the Winter Palace. But Reed-Beatty, all-American hero of the Revolution, also remains Beatty-Reed, all-American movie star; and so, on a par with *Reds*' other Hollywood effects like the over-sentimentalised dog and the Sondheim score, we get a bathetic scene in which Reed is seen joking around in a Petrograd square with a Christmas tree: an absurdly domestic image given the circumstances. But then the entire film contains a strong domestic pull – the house at Croton, its garden and its dog; the desperately unfunny and grossly sexist scene in which Beatty spectacularly fails to cook dinner; Bryant's increasingly wifely characterisation as a woman who doubts the Revolution, in America at least ('not here'), in the name of what looks suspiciously like good old-fashioned bourgeois marriage.

True, there are productive tensions here, and *Reds* is often at its most effective when dealing with the problems of integrating a personal life into one of political commitment. (In this sense the geography of *Reds* – all those panoramic sweeps across the landscapes, from perma-frost to desert, that separate Reed from Bryant – goes a long way metaphorically to make up for the loss of the much more precise topography of *Comrades* and its almost cartographical approach to describing where the Revolution took place.) Yet it also has to be said that the all-Americanism of both Bryant and Reed works against any real exploration of contradiction in them. Beatty may have told Griffiths that the *Comrades* script would not do because it was a 'religious text' that turned a communist into Christ in a way unacceptable to American audiences,[18] but that did not prevent him from turning Reed into a hero anyway – the romantic idealist of Rosenstone's biography – and Hollywood heroes just do not have contradictions.

What Griffiths has called 'the correspondences and disjunctions between . . . the private man and the public political life'[19] are explored in *Comrades* through scenes like the one in which the young *Pravda* journalist points out the contradictions in Reed's class background: 'Reed spent time with the rich and the pampered to whom he was, of course, no stranger.' *Reds* collapses most of these considerations into the central relationship with Bryant, where because of the romance tradition they are more acceptable. The notion of Reed having a 'role crisis' – a phrase that crops up several times in the manuscript notes for *Comrades* – is not developed. Nor, for that matter, are the tensions between Reed the 'artist' – a phrase that gets bandied around a lot in *Reds* – and Reed the activist. Bryant, too, is allowed few contradictions. In *Comrades* her politically incongruous affair with the misogynistic Eugene O'Neill is treated in some detail, with Griffiths even making him the father of a child she has aborted (based on a rather hazy account in Rosenstone). In *Reds*, it is much more a casual fling which does not question her in any way.

One final striking difference between *Comrades* and *Reds* is the way the latter refuses to give a voice to the historical figures who have *scripted* parts in the former: notably Lenin and Trotsky. Griffiths gives major speeches – if only cameo roles – to both, but in *Reds* they are reduced to visual images only, and clichéd images at that, with Lenin in particular being cast in classically conspiratorial poses. This absence is made all the more glaring by the *presence* of Zinoviev in a superbly realised performance by Jerzy Kosinski. At one level this is merely a further indication of Beatty's reluctance to engage with history rather than legend, the same kind of unwillingness or uneasiness that led him to cut so many of Griffiths' detailed 'quotations' from *Ten Days*. At another level it is even more fundamental: Trotsky and Lenin are bad box-office in the United States at the best of times, but Beatty was shrewd enough to recognise that *Reds* would be received in the ideologically fraught atmosphere of a new cold war. We're a long way, indeed, from *Absolute Beginners* and the days when Griffiths could write not just a few scenes but a whole drama about a fully-rounded character called Lenin.

THE WRONG MOMENT AT THE RIGHT TIME

Yet for all that *Reds* distorts and deforms *Comrades*, the film which eventually went into theatrical distribution still has a clear and recognisable provenance in what Griffiths originally wrote. The author himself agreed as much when he allowed his writing credit to remain in the opening titles after having threatened to remove it. There is on the whole, we suspect, a much more complex relationship between *Reds* and *Comrades* than most of the personnel working on the project or any of the press who reviewed the completed film recognised at the time.

It has already been noted how a 'domesticating' process is at work in *Reds'* treatment of the Russian Revolution. One of the symbols of this is Reed's habit of accidentally hitting his head against a low-slung ornamental glass lampshade in the Petrograd apartment: a small thing, but along with the Reed-Bryant badinage very much the sort of thing audiences associate with Hollywood. Clearly it is one of those elements Beatty added on set. But is it? The 1979 step outline contains a similar running gag, the only difference being that it involves Reed bumping his head against a low ceiling rather than a lampshade. There is, too, the train scene, where Reed and Zinoviev almost come to blows over the direction the Revolution is taking. Here not only does Beatty for once retain the dialectical structure of the original scene – Reed arguing for 'truth' against 'propaganda', whatever the consequences ('revolution *is* dissent'); Zinoviev countering with the need to defend the Revolution by supporting the Party, right or wrong; and then a shell exploding against the side of the carriage and 'carrying the dialectic on in a very powerful way'[20] – he actually improves on it. In *Comrades*, the carriage where Reed finally runs Zinoviev to ground has been the scene of an orgy between Comintern members and a group of Daghestani prostitutes. The aim, presumably, is to hint at the Revolution betrayed: already incipiently Stalinist and now, too, already falling back into a bourgeois sexual economy. But it does not really work, serving only to clutter the scene – and to spectacularise it voyeuristically – and Beatty was right to drop it. The fact that the resulting scene is probably one of the most effective in *Reds* and that Beatty also retained similar exchanges between Reed and the anarchist Emma Goldman (with this time Reed defending the Revolution against her scepticism) suggest that the view of Beatty's contribution as merely the bowdlerising of *Comrades* is in need of some revision. And clearly this will have important implications for any attempt to offer a comprehensive reading of *Reds*. In the space remaining, however, we will restrict ourselves to a number of observations on the context in which the film eventually appeared.

Reds ran into an overwhelmingly hostile ideological climate. The right-wing resurgence that was to bring Ronald Reagan to the White House (and Margaret Thatcher to Downing Street) was already under way when Griffiths began work on the project. By the time Beatty started filming, all kinds of pressures were beginning to militate against the film: not least renewed East-West tension following the Soviet intervention in Afghanistan, the American boycott of the Moscow Olympics and, more latterly, the appearance of the Red Army on the streets of Warsaw. Under these circumstances, it was hardly surprising that a screenplay which set out to recover the impact of the Russian revolutionary experience on a generation of American socialists and intellectuals should have finally reached the screen in a muted form. Nor that it should have been promoted largely as a historical romance. Indeed, given the connotations of the word in the 1980s – the President of the United States would soon be averring that it was 'better to be dead than red' – it was a minor miracle that the film retained the title *Reds* at all. What remains surprising, and very significant, is that Griffiths should have decided that, in his own words, there would be a 'yield for [his] sort of cultural politics' in such a film *at such a time*.

It is not just that politically it now seems entirely the wrong moment to have attempted to 'recover' the resonance of Russian revolutionary experience. Or that the focus was on America and Americans and hence remote from the specifically British concerns that had previously occupied Griffiths. It is also, crucially, that the

138

film physically removed him from Britain and its deepening social and political crisis just at a time when he seemed, with *Comedians*, to have found new forms to deal with it. He had in effect turned full circle: *Reds* was a return to the earlier 'historical' work on revolution he seemed to have left behind. But such were the conditions of the film's production, much of it being redrafted in the anonymous suites of some of the most expensive hotels in America and Europe, that it seemed, in Marx's phrase, as if Griffiths might be in danger of beginning to repeat history as farce.

7 'Working in a factory': *Sons and Lovers* and *The Cherry Orchard*

After the intensive work with Beatty on the second draft of *Reds*, Griffiths returned to Britain in the autumn of 1978, by all accounts relieved to have put the experience behind him. But as it turned out, his Hollywood connection did not end there. While Griffiths had been working on the Reed screenplay for Paramount, Stella Richman (executive producer on *Bill Brand*) had been negotiating with another Hollywood major, 20th Century-Fox, for the rights to D. H. Lawrence's novel *Sons and Lovers*. Fox were one of a number of Hollywood majors to have taken out options on Lawrence novels following the notorious *Lady Chatterley* trial in 1960. Richman, still working as a freelance producer, was trying to put together a package that would mark the 50th anniversary of Lawrence's death in 1980 with a first-ever adaptation of one of his novels for television. She found a ready taker for the project in ATV, then the IBA franchise holder for the Midland region. ATV were not renowned for their drama output – these were the days before the arrival of producer Margaret Matheson – but it was not difficult to fathom the reasons for their interest in the project. 1980 was also the year in which the IBA were to conduct a major franchise review. ATV were facing a serious threat from a consortium based in the East Midlands – very much Lawrence country. The opportunity to impress the IBA with a piece of prestige 'cultural' programming which at the same time, because of its strong 'regional' element, would take the wind out of the sails of its competitor, Mercia, was too good to pass up.

Although slightly hesitant because of other commitments, Griffiths actually needed little persuading to work on a version of what, as we have seen, had been a key text in both his personal and political development. Meanwhile, Stuart Burge, producer/director on *Bill Brand,* was drafted in to direct and a cast including Frank Finlay as Walter Morel and Anton Lesser as Paul was contracted. But with pre-production well advanced, the project ran into an industrial dispute involving ACTT personnel throughout the ITV network. Filming was held up for nine months. Weeks after rehearsals began again the following spring, ATV unexpectedly dropped its commitment to the production. Stuart Burge recalls thinking at the time that the reason for this (unexplained) decision was that 'by then, because of the strike, ATV knew they weren't going to be able to get it out in time to influence the franchise reallocation – in my view, their main reason for doing it in the first place.'[1] Richman, Griffiths and Burge now took the unprecedented step of offering the more or less ready-to-shoot project to the BBC. Jonathan Powell, producer of the 'classic serial' slot on BBC2, and who had worked with Griffiths before on the television version of *Occupations*, quickly secured the resources required to take it on and, after some re-casting, filming began in the summer.

The pairing of Griffiths, a socialist playwright with an absolute belief in the radical potential of television, and Powell, the producer whose stylish and innovative approach to adaptation had given a new respectability to 'classic' serialisation, was always going to be intriguing. And so it proved. From the start, Griffiths was uneasy about the way the assembled expertise of the BBC's design departments and the working methods associated with the production of period drama seemed to be subtly deforming his script, shaping it in ways he had not intended. 'I never anticipated just how difficult it would be to break the mould of the classic serial. You are basically working in a factory where these things are being turned out one after another. Methods of working have evolved geared to a certain kind of period look and once the logistics of the operation take over, a totality of effect is set in motion that becomes almost unstoppable – it's like a juggernaut, once you are on it's very difficult to get off. Let's be clear though, a tremendous amount of skill, expertise and personal commitment goes into the reproduction of historical detail – accuracy is never in question. But it's frequently an accuracy that is skewed in important ways. What is right in period terms can often be wrong in class terms, and in the case of *Sons and Lovers*, where I set out to reproduce the *material* reality of a nineteenth-century mining community, this had damaging effects.'[2] The debates, disagreements and compromises through which the production evolved tested the limits both of period drama itself and of Griffiths' own optimism about his ability to politicise it.

What was basically at issue was naturalism versus realism – a materialism of detail versus a materialism of forces, history as backdrop versus history as agency. Implicitly at stake, too, were differing assumptions about the nature of the television audience. Griffiths' script aimed to reinstate Lawrence's distinctive working-class voice specifically in order to stress its continuity with the shared experience of a contemporary working-class audience, in, as he wrote in the *Radio Times,* 'the year when unemployment will reach three million'.[3] This, however, was always at odds with a period format that had evolved precisely to meet the needs of an undifferentiated, 'classless' audience. An audience which, it is assumed, regards history itself as simply an undifferentiated *past* devoid of any purchase on the present. At bottom, the argument was: Lawrence for whom and – to some extent inseparable from this – *by* whom?

What is immediately striking about this struggle over Lawrence's 'meaning' – and indeed about the whole production history of *Sons and Lovers* – is the curious way it seems to reproduce the *Reds* experience, albeit in the different, and to Griffiths more familiar, context of British television. Griffiths could again be found explaining to the press how his original intentions had not survived a production process. There was even a Hollywood major in the background, 20th Century-Fox's television division having retained an interest in their original property as part of the deal. In fact, this 'interest' extended to interference in the 'artistic' decision-making of the Burge/Powell tandem. Contrary to the usual assertion that co-producers have no 'creative' input in the productions they buy into, Fox insisted that a number of scenes of a sexually explicit nature be reframed in mid-shot so as to render them more ambiguous. Perhaps even more striking, notwithstanding Griffiths' long personal involvement with Lawrence's novel, is that he should again have entered on a 'historical' project of recovery rather than returning to the contemporary concerns of his mid-70s work. *Sons and Lovers* pre-dates in period even *Reds,* having been written between 1910 and 1912 and published in 1915, and although it is decidedly 'modern' rather than pre-World War I in its concerns, its dominant theme – class translation – found a much greater contemporary resonance and relevance in the decade 1956–66 than in the decades that followed.

Thus, fascinating and important as Griffiths' 'counter-reading' of *Sons and Lovers* is, its principal interest now probably lies in what it tells us about how television adapts novels and, more crucially, about how it is industrially geared to produce period detail to order. Costume

142

drama, often allied to literary sources, has been a staple of British television's output since the phenomenal success of *The Forstye Saga* in the late 1960s. But by the 1980s a combination of recession and right-wing government at home, generating a climate of cultural nostalgia, and new patterns of co-production financing abroad, generating a drive towards high-gloss 'prestige' drama, had helped to accentuate it into something approaching a *dominant* style: *le style retro*, as it has been dubbed.[4]

It is in this context, the context of an industry that permanently ties up vast resources and studio space in the production of an essentially anodyne version of the past, that Griffiths' achievement needs to be measured and his critique of its working methods assessed. Period drama, whether 'literary' or populist in impulse, not only fails to produce any understanding of history, but positively inhibits it. This is particularly so in the case of working-class history. In countless series, from Granada's *Sam* through to, say, the BBC popular success, *When the Boat Comes In*, video and the aesthetics of design have conjoined to sanitise and deform a whole area of experience – of political, cultural and class struggle – by presenting it within a framework that is at best purely personal, and at worst merely picturesque. Passed through the primetime prism of period drama, that experience emerges unrecognisable, its threads of continuity unpicked and effectively rendered invisible, *unusable*.

In 'classic' serialisation, the conventions of period drama combine with the dominant readings of a literary tradition to produce further distortions. So that for all Griffiths' emphasis on Lawrence's detailed portrait of Nottinghamshire working-class culture at the turn of the century, *Sons and Lovers* is still 'packaged' to suggest a very different reading in which the novel is valued principally as a fable about the artistic impulse – a portrait, rather, of the artist. The opening title sequence, featuring a soft-focus watercolour being painted, directs us towards an interpretation of Lawrence's autobiographical hero, Paul Morel, as a study in sensibility. Similarly, BBC press releases made repeated references to his miner father – in Griffiths' version the major repository of working-class values – as 'uncultured' and 'uncouth'. This was how one such press release constructed the series for journalists: 'Gertrude Morel, high-principled and refined, is embittered by her marriage to Walter Morel, a miner who has taken to drink since he cannot live up to her standards. All her hopes centre on her artistic son Paul. Eileen Atkins plays Gertrude Morel and Tom Bell plays her uncultured and frequently drunken husband, Walter.'

Griffiths has described in detail how the design process works to produce this kind of distortion. 'Designers determine the "look" of a

Paul Morel (Karl Johnson) and Miriam Leivers (Leonie Mellinger), bewigged with a meticulously replicated, yet inappropriate, period hairstyle.

production on the basis of highly selective photographic evidence, which is really a poisoned witness to the past. Photography, as it developed in the nineteenth century, was a middle-class practice conducted by outsiders who didn't necessarily understand their working-class subjects. They produced *posed* images which convey very little about how lives were actually *lived*. Once you accept such images as representative and the design process takes over, it becomes

144

very difficult to retrieve any sense of just how hard those lives really were. For example, the decision to use wigs for some of the characters in *Sons and Lovers*, and in particular for Miriam Leivers, was a logistical decision taken early on which had deep repercussions as the series developed. Though they meticulously replicated period hairstyles, their appropriateness for the daughter of a subsistence farmer who would have had neither the time nor the money to devote the amount of attention to her appearance they suggest is highly questionable. Yet, given the production resources, if you want an actress to rehearse on the set she must be free to do so, i.e. she can't be in make-up having her natural hair done.'[5] The cumulative effect of these small distortions – a child's doll that is just too expensive to belong in a miner's home, a parlour that looks just a shade too lower middle-class – leads to a loss of overall material texture. The result is inevitably a safer, blander version of history: 'How can you convey the full weight of the tensions and stresses of a working-class community, where money is short, exploitation rife and life crushingly hard, if the material conditions have been diluted and softened? At least 25 per cent of the historical reality, the "truth" you are aiming at, simply drains away.'[6]

Part of the problem lies in the nature of studio production itself. Griffiths, for instance, notes the damaging effects of an increased *pace*: 'You are expected to produce 40 minutes from a day in the studio – when I came into television a decade ago, it was 10–15 minutes.'[7] The paraphernalia of illusion – pasteboard, hardboard, multi-camera presentation, lighting constraints – also has a standardising effect, making period dramas resemble nothing so much as other period dramas. Griffiths had originally hoped that *Sons and Lovers* would be shot entirely in the more distinctive medium of film, but budget limits demanded a 50:50 studio/film ratio. The film footage includes exterior shots of miners' houses dating from the 1880s that would have been ideal for the interior of the Morel home, where most of the key encounters take place, had not the decision to go for studio presentation already been taken. The location work in semi-rural Nottinghamshire, and Stuart Burge's direction in general, rigorously eschews the formal lyric sequence that is normally the hallmark of period drama. This was partly an acknowledgment of the extent to which nature in Lawrence is never simply picturesque. But it also has an important dramatic function, buttressing the novel's central obsession with crossing borders – town/country, male/female, and ultimately the boundaries between *classes* – by locating it in a symbolic landscape. This search for a non-lyric style is greatly helped by John Tams' minimal score, which avoids that other period signature –

music as emotional manipulation. Tams, who also has a small acting part as a clerk in the factory where Paul works, was at the time musical director of the Cottesloe Theatre and had worked extensively with the folk revivalists, the Albion Band. He based his *Sons and Lovers* score on traditional music for concertina, trumpet and euphonium culled from the Nottingham area and dating back to Lawrence's own time.

'OBJECTIFYING' LAWRENCE: COUNTER-READING

Griffiths' version of *Sons and Lovers* also differs crucially from most other classic adaptations in its willingness to go beyond mere replication and offer a genuinely *interpretative* reading of the novel. It asks questions both of Lawrence and of the various critical discourses, particularly the dominant Leavisite meanings, that the text had been made to sustain. Partly this involves a literary-historical 'recovery' of Lawrence as a specifically working-class writer; and partly an 'objectifying' of the novel's classically realist procedures through the dramatic process itself. Both come together in the central plank of Griffiths' interpretative strategy: its counter-reading of Walter Morel.

Sons and Lovers belongs to a series of early autobiographical novels and its highly subjective narrative reflects this. Lawrence's authorial voice is heavily biased – he loads the dice, particularly when it comes to Paul's parents, who are closely modelled on his own. He seems to want to resolve some deep psychological conflict by getting the reader to side with the mother against the father. Like the BBC's publicity material, generations of critics have gone along with this, equating intentionality with effect. But Lawrence was also writing in a realist tradition which assumed a dialectical relationship between character and society, and his intentions vis-à-vis the father are consistently undercut by what the text tells us in addition to what Lawrence himself thinks it is telling us. Thus the detailed descriptions of the Bestwood (i.e. Eastwood) community are so acute, so typical in a sociological sense, that they incorporate historical and class forces which place the Morels' marriage in an entirely new context. Gertrude's antipathy towards her husband emerges as deeply rooted in their straitened economic circumstances; their emotional rift becomes a measure of a profound gap in consciousness, a class tension that separates her lower middle-class aspirations from his militantly working-class identity. Paul's dislike for his father is, in fact, the prelude to his rejection of the working class itself.

The presence of these underlying patterns, this setting in motion of forces beyond the merely personal, is what Lukács had in mind when he talked about the great nineteenth-century novelists being realists *in spite of themselves*. In a sense what Griffiths does is to *dramatise* this effect. Walter Morel becomes a study in resistance, an assertion of the positive values of the culture Paul rejects. Considerably aided by a performance of great power by Tom Bell, full of nuanced use of dialect and gesture, Morel becomes the working-class voice suppressed in the text. As with the father figures in the plays of David Mercer and the novels of David Storey, Morel's overbearing presence is something that his sons have to escape, but it is an escape that entails a loss – their 'education' tragically closes off his experience, making it redundant in the class translation they undergo. Morel hardly features at all in the last two-thirds of the novel, but Griffiths keeps open the perspective he represents by amplifying the role of a character most critics relegate to minor status – Baxter Dawes, the metal-worker with whose wife Paul has an affair. With a major actor – Jack Shepherd, veteran of *Occupations* and *Bill Brand* – in the part, the production plays up the curious intimacy that develops between the two men, and Shepherd's abrasive presence from episode four onwards contributes a hard-edged quality that keeps the class issue to the fore.

In his introduction to the published *Sons and Lovers* script, Griffiths explained his Lukácsian method – of extending and developing the typicality of Lawrence's characters, and asking questions about them the novel itself cannot pose – in the following terms:

> Realistic novels, especially by Lawrence, work differently from realistic plays. *Sons and Lovers*, though ostensibly a third-person novel, frequently presents events, relationships and people through the consciousness of its central figure Paul Morel (who, as we have seen, is a version of the author himself). Since no comparable relationship to Paul existed for me in the dramatic re-working, it proved pointless to seek a dramatic device that would support one. My interest in the difference I'm trying to account for lies in the way Paul – and all his social relationships – become *objectified* within the form of realistic drama. (Put another way, realistic drama demands that characters shall be both subjects and objects. Hence, as Paul's subjective view of the social reality is de-centred, so the other characters' perceptions acquire a newly charged subjective dimension.) Revelations ensue, each one a subtle shift in the flow of meaning, a redistribution of effect, a rupture with the prevailing protective empathy that urges the reader to see Paul as the subject and perceive his world – family,

work, friends, lovers, problematic – through his eyes and, often unthinkingly, at his valuation.

And the shift in formal focus affects, in some cases as crucially, all the other characters in the piece. The Walter Morel that emerges, for example, is now as much victim as anyone else and, incidentally, much closer to the 'father' that Lawrence revalued towards the end of his own life. Gertrude, Clara, Miriam, too, all undergo a significant re-making in our minds, as the plays centre them for the first time as subjects within the structures of their own lives.[8]

This 're-making' of the women characters is, however, much less marked than that reserved for Morel. Griffiths makes much of Clara's involvement in Women's Rights to produce a contemporary resonance, but there is more than a hint of the fashionable feminism of *Reds'* Louise Bryant in the way this is achieved, and, equally, Gertrude and Miriam do not benefit from any corresponding feminist gloss. Significantly, Stuart Burge recalls that in certain areas the adaptation 'tended to be *too* faithful. There was a quite different, special slant as far as the father is concerned, but some of those other scenes – a lot of them are just pages out of the book, and they're quite difficult to do . . . I think he should have gone further; there's an enormous area concerned with Paul's relationship with Miriam . . .'[9]

Son and lover: Paul (Karl Johnson) and Clara (Lynn Dearth).

148

In fact, it is difficult not to feel that in terms both of what he was attempting to 'recover' and of what he was seeking in the way of contemporary relevance Griffiths was working within a rather limited politics here. Certainly the lessons of *Comedians* seem to have been forgotten: what *Sons and Lovers* celebrates essentially is traditional working-class culture and its overwhelmingly *male* values. Morel's hardness, violence even, becomes one of the serial's major indicators of what is to be valued and what not.

Tellingly, in his introduction Griffiths actually appears to weigh Lawrence's 'incipient derogation of women' against his 'celebration of dignity in resistance within working-class culture'[10] as if the one were somehow *worth* the other. This is perhaps a little harsh. Yet the extent to which *Sons and Lovers* did operate within notions of 'progressiveness' increasingly inadequate to a changing political climate was well illustrated following the censorship battle over the serial's last episode. Ironically, given Lawrence's own history with the censor and the fact that in 1980 the BBC had itself mounted a dramatisation of the *Lady Chatterley* trial, Alasdair Milne, Managing Director of BBC Television, ordered that 22 seconds of a fairly brutal sex scene should be cut. When *Time Out* ran an article about the incident, quoting Griffiths as denying 'any interest in pornographising sexuality' and expressing concern about the possibility of growing censorship under the Thatcher government,[11] it received – and printed – a number of letters from feminists arguing against the liberal-progressive consensus on censorship and expressing support for the BBC's action: 'I am a socialist feminist and opposed to censorship on principle, but I felt positively grateful for the painful sexual scene in the final episode not being dwelt upon at unnecessary length. The point was made quite strongly enough!'[12]

Griffiths' interest in sexuality in *Sons and Lovers* remains largely Reichian. As he told one interviewer, what exercised him about the character of Paul was the way Lawrence had demonstrated 'the subtle and pervasive inhibition on human growth that characterises industrial societies. . . . From the eighteenth century onwards there has been a controlling attachment of sexuality to time and work discipline. Paul's sexuality is arrested in the contradictions of his relationship with his mother, but it is also arrested – like that of his father – in the contradictions of industrial social life, where getting up and clocking on prohibit lapses into passion. And it's all there – Lawrence, in his as yet untheorised passion for what *is*, knew this intuitively'.[13] It was this long perspective, this carefully thought-through historical input, that finally makes *Sons and Lovers* more than just another classic serialisation. For behind Karl Johnson's fragile performance as Paul Morel, and its suggestion of an infinite social *malleability*, lies a process – a shared experience of dislocation – that is still being played out: 'Lawrence projects something in this novel which runs like an arrow throughout the century: the demand on the individual for a class translation, a transference out of the working class and into the bourgeoisie. It is frequently mystified as an entry into the "autonomous" realm of art – that's why so many working-class writers are to be found propping up bourgeois culture.'[14]

RECOVERING 'THE BEST PLAY OF THE TWENTIETH CENTURY'

The very considerable achievement of *Sons and Lovers* should not, however, be allowed to obscure the fact that the project prolonged Griffiths' retreat from contemporary subjects which began with *Reds* and continued with the other adaptation he worked on during this period, *The Cherry Orchard*. He himself would undoubtedly have been aware of this, since he once differentiated for an interviewer between writing 'that is clearly out of me and *now*' and writing 'that is mediated by historical correlatives'.[15] Yet he seems to have remained curiously blocked from that 'now', in flight from contemporary politics and having to push further and further back into history for material: 1917, 1913 and, with *The Cherry Orchard*, 1903.

Griffiths' version of Anton Chekhov's masterpiece was, like *Sons and Lovers*, commissioned by a colleague with whom he had previously worked on an original text. Richard Eyre, who directed *Comedians* in 1975, had mounted his first production of Chekhov's play in Edinburgh in 1971. At Nottingham, he longed to tackle again what he felt was 'the best play of the twentieth century'. And after *Comedians* he also wanted to renew the working relationship with Griffiths. So in 1976, as Griffiths was being drawn into *Reds*, he suggested the project to the writer, who was immediately engaged by it. On several occasions, Griffiths has spoken of the importance of Chekhov to his own writing; asked at the time which dramatists had influenced him, he replied, 'Ibsen, I suppose, Strindberg certainly, Chekhov more and more.'[16] He recognised that a new translation, prepared for a performance to be directed by Eyre, could recover meanings within the text which had been submerged in the English theatrical tradition. So just as two years later he was to approach Lawrence, he tackled Chekhov's final play with a specific strategic intent. The new version was premiered at the Nottingham Playhouse in March 1977, where it ran for four weeks. Just over three years later, Eyre had the opportunity to produce it again, this time for BBC1. The resulting performance, screened in October 1981, is a lucid and compelling realisation of the text, and was recorded with a particularly innovative use of studio videotape cameras. Indeed, Eyre approached this production intending to parallel Griffiths' recovery of Chekhov with his own recovery of the dramatic potential of the normally intractable television studio.

At the start of rehearsals for this television version, in December 1980, Richard Eyre introduced the play to the cast and placed it against a detailed historical background.[17] He stressed how important it was to understand the specific references within the work, particularly those related to the emancipation of the serfs in 1861. This act, carried through by the Tsar and a small grouping of liberal nobility, forced the gentry to cede half their land to the peasants whom they had previously owned. In return the peasants had to pay redemption money, which caused much bitterness. Years of terrorism, culminating in the assassination of the Tsar in 1881, had increased the regime's repressiveness, so that by the time Chekhov wrote *The Cherry Orchard* in 1903 the country was effectively a police state. At that moment too there was growing unrest among the peasantry; and this, coupled with the gradual emergence for the first time of a petit bourgeoisie in Russia, foreshadowed the imminent breakdown of the previously rigidly ordered class structure. But as Richard Eyre stressed, that class structure was not to be equated with a British experience; it had to be understood within the historical development of Russia. This structure is presented fully in the panoramic reach of *The Cherry Orchard*, and is organised round the household of a land-owning family fallen on hard times. Madame Ranevsky returns from Paris to her bankrupt estate but refuses to recognise the impending sale of her family's vast and precious orchard. The title, however, refers not only to this but to the young Trofimov's line in a visionary speech to the dreamy Anya: 'Our orchard is all of Russia.' Chekhov looks to the future as well as to the past, anticipating the changes the new century will bring.

When he began work on his text Griffiths was concerned to inscribe this history and politics throughout a subtly interpretative reading of the play. Yet he was not interested in rewriting Chekhov, only in pointing up the meanings which he had recognised were 'screaming out to be realised'. So he determined to remain 'faithful' to the original and, since he did not speak the language, he commissioned a new, strictly literal translation from the Russian scholar Helen Rappaport. Once this rendering was delivered, accompanied by quite extensive linguistic notes, he and the translator went over it in detail.

Their discussions are evidenced by the copious marginal notes on the typescript of the translation in the BFI collection, and illustrate

Griffiths' concern to find the precise metaphorical echoes of key phrases. So, for example, after the merchant Lopakhin has bought the orchard, he speaks to the shocked Ranevsky family. In Helen Rappaport's text, one sentence reads: 'I must be asleep, it's just a dream, I'm imagining it. . . . It's a figment of your imagination, enveloped in the gloom of obscurity.' Griffiths notes here of the latter phrase: 'Lit: it's the fruit of your imagination covered by the gloom/darkness of ignorance/incertitude/uncertainty/not-knowingness.' Lopakhin is stressing his social and intellectual distance from the Ranevskys by drawing on an attitude which they have often ascribed to him from their 'superior' position. Other translations ignore this delicate reference. But in his final version Griffiths gives expression to this quality of 'not-knowingness' by having Lopakhin say, 'You think I'm imagining it, dreaming it . . . oh these ignorant yearnings . . . is that it?' The 'faithfulness' reflected in this detail extended throughout Griffiths' work on the play. As he wrote in a penetrating introduction to the published text: 'The simple *facts* are that (a) I *edited out* next to nothing, save for some patronymics (though I debated hard about the often unplayably expository structure of Act One); (b) I *added* fewer than fifty words of dialogue to a play that has approximately 21,000; (c) not a single line or action was transposed to another part of the play.'[18] Yet within these self-imposed constraints, Griffiths finds a direct and immediate language which one critic described as 'the most idiomatic and speakable Chekhov I have experienced'.

In the same introduction Griffiths wrote of how he intended his version to act on the tradition of Chekhov production in the English theatre. Raymond Williams has succinctly characterised the dominant interpretation: 'The devotees of Chekhov in the theatres of England . . . acclaim his work as "really lifelike and free from any tiresome moralising". Taken over, as he has been, by a sentimental sect, he has even been welcomed, astonishingly, as "naturalism without politics".'[19] Griffiths developed this argument: 'For half a century now, in England as elsewhere, Chekhov has been the almost exclusive property of theatrical class secretaries for whom the plays have been plangent and sorrowing evocations of an "ordered" past no longer with "us", its passing greatly to be mourned. For theatregoers . . . Chekhov's tough, bright-eyed complexity was dulced into swallowable sacs of sentimental morality. . . . Translation followed translation, *that* idiom became "our" idiom, that class "our" class, until the play's specific historicity and precise sociological imagination had been bleached of all meanings beyond those required to convey the necessary "natural" sense that the fine will always be

Characters oriented to the future: Lopakhin (Bill Paterson) and Trofimov (Anton Lesser) in *The Cherry Orchard*.

undermined by the crude and that the "human condition" can for all essential purposes be equated with "the plight of the middle classes".[20] So just as Griffiths was later to attempt to recover Lawrence as a specifically working-class writer, here he was concerned to recover the specificity of Chekhov. Working within the mature modes of nineteenth-century European theatre, Chekhov, like Lawrence, was a realist writer, presenting a sociological portrait of a family in decline, and analysing through that the historical and class forces of a critical moment in his country's history. And as has been suggested at several points in this book, it has been within this realist tradition that Griffiths has identified his own work.

With *The Cherry Orchard*, Griffiths saw that the text was not, as it has so often been interpreted, solely a lament for the loss by languid aristocrats of both property and values. '*The Cherry Orchard*,' he wrote, 'has *always* seemed to me to be dealing not only with the subjective pain of property loss but also and more importantly with its objective *necessity*. To present it as the first is to celebrate a pessimism; as to see it as both is to redress an important political balance potent in the text Chekhov wrote but in *practice* almost wholly ignored.'[21] Redressing this balance involves inflections throughout the play, but it can be seen most clearly at work in Griffiths' presentation of the characters of Lopakhin and Trofimov. A grandson of serfs, Lopakhin is a self-

153

made businessman who has earned enough to buy the orchard, which he now intends to cut down. Like the radical student Trofimov, Lopakhin is a character oriented to the future, and it is the tension between their differing hopes of the world to come that Griffiths locates at the centre of the play. (Again, it should be stressed, in line with the intentions of Chekhov, who wrote of Lopakhin that he was 'the central character of the play'.)

The entrepreneur's vision of liberation is a private family idyll: 'Lopakhin will take his axe to the cherry orchard,' he promises, 'and send the trees whistling to the ground! And . . . summer cottages we'll build in their stead and our children's children's children will hear the distant music of a new life blossoming about them.' Trofimov, in contrast, foresees a *social* change: 'There *is* a discernible future in which we'll find solutions to the problems that confront us now.' Griffiths' sympathies rest with Trofimov, whose radicalism is underlined. In Chekhov's text there is the implication that he is a 'perpetual' or 'eternal' student because of official disapproval of his views. Griffiths actualises this by adding 'If the authorities have their way' to his early admission that 'I suspect I'll always be [a student]'. Chekhov himself could not have got such an explicit statement past the censor.

More fundamentally, Griffiths strengthens Trofimov's political consciousness. His most passionate expression of his belief in the future is in a speech delivered to Madame Ranevsky and her daughters which *can* be expounded in purely intellectual terms. The beginning of this speech in Elisaveta Fen's translation for the Penguin Classics series is rendered in this way: 'Humanity is perpetually advancing, always seeking to perfect its own powers. One day all the things that are beyond our grasp at present are going to fall within our reach, only to achieve this we've got to work with all our might, to help the people who are seeking after truth.' This is rarefied discourse, obsessed with ideas, metaphysics even. Helen Rappaport's literal translation has only a slightly different emphasis: 'Mankind is marching ahead, consolidating its strengths. Everything that is unattainable at present, will one day be easily discernible and within our grasp. Only, to achieve this, we must work, and use all our strength to help those who are searching for the truth.' But Griffiths' Trofimov wants action, concrete and meaningful *answers*, not an abstract 'truth'. And this Trofimov knows exactly where these answers are to be found: 'Mankind can make progress, *struggle* for perfection. There is a discernible future in which we'll find solutions to the problems that confront us now; but we'll achieve it only through unremitting *struggle*, by working with all our strength to help

154

those who even now are seeking the answers.' (Emphasis added.) For this Trofimov, those *even now* seeking the answers would surely be the nascent Bolshevik party.

Griffiths recognised throughout the preparation of his version that his language could only contribute one element to the recovery of 'that lively class heretic', Chekhov. The meanings he was uncovering could only be fully expressed in performance. 'Readers will judge for themselves,' he wrote, 'whether the version I've written speaks to them more pertinently about the world they live in than other versions they've encountered; but they would have had to *see* it, in a production as truthful as Richard Eyre's at Nottingham, to feel that relevance bite into the flesh.'[22] In the later television version, which was completely re-cast, the performances were again critical. In Nottingham, Lopakhin had been played by Dave Hill, a frequent presence in Griffiths' television work. Michael Coveney wrote of him in the *Financial Times*: 'He might be recognisable as the sort of person hoping to build a leisure centre on the dying Thames. Or, in his fur-collared overcoat and forthright manner, as the proprietor of a northern club.'[23] Now the actor was Bill Paterson, offering the character as an equally familiar bluff, sympathetic Scot. Anton Lesser, who had been the first choice for Paul Morel, was chosen for Trofimov, and found precisely the right level of idealism and commitment. As Griffiths had intended, Madame Ranevsky, magnificent yet deeply vulnerable in Judi Dench's portrayal, was not the sole pivotal focus, but she remained as one of several significant psychologies and social positions which the play explores in full. Indeed Eyre, as he began rehearsals, told the cast that each of the twelve characters was equally important, that each should hold the audience's identification and sympathy as they spoke, but then be undercut by an entirely persuasive reply. Here was the dialectical structure of *Comedians* extended across an even greater range.

LIBERATING THE STUDIO

The Cherry Orchard was produced for television almost by accident. After leaving Nottingham in early 1978, Richard Eyre went to the BBC as a producer on 'Play for Today'. At that point he had not directed for television, but he intended to rework for the medium both *Comedians* and Griffiths' version of Chekhov. The former was accommodated in his first season and the script of the latter was given to Keith Williams when he became Head of Plays in 1979. Williams was excited by the text but knew that all the slots for classic plays were filled for the following twelve months. The idea rested. Nearly a year later Eyre and the producer Ann Scott contracted with the BBC to work on the six-part series 'Tory Stories', to be written by Griffiths. But the scripting of the first film took longer than they had all anticipated. Eyre and Scott made another film – *Pasmore* from the David Storey novel – and then Scott was offered two 'Play for Today' slots for studio productions. *The Cherry Orchard* was suggested again, and despite expectations that the productions would be contemporary in subject, adjustments were made and it was accepted. The necessary extra facilities were made available and the production given a final go-ahead in early October 1980.

By this point Richard Eyre had already directed two films for television (*Pasmore*, and the earlier *The Imitation Game* from an Ian McEwan script) and was consequently uncertain about returning to conventional studio production on videotape. Like the majority of writers and directors, he believed in the superior expressive qualities of film, which David Hare has encapsulated in this way: 'Film is free. By angling, by heightening, by the slightest visual distortion your view of your material may alter in the passage of a single shot. Film is fast. It cuts well. You create your work like a mosaic out of tiny pieces, each one minutely examined as it's prepared, and then slipped into the stream of images you are preparing in your head.'[24]

By contrast the studio, with electronic cameras recording images on videotape, is seen as inevitably destroying any attempt to create distinctive drama. It is held to be less 'realistic' than film and impossible to use expressively. Because a number of shots are recorded together in sequence, cutting from camera to camera, precise framing, movement and lighting are difficult to achieve. In addition, the pressure of time in the studio is immense and, under such rigid working practices, a good studio director is held to be someone who can simply meet tight deadlines. Real costs on an average programme are roughly comparable between film and studio videotape, but the massive capital investment in the 50s dictates that the studios built then must be fully used. Consequently most television drama is still made in the studio.

From watching productions being taped, Richard Eyre saw the problems but also felt that the process did have a largely unexplored potential, which only a few directors had attempted to unlock. (His own examples of successful studio work included Jonathan Miller's productions for the BBC Shakespeare cycle and Alan Clarke's production of Büchner's *Danton's Death*.) Discussions with Geoff Feld, the senior cameraman on *Comedians* who had also been attached to the unit of *The Imitation Game*, suggested that film techniques could be applied in the studio. Small, light cameras with comparable mountings were available and were capable of operating within an enclosed, four-wall environment. Such electronic cameras had been used on location for more than six years, but only recently had they begun to approach the quality of image and colour expected from studio cameras. Restricted studio time would still remain a central problem but with full rehearsal and detailed preparation, the project did seem feasible. With the committed co-operation of Geoff Feld and lighting designer Howard King, the technique was made to work. Each shot was framed and lit individually, mostly using just a single camera, and these brief sequences were then edited together in the post-production process.

The advantages of the technique are clear from the completed drama which, for a television production of a classic play, achieves a rare intensity. At each point the meanings and implications of Griffiths' text as well as the shadings of performances are complemented by precisely appropriate images. Chekhov is released from the clench of tradition and the studio is liberated from the equally deadening weight of traditional style and working practices. Yet the project remains an exception, since few directors have attempted to exploit further the experience gained. Eyre himself has done one other such production – a recording of his National Theatre staging of *The Beggar's Opera* – but he has continued to devote his principal energies to the theatre and to film.

As is the case with *Sons and Lovers*, the achievement of *The Cherry Orchard* was considerable. But there remains the concern that Griffiths was avoiding the challenge of the 'now'. As the writer wrestled with John Reed, Chekhov and Lawrence, contemporary struggles seemed to others particularly important, with a right-wing resurgence bringing the new Toryism to power in May 1979. In the week of *The Cherry Orchard*'s transmission, the critic W. Stephen Gilbert raised the related question with Griffiths of whether adaptations were a dilution of his work. 'If you look at the whole of a year's drama output on ITV and the BBC,' Griffiths replied, 'over half of that will be re-workings in dramatic form of other literatures. Brecht knew about this. A good half of what Brecht wrote was re-working other people's work, to point it, to give it a particular relevance and resonance for the conjunction of social and political forces in that society. Frankly *Sons and Lovers* could have been done by any of 300 writers. But not *that Sons and Lovers*. And *Cherry Orchard* too. I did *Cherry Orchard* because I felt that its meanings had been seriously betrayed, almost consciously betrayed, over forty or fifty years of theatre practice in this country.'[25]

The Cherry Orchard, then, was primarily a *theatrical* intervention. Yet

157

the play reflected a significant shift in Griffiths' writing, away from a concentration on working-class experience and towards an analysis of the ruling class. This shift was to be fully realised with his next major project, the film *Country*, which was shown on BBC1 a week after *The Cherry Orchard*.

8 'A Tory Story': *Country*

'When I sat down in 1979 to start a new play for television I asked myself what I had learnt most about in the previous few years. The answer was wealth!'[1] 1979 and the writing of *Country* marks probably the most decisive shift to date in Trevor Griffiths' strategy as an author. From a concern with working-class experience, from an analysis of revolutionary politics, and from an interrogation of the failures of the Left, he turned to an engagement with the Right. 1979 is also identifiable as the moment of a further stage in his own class translation. The worldwide success of *Comedians* and the commission for *Comrades* had provided substantial financial security; in 1981 he reflected that he was 'almost necessarily . . . divorced from the condition of [my] earlier life'. If he wished to retain his integrity as a writer, this inevitably involved a realignment of his focus: 'If you can fake it, you can still write about the working class as if you were having that experience. But *Comedians* was the last play where I felt I could honestly occupy their space, directly and without going back.'[2] 1979 was also the year of the first victory of Thatcherism, when the Conservatives were elected with a commitment to the most far-reaching programme of social change since the 1945 Labour government.

Set over two days at the end of the Second World War, the television film *Country* is a portrait of the English upper class responding to that Labour triumph. The prologue is set against one of Churchill's election broadcasts, in which he attacks the 'formidable machine' of socialism: 'Here, in Great Britain, the cradle of free democracy throughout the world, we do not like to be regimented and ordered about and have every action of our lives prescribed for us . . .' Counterpointed with this are shots of a fire drill at Eton with boys jumping, senselessly or so it seems at first, from a window to a prefect's sharp, unconcerned commands. The ironic tone established here is crucial to the film which follows. A slow motion shot similarly prefigures the dreamlike quality which inflects many of the later scenes where 'reality' seems to be a frame or two out of joint. A gunshot cuts the action on the titles sequence to the Carlion estate in

159

Kent, where a huge, predominantly Regency mansion dominates and possesses the landscape of the weald around it. Sir Frederic Carlion (Leo McKern) is summoned from pigeon shooting for a family christening. He is distracted, recessed, broken – as becomes clear – by the recent death of his eldest son and heir. Along with the 'clan' of related but subsidiary families, the christening and Lady Carlion's birthday celebrations have attracted the Carlions' second son Philip (James Fox), a gossip columnist living in London, and his errant sister Virginia (Penelope Wilton). Philip arrives for the church service and is immediately apprised of his father's wish, which he resists, that he should take over the Carlion brewing concern so that 'things will go on as they have done'. Virginia approaches the house far more circumspectly, watching and weighing it and taking numerous photographs.

The world of the Carlions as revealed is a world out of its time yet still one of enormous power, a world with a language of its own, and with a distinct morality. To an outsider its rituals and customs may seem bizarre, but it is not a decadent world, or only partly so. Although, as exemplified in Sir Frederic, it is aged and diseased, it will be almost effortlessly reinvigorated by Philip and his opportunist New Toryism. On the night of the christening the Carlions' ball goes ahead, despite the sudden arrival in the stables of East End families, homeless after the London bombings and now down on the estate for the annual hop-picking. Emboldened by recent events, they turn the horses loose and move in. As one of them says in a confrontation with Sir Frederic, 'This is the best place I've put my head down all year. You treat your horses better than you treat us . . .' To which Carlion replies, 'My horses have names . . .' The night also brings the first news of the Labour election landslide, news which is greeted the following morning with blank disbelief by the assembled families. Recognising that action will now be necessary to ensure the continuance of his world, of its power and privilege, Philip understands where his duty lies and accedes to his father's wish. Fighting off the competing claim of his nephew, and making the necessary adjustments to his 'deficiencies' – 'wife, clubs, clothes' – he snatches complete control of the brewing business.

UNDER THE INFLUENCE

One acknowledged influence on the writing of *Country* was *The Cherry Orchard*, and – even from this sparse summary – certain parallels are obvious. Both offer a class analysis of a society in microcosm centred on a country house and its estate, both feature families faced with the

Country: the old order and the new. Leo McKern as Sir Frederic Carlion and James Fox as his son, Philip.

loss of property and position. At the centre of both is a ball, and in both the gentry has a brief, hostile encounter with the working class. Chekhov encompasses a broader social range and the depiction of all his characters is far more sympathetic than the later writer's implicit critique. But the most significant difference is that in *The Cherry Orchard*, the orchard itself is sold and felled. In *Country*, home and business are preserved. Russia was to experience fundamental social change; despite the intentions and achievements of its 1945 government, Britain was not. *Country* addresses itself to the reason for that failure.

Even more fundamental to *Country*'s composition was Dodie Smith's *Dear Octopus*. An exemplar of what Griffiths calls the 'country house drama', this 1938 West End hit is also the tale of a family reunion at a rural mansion. When *Country* was transmitted several critics commented on the more than superficial closeness, and indeed, when the plays are read together, the similarities are striking. In Act 1 of *Dear Octopus* the Randolphs are assembling to celebrate with a dance the Golden Wedding of Charles and Dora. Their children are returning home, first Nicholas, who works in publicity in London, and later Cynthia, a woman with 'a past'. Like the Carlions, the Randolphs are not aristocrats with a lengthy lineage, but more recently elevated gentry, having acquired their modest fortunes from industry and mercantile interests. Much of the play's mostly inconsequential dialogue hinges on Nicholas' marriage prospects, as does the main thread of the plot. Just as Philip does in *Country*,

161

Nicholas meets first on his return the faithful companion of the household, Grace, known to everyone as Fenny (Faith in *Country*), and subsequently bickers with the wife of his late brother, who was killed in the last war (Alice Carlion, and the dead Major Frederic).

Act 2 takes place in the nursery with Nicholas and Cynthia reminiscing, together with their sisters Margery and Hilda (who have no equivalents in *Country*). All four look back to an idyllic childhood, and reflect on their problems in life since then. Which is precisely what Philip and Virginia do in scene 52 of *Country*. Other scenes and characters are similarly paralleled before the dramatic climax (Act 3 in *Dear Octopus*, scene 57 in *Country*) where Nicholas/Philip proposes a toast to 'the Family'. In Dodie Smith's text this toast is a saccharine celebration: 'It is, like nearly every British institution, adaptable. It bends, it stretches – but it never breaks. And so I give you our toast . . . to the family – that dear octopus from whose tentacles we never quite escape nor, in our inmost hearts, never quite wish to.' For Griffiths it is capitalism which bends, stretches, and perhaps never breaks, for Philip's address over the port indicates how even an outdated autocracy is, in Smith's words, 'like nearly every British institution, adaptable', even when faced with the strong challenge of socialism. Finally, to cement a continuity in both plays, Nicholas proposes to Grace and Philip offers his hand, and fortune, to Faith.

Griffiths' intent in working with a pre-existing text was also partly to put forward a critique of the genre which it represented. *Country* was conceived to indicate and expose the silences in such plays, and to make them less seductive for future audiences. As he has explained, 'One of the things which is never discussed in country house drama is the economic base of the class portrayed, and its exploitation of other classes. What we're asked to see as the truth is that rich, powerful people share a common humanity with those who are less rich and less powerful . . . *Country* deals centrally with the question of succession, with wealth and the perpetuation of wealth and privilege. So it challenges the inbuilt but never spelt out assumptions of a genre.'[3] That genre may be moribund in today's West End, but it undoubtedly thrives within the dynastic sagas of television costume drama. So that *Country* is as much directed against, for example, the distortions of *The Forsyte Saga* as it is against a theatrical tradition of the 30s. Ironically, *Country* was actually transmitted at the same time as the second episode on ITV of Granada's *Brideshead Revisited*, a much-hyped and extraordinarily lavish adaptation of Evelyn Waugh's novel, which celebrated the human and spiritual qualities of the Marchmain dynasty. As one critic remarked, 'There could be no more comprehensive corrective to Waugh's romantic vision of

162

opulence than Griffiths' rigorous class analysis.'[4]

One further aspect of *Country*'s complex relationship with genre is the integration of references to the family saga of *The Godfather*. More obvious in earlier versions of the script than in the final film, these include the play on the family name, Carlion, phonetically only one sound removed from Corleone. There is also the centrality of family ritual and celebration, which is fundamental in Mario Puzo's book and Francis Coppola's film. Without over-stressing the parallel, Griffiths identifies Britain's controlling Mafia.

CINEMATIC STYLE: THE TEXTURE OF DETACHMENT

Griffiths' writing in *Country* is materially different from all his previous work. Far more than in his earlier scripts, there is a reliance on gesture, glance and movement to convey meaning. This was partly dictated by the new subject matter. For in extensive research and study of the upper classes, Griffiths came to recognise the lack of what he described as 'any serious ideological thought that needs airing and debating'. And he added, 'I feel I also discovered that one of the other extraordinary absences within that class is inner dialogue, or interior life. For them there is precept, there is duty, there is opportunity, and there is power – these seem to occupy all the space within these people's lives . . . In a sense they see themselves instrumentally.'[5] These considerations indicated that spoken debates about thought, emotion and action would be inappropriate, and indeed inaccurate, for the representation he envisaged.

Also critical to the shaping of *Country*'s writing was the experience of *Comrades*. Wrestling with that script, Griffiths for the first time had to reach an intimate understanding of *film* as a medium. *Country* was then his first film for television, and the medium's potential for far greater visual expressiveness than is possible on studio videotape complemented the requirements of the subject.

There were dangers. A lavish production (the budget was £400,000) and the eminent cast could easily swamp the text's critique and offer little more than a celebration. Griffiths wanted to present the precise *texture* of his characters' lives, and to achieve both a sociological accuracy and the sense of a concrete world, inhabited by believable beings. But he also saw the necessity of a critical, ironic distance from them, and this is achieved through the character of Virginia, through certain filmic strategies and through the subtle stylisation of performances. Virginia is introduced taking photos of the Carlion estate, a device which establishes the idea of the families and their tribal rituals being dispassionately watched by the viewer.

163

References to observation also recur throughout the text. These are complemented by director Richard Eyre's handling of the cast and of the camera. For his employment of movement, of framings and the placing of characters within environments always contributes to, and never undercuts, the meanings of the script. As Griffiths says, there is 'the sense of real life being lived, real space being occupied and yet a very cool, detached and mobile camera seeing them from another point of view.'[6]

The operation of this is clear in the comparison with *Brideshead Revisited*. There the camera of director Charles Sturridge embraces the world of the rich, enters into it and surrenders all detachment. By contrast, Eyre cites the continuously moving, watching camera of the Hungarian film *Angi Vera* as an influence on *Country*. For his camera is similarly fluid and sweeping. One shot, for example, tracks along the balustrade of a balcony, eavesdropping on the several after-lunch conversations. Another long developing track catches the family entering the dining room, and gives a sense of the scale of the house and their complete self-assurance within it. These shots illustrate the elegance and opulence of the mansion but are neither seductive nor admiring. Throughout the film the house is integral, dominating (though never dwarfing) the characters and developing a 'life' and a history just as important as any of the characters. Eyre describes as 'expressionistic' the bold style and often striking use of light which he used to catch this (and stresses how important were the contributions of the cameraman Nat Crosby and designer Geoff Powell). This 'expressionism' he defines as the correlation of appropriate images with statements about the moral, political and social concerns of the drama.

One example is a wide-shot of Sir Frederic's study towards the close of the film. The tones are dark and suggestive of age and the frame is entirely dominated by two huge portraits of family ancestors – the past remaining in the present. Before the pictures Leo McKern's Sir Frederic bends over his desk, bowed down by the collapse of the order of his world and by a realisation of who Virginia has become: 'She was my daughter.' Philip stands easy and erect by the window, aware of but relatively independent of 'the past'. Side-lighting picks out his profile, glamourising his mastery of the situation and illustrating the confidence which permits the easy irony of his description of the election result: 'I think it's what they call Letting the People Speak.' Sir Frederic's line is static, heavy, defeated: 'Everything passes.' Philip's is casual, relaxed, aware that this is not Armageddon: 'It's possible.'

In its understanding and analysis of World War Two, *Country* adopts a direct relationship with a distinct group of recent plays, many of which have been commissioned and directed by Richard Eyre. One of the most important is the film *The Imitation Game*, which Eyre directed from a script by Ian McEwan in 1979/80. A rigorous analysis of patriarchy, it is also set during the war and describes how a young middle-class woman, Cathy (played by Harriet Walter), joins the ATS and is posted to the code-breaking centre at Bletchley. There she is drawn towards the centre of the highly secret, male-run Ultra operation, and is destroyed by it. A severe, precisely calculated study of the relationship between secrecy and power, the film works in a similar way to *Country* by offering an analysis of the past to reach an understanding of the present. Resonance with contemporary experience issues in a potent feminist text. Other plays which adopt this project include *Brassneck* by Howard Brenton and David Hare (directed at Nottingham by Eyre), Hare's film for BBC Birmingham *Licking Hitler* and his related stage play *Plenty* mounted by the National Theatre, Stephen Lowe's *Touched* (premiered by Eyre at Nottingham), and another BBC Birmingham drama, *Clapperclaw* by Jack Shepherd. The interest and importance of the time is summed up by Eyre: 'It does seem to me to be the most significant period in my life, even though I was only born in 1943.'

The major influence on all these works was Angus Calder's seminal study *The People's War*, a 'history from beneath' of the Home Front during World War Two. Calder's book, which was first published in 1969, culls from a wide range of sources an account of life in Britain between 1939 and 1945 that dismantles many of the myths that have grown up since, and which are perpetuated in popular journalism and fiction, particularly nostalgic television series. Calder exposes the false understanding of the country as united, 'classless', equal. He illustrates how privilege remained entrenched and how the aristocracy stayed a great deal more equal than everybody else. And it is this analysis which Griffiths elaborates in *Country*. He remembers, for example, how until he read Calder and began his research in books such as Waugh's diaries, he really believed that the rich suffered from rationing and austerity just as much as his own Northern working-class family. *Country*, then, again in line with his earlier work, represents an engagement with other representations of that history in the cinema and television, the views of series like *Danger UXB* or *A Family at War*.

Challenges within the film to the class portrayed come from both Virginia and from the hop-pickers who have moved into the barn. Virginia was once inspired by Philip's early socialism to fight in Spain and to reach a class-based hatred of the world which bred her. She and Philip, indeed, are the drama's only truly vital characters. She has lived a full life, symbolised in a typical Griffiths reference to her free and strong sexuality. Almost everyone else is old and tired, morally and sexually corrupt, or foolish and ineffectual; apart, that is, from Philip, whose movement into the family and the firm also has a dubious and in many ways reactionary sexual parallel, since he moves from a homosexual lover in London to the 'healthy' heterosexuality of marriage to Faith. After uneasy meetings with the family and after Philip's accession to the Carlion throne, Virginia bursts out at the assembled male diners: 'One day – soon, I hope – there'll be a banging at your door. It will be the people. Because they'll be English, they'll probably give you a third-class rail ticket to Dover or Southampton, when they ask you to go. Personally, I would not object if they simply disembowelled you in front of your children and fed your bits to the chickens. Because I feel that, were there a God, he would want you to suffer for the suffering you cause.' But her hostility appears futile, and her speech is undercut by a throwaway remark from her own son, who is clear about his place with the Carlions.

The working-class challenge is one of the least achieved elements of the film. For the East Enders are shown as little more than cyphers, bluff and inarticulate in their confrontation with Sir Frederic, or heavily romanticised in scenes around the camp fires. It is arguable that they are presented as they are observed by the family, from the point of view of the upper class. Even so, their challenge is no more effective than Virginia's. In the final scene Philip and his father watch the celebration of the Labour victory. Round a crackling bonfire topped by a dress-suited effigy, the men sing 'Roll out the barrel' and crack a cask of Carlion ale. Sir Frederic is puzzled: 'What is it? Is it a funeral?' To which Philip replies: 'I rather think it is, Father. They have not yet noticed that the grave is empty.' It is Philip's perception which dominates the scene, providing the closing note of the film and presaging the ultimate failure of the Labour government and of effective socialism in the post-war period. So if it is granted that the working class is seen through Philip's eyes, does this preclude an indication of directions to change the society? Griffiths' response is: 'You have to remind people that their power is almost unlimited, but you can't do that by waving slogans in the air.'[7] That reminder may be present in *Country*, but should an audience not look for something more positive?

The sense of incompleteness in the political project of *Country*, as well as the lack of resolution of several sub-themes, is explained by the fact that it was originally intended as the first of six such stories following the fortunes of the reinvigorated Carlion family through the post-war period and into a near future of extreme Thatcherism. Before this, it had been conceived as six contemporary plays about Conservatism, addressed to the rise in the late 70s of a new Toryism and set in various sites including Ulster Unionism and the Barnsley working class. But it evolved into a historical series, 'Tory Stories', or as Griffiths half-jokingly referred to it, 'The Working of the English Making Class'. The next film, with many of the same characters, was to be set in 1957 and to be focused on the bank-rate leak of that year, an event which Griffiths feels has been totally submerged in contemporary history. Next was to have been the Profumo affair, then 1968 and the attempted Zuckerman putsch planned in response to the May 'events'. The 1973–4 toppling of Heath was to be the fifth key historical moment, and then the strands were to be projected into the late 80s.

All these films would have developed a central metaphor introduced towards the end of *Country*. Philip celebrates his new position with 'something special sent down from town . . . something the Carlion lab boys have been working on.' This early keg beer – 'half the price, travels, keeps forever' – is described as 'weasel piss'. But as Philip points out, 'All we have to do is make it taste a little less like weasel piss and we could be in clover . . .' As one of the present authors wrote in the *New Statesman*: 'Changes in the brewing industry – first keg, then lager, then multi-national mergers – were to have served (in the full series) as a metaphor for the restructuring of British capital. But beer was also chosen because of its importance within working-class culture, the area where consumerism, the multi-nationals and, eventually, monetarism were to wreak the profoundest changes of all.'[8]

The plan for such a major series is daring and exciting. Yet the other five film scripts have remained unwritten. The reasons for this are complex, but perhaps it is most significant that, in some fundamental way, and not at all because of censorship, such scripts *could not* be written in the repressive social and political climate of

Britain at the start of the 80s. No contemporary dramatist seemed able to deal properly with the immense impact of Thatcherism and the disillusionment of the Left. Those from whom such a script might have been expected, retreated, even if only temporarily: David Edgar occupied himself with a mammoth adaptation of Charles Dickens' *Nicholas Nickleby*, a direction also followed by Howard Brenton with *Galileo* and *Danton's Death*. David Hare, like Griffiths, sought a way forward in the past, in *Licking Hitler* and *Plenty*. At the end of 1983, there are signs – the feature film *The Ploughman's Lunch*, written by Ian McEwan and directed by Richard Eyre, Brenton's *The Genius*, Edgar's *Maydays*, and Griffiths' renewed interest in the present – that this 'block' has been broken. (Though Brenton recently confided to the *Guardian* that he had been trying and failing to 'write a Utopian play for five years'.) In retrospect, however, it will be seen to have exerted a remarkably strong hold on many of the most vigorous and significant writers of the moment, Griffiths himself being no exception.

9 'Nothing more urgent': *Oi for England*

A Moss Side cellar. Outside, the cacophony of riot: breaking glass, police sirens, exploding CS canisters. Inside, a four-piece skinhead band hammers out its 'Oi' repertoire: lumpen, backs-to-the-wall youth finding an angry voice in no-frills music and mob lyrics: 'Law and Order/Up your arse/The rules are bent/The law's a farce.'

The frenetic urgency of the all-video *Oi for England* could hardly have been further removed from the measured nuances of the eminently cinematic *Country*. One commentator, picking up on the musical element in *Oi for England*, likened the difference between the two pieces to that of 'a three-minute punk single recorded in a garage, set against a multi-track concept album'.[1] And that, of course, was exactly the effect Griffiths was aiming for. As he told *City Limits*: 'After a long involvement with nuanced scripts like *Country* and *The Cherry Orchard*, not to mention the *Reds* saga, I felt the need to write something more urgent and immediate – and there's nothing more urgent than racism.'[2] Yet at another level, *Oi for England* can be seen to offer a curious telescoping of one of *Country*'s central themes: the post-war erosion and deformation of traditional working-class culture under consumer capitalism. The history of this process, which was to have been explored through to the late 70s in the five other 'Tory Stories' of which *Country* was merely the first, is as it were reprised and concentrated on its most ugly moment: the appearance of an aggressively racist skinhead subculture, described by its most reliable chronicler as precisely based on 'a mythically conceived image of traditional working-class community'.[3]

At the same time, *Oi for England*'s significance within Griffiths' overall output clearly lies in the fact that it signals a return to contemporary concerns. The project had a highly specific genesis. In 1981 Griffiths, who had previously been associated with the work of the Anti-Nazi League in Leeds, was invited to attend a conference on 'Race in the Classroom'. Appalled by the racist incidents he heard recounted, Griffiths conceived of writing a short classroom drama

169

that could be used as part of a wider campaign to combat the attempts of racist organisations to recruit members within Britain's secondary schools. However, the riots of the summer of 1981 intervened and the project took on a different, more urgent complexion.

The Oi phenomenon – basically a musical style with strong racist overtones that had emerged from earlier forms of skinhead subculture – seemed to focus the summer's social and racial tensions. In Southall, street disturbances involving Asian youths followed a racially provocative Oi gig in the area, and the venue itself, a public house called the Hamborough Tavern, was badly damaged by fire. Meanwhile, the widely available rock album, 'Strength Through Oi', made it easier for neo-fascist organisations like the British Movement to exploit what was really a highly ambivalent subculture (Oi's exponents were by no means all racists). It was partly this ambivalence that drew Griffiths to Oi, since in writing about racism in the classroom he would necessarily have had to confront the fact that the problem was largely a working-class one. Oi provided him with an extremely potent image of a debased working-class culture: at once deeply reactionary *and* capable of regeneration. It also enabled him to explore more fully the notion of politics as resistance developed in the characterisation of Gethin Price in *Comedians*: Oi was nothing if not a 'ritual of resistance', a symbolic negotiation of the contradictions of being white, working-class and unemployed in Britain in the 1980s.

The skinhead phenomenon, in fact, was 'the rendering back of a particular experience – the no-hope, nothing-to-lose response of urban dole boys'.[4] It was this experience that Griffiths attempted to flesh out in the story of four Mancunian skinheads and their Oi band, Ammunition. The refrain to one of the numbers added for the touring version of *Oi for England* runs as follows:

> Dole boys
> Black and white
> All getting buried
> Under Thatcher's shite

But Stuart Cosgrove, *Oi for England*'s most perceptive critic, was surely right to point out that Griffiths was also simultaneously attempting 'to interrogate the dominant images of social violence that had been in general cultural circulation over the previous twelve months'.[5]

The urgency of *Oi for England*'s subject was reflected in the production's remarkable turn-around time once Griffiths had made

170

the initial approach to Margaret Matheson at Central Television in the autumn of 1981. The script was only delivered at Christmas but the finished tape was ready for transmission by the following April. Matheson, now Head of Drama at Central, had slotted the production into gaps in the studio schedule of the thrice-weekly, Birmingham-based soap opera, *Crossroads*. The technical results achieved by the *Crossroads* crew were often rough and ready, but producer Sue Birtwistle – the wife of Griffiths' long-standing collaborator Richard Eyre – clearly felt that the lack of polish assisted rather than hindered the piece's overall effect by underscoring its immediacy. As did blood-red fusions of actuality riot footage and newspaper headlines in the opening and closing video mixes, and the fact that none of the skinhead cast had done any television work before. These arrangements do, however, produce a major restriction: the naturalistic, single-set locale in which every exchange has to take place. In particular this means that the absolutely central theme of a temporary breakdown in the social order is reduced to a few 'off-stage' special effects: shattering glass, dull thuds, wailing sirens. As Cosgrove put it so succinctly: there is no 'outside social landscape'.[6] Instead what we get is a piece of accentuated slice-of-life naturalism, which in the end disintegrates into a pseudo-symbolic register under the palpable pressure of what it simply cannot represent. More of which later.

Contradiction is built into the very texture of *Oi for England*. Napper, Finn, Landry and Swells ironically owe their existence as an Oi band entirely to the rioting of the summer of 1981: all their equipment is looted. Moreover, they practise in a bunker-like basement owned by a black landlord. In the first of many contradictory exchanges, we see British Movement supporter Napper paying the rent from the wage packet of an Asian worker he has mugged earlier in the evening. As a group, the four form a curious relationship to the rioting going on in the street above them. Instinctively drawn to a confrontation with the police ('The Law's out there cracking heads'), they are both of it and not of it – their watering hole, 'The Union Jack' pub, echoing the Hamborough Tavern incident, is being besieged by a black crowd. This contradictory relationship to their own locality is reflected in the growing tension between the tattooed Napper and the more withdrawn Finn, Irish by extraction and anti-fascist in inclination. It is brought to a head when Napper announces that he has secured a gig at a 'skinfest' organised by Music Movement Inc – a British Movement front masterminded by a well-heeled local fascist known simply as 'The Man' (Gavin Richards reprising the role of the

171

northern Nazi he had perfected with such icy precision in David Halliwell's 1981 stage play *Creatures of Another Kind*).

The offer of the gig comes complete with a set-piece speech of such sinister power that the production – like all naturalist attempts to grapple with racism – runs dangerously close to allowing the vehemence of its rhetoric to go unchallenged: 'Listen to it out there. Listen to the sound of England – Chocolate England – coons and Anderton's puff-balls . . . they're going to burn.' White supremacist bile dressed up as a beguiling form of working-class politics. Isn't there, one interviewer wondered, a problem here, realism caught with its political pants down? 'There always is with realism,' agreed Griffiths, 'especially in a studio production like this. With only six characters and a single set you have to allow them to develop a credible space of their own – and in the case of Napper and the Gavin Richards figure this meant giving a dramatic logic to some pretty unsavoury types. Otherwise you're dealing with cartoon cutaways. But their position is, I think, quite clearly challenged from within the piece by the Finn character.'[7]

This challenge significantly centres on the question of representation. The band are called Ammunition – but for British Movement purposes they are to be marketed as White Ammunition in a 'carnival' designed to draw a fascist show of strength on local government election night in Greater Manchester. Finn baulks at this, taunting 'The Man' with a very different kind of ammunition: 'Politics, eh. What, "Black and White Unite" you mean?' Supported by the drummer – 'I don't understand, but I'm taking your word for it' – he scuppers the gig and is left alone in the basement for what proves to be a somewhat uneasy symbolic climax. The black landlord's daughter returns to lock up and together they prepare to join the riot by arming themselves with looted martial arts masks and guards. But not before Finn, in deadly serious pastiche of a Townshend or a Hendrix, has smashed up all the musical equipment in a highly charged hand-held sequence, which concentrates the play's central concern with cultural and political co-option as a struggle over representation – the instruments can no longer produce any meaning he wants to be associated with.

This spectacular display of symbolic violence is, however, counterpointed by a string of references to a suppressed 'lyrical' element in Finn, mostly defined in relation to his Irish descent. The discourse around Finn's Irishness, evident from early on and used throughout to emphasise his political differences with Napper and the others, now signals an *emotional* separateness. Surrounded by the sartorial and technological appurtenances of urban Oi, and to the

Dole boys: *Oi for England*'s band, Ammunition (Adam Kotz, Neil Pearson, Richard Platt, Ian Mercer).

sound of rioting in the inner-city street above, Finn switches on a tape of a nineteenth-century Irish rural ballad. The suggestion is that the 'hardness' of his skinhead persona has been achieved only by suppressing another area of his personality – and that this other Finn can be won for something other than Oi: Griffiths' political understanding of the Oi-skinhead phenomenon being that it represents an essentially 'pre-political phase' which 'can develop either way or not at all' and which hence 'has to be contested'.[8] Griffiths himself has described these final scenes in the following terms: 'Finn is blocked. There's a potential tenderness there that is being denied in the subculture. I had a real problem with the language – skinhead vernacular is detached from most forms of working-class speech. It's a display of aggressiveness for its own sake, uncontexted in other things like solidarity, gentleness, tenderness. I tried to show this through Finn's indistinct awareness of his Irishness. When he turns on the tape it's his frustration at having to deny that more tender, lyrical side of himself that, as much as anything, provokes his violent outburst.'[9] Yet these scenes remain somehow unsatisfactory. Their awkward symbolism exposes the limitations of the naturalism that has preceded them; they constantly run the risk of slipping into an inappropriate sentimentalism and, worse, a mythologised 'Irishness'; and, as was pointed out at the time, they raise doubts as to whether a discernible equivalent for the Finn character really could be found in the skinhead subculture.

173

Moreover, they fail to provide the kind of resolution Griffiths was obviously seeking.

THE POLITICS OF SOCIAL DECAY

Oi for England continues Griffiths' long engagement with the various forms taken by working-class resistance during different periods of history. As such, it clearly constitutes his most 'extreme' statement to date: the 'hardness' on display tops Gethin Price's 'hate' in *Comedians* by some considerable degree and is, of course, deeply racist to boot. If it had been allowed to go unchallenged dialectically within the piece, it would have invalidated that 'hard' quality in working-class culture which Griffiths had celebrated in *Sons and Lovers* and in countless other works and other ways – politically in *Occupations*, industrially in *Such Impossibilities*, aesthetically in *Comedians*. It is effectively challenged in terms of racism: Finn wins all the arguments. But this still leaves a residue of violence that seems to induce a double wariness on Griffiths' part: too obviously macho to be incorporated into a socialist politics for the 1980s and too close to the social violence that forms the piece's backdrop to be unequivocally presented, it demands some kind of softening. Hence Finn's 'lyrical' interlude and the essentially false resolution it offers. And one senses here something more than just a project that is, as Cosgrove would have it, 'ill-conceived'[10] in its own terms.

Not to put too fine a point on it, *Oi for England* is ill-conceived in terms of the rest of Griffiths' work. It lacks the kind of dialectical control between the 'hard' (Kabak) and the 'soft' (Gramsci) demonstrated in *Occupations* and it retains none of the conviction of *Comedians*, where Griffiths had been prepared to push notions of working-class resistance through to their logical conclusion without feeling the need to qualify what he, or Gethin Price, was about. The fact that in this sense *Oi for England* seems to contradict *Comedians* is, we would argue, deeply significant as far as Griffiths' future direction is concerned. What it specifically suggests is that his politics are steadily becoming detached from his practice as a dramatist. Having returned to pressing contemporary concerns in *Oi for England,* he discovers that the kind of working-class 'resistance' he has celebrated in the past is, in circumstances of social decay, capable of becoming racist in character. But rather than attempting to integrate this perception into a new understanding of the extent to which 'resistance' under Thatcherism embraces a far wider, far more contradictory constituency than that encompassed by the traditional working class, Griffiths merely tries to soften the blow of recognition

174

with Finn. The result is dramatically clumsy and politically retrograde. *Oi for England,* already clearly the inferior work, represents no significant advance on *Comedians* in this sense, even though seven years separate them.

And yet in television terms *Oi for England* was still a major landmark. Coming so soon after Jim Allen's *United Kingdom* (1982) and its version of the working class as the 'natural' repository of progressive values, it at least registered that the terrain of class politics in Britain had shifted. It also showed that working-class politics is a battleground, a disputed area of contending representations that has to be fought over – and nowhere more so than in the case of Oi, where the gut radicalism of unemployed youth became easy meat for the British Movement. But, as it turned out, *Oi for England* was to be more than just a television drama.

Returning to his original notion of a *performance* drama that could be used (and re-used) in specific contexts, Griffiths decided to extend the life of *Oi for England* by reworking it for a touring version that would take it to non-theatrical and non-fringe venues in the big multi-ethnic communities: London, Birmingham, Manchester, Leeds and Sheffield. The idea was to break down the sensationalising effect of TV transmission by providing a context in which the issues, particularly racism, raised by the play could be discussed with its target audience: young teenagers. In this respect, it followed the kind of model already developed in the trade union movement whereby videocassettes of material relating to, say, the introduction of new technology or redundancy schemes are shown to workers and then collectively discussed. A model also pursued by independent film-makers Sue Clayton and Jonathan Curling in their non theatrical screenings of *The Song of the Shirt* for women's groups. The difference was that rather than simply screening the TV version, Griffiths envisaged a live performance each night.

The reasons for this were fairly obvious – the prospect of live performance and live rock music from performers already touched by TV's 'star' system was a much more attractive proposition to prospective audiences than the idea of congregating in a group to watch some warmed-over TV. None the less, it still seemed a curious undertaking for Griffiths to be involved in since he had previously rejected theatre precisely in favour of the kind of mass audiences television could deliver. The key, of course, was that the venues for the *Oi for England* tour were not to be the conventional theatrical spaces of the bourgeois stage but the community centres, youth clubs and school halls of the inner-city working class. In this sense, Griffiths was pushing not just television beyond its usual parameters, but the theatre as well. Ironically, in view of the content of *Oi for England*, Griffiths had once described writing for the theatre as like watching football from the covered stands: 'You stay dry but there's a pitch dividing you from another possible, possibly decisive, action on the terraces.'[11] Given the fragmentation of the mass television audience already evident since the advent of Channel 4 and soon to be accelerated by the proliferation of cable and satellite systems, the *Oi for England* experiment may well have been the shape of TV drama to come. Certainly it created a *new* cultural space that moved beyond the limits of both broadcast television and conventional theatre. The results in performance, however, were often mixed.

PEOPLE'S THEATRE: THE TOURING VERSION

The 'pilot' tour, produced from London's Royal Court and directed by Antonia Bird of the Theatre Upstairs, covered seventeen venues, mainly in the Greater London area.* This was how one of the present writers described its progress in an article in the *Guardian*:

> Eastlea Youth Club, nestling between high rise flats, streets of derelict houses and the run-down industries of the Lea Valley. Hardly the likeliest venue for a play by one of Britain's leading dramatists. But the cast of the Royal Court's touring version of Trevor Griffiths' TV play about skinheads are inside doing a sound check for their repertoire of Oi numbers.
>
> Outside, the local kids seem a bit bemused by this experiment in bringing theatre to a more popular audience. Hardly anyone will admit to having seen *Oi for England* on TV and many of them are obviously miffed because it means they won't be able to play snooker. Then, with 20 minutes to go, someone recognises one of the older actors from his TV role in *The Gentle Touch*. Suddenly a buzz goes round for the evening ahead.
>
> When the guitar-toting, head-shaved actors – sartorially decked out in Fred Perry shirts and Doctor Martin's boots – finally make their way on to the makeshift stage, they are greeted with cries of 'We want the baldheads!'. The Marlboro-smoking 14-year-old next to me wants to know if the actors come from Canning Town. If not, why not? There's no

* Running from 12 May to 5 June, before beginning a season Upstairs at the Royal Court, the production played the following London venues after a one-off performance at the Birmingham Arts Festival: Jackson's Lane Community Centre; Bushill Park Y.C., Enfield; Eastlea Y.C., West Ham; George Green Centre, Millwall; Bramton Y.C., East Ham; Hoxton Hall; Walthamstow Y.C.; Wellington Avenue Y.C., Chingford; Cedars Youth and Community Centre, Harrow Weald; Oriel Y.C., Northolt; Castle Y.C., SW6; Hounslow Youth Centre; Plumstead Adventure Playground, Woolwich Dockyard Estate; Albany Empire, Deptford; York Gardens Community Centre, Clapham; Nettleford Hall, West Norwood.

sense at all that we are watching a piece of theatre. It's assumed that the actors are real-life skinheads. There's also a constant banter going on in the background as the cast struggle to hold the attention of an audience that clearly doesn't know quite how to react to what is happening on stage. On TV, *Oi for England* went out with an IBA warning about 'offensive' language and its depiction of a neo-fascist undertow in skinhead subculture is a complex affair. The rough-and-ready musical numbers performed by the novice band provide an easy enough way in, but most of the kids seem to find the rest of it heavy going.

Halfway through the performance a scuffle develops in the entrance hall. A rival youth club in the area has got wind that there are some skinheads around and have arrived to 'do' them. Although they are mistaken – the only shaved heads among the gathering of 40 or so are on stage – the police still have to be called and the evening never really recovers. The music continues to go down well – but the piece's politics seem to go right over the heads of what is a very young audience, and when it ends there is a good deal of puzzlement: 'Is that it?' Only a handful remain for the discussion with the cast and director, and the hoped-for debate around the issues raised in the performance – racism, unemployment, police harassment – doesn't materialise.

This rather muted response, in a borough where the National Front polled more votes than anywhere else in London in the recent GLC elections and where unemployment is high, surprises everyone. Director Antonia Bird begins to think about changes to make the production more accessible. The original TV script had already been extensively reworked by Griffiths himself – the Moss Side setting becoming Hackney; the guitar-smashing finale dropped; and two additional musical interludes inserted. Now there is talk of compressing the ending and simplifying its drawn-out symbolism; 'softening' the role of the British Movement supporter and firming up that of his anti-fascist protagonist; and restructuring the whole discussion format at the end.

As expected, things go much better down in the Isle of Dogs, where the George Green Centre has a proper auditorium and the slightly older audience seem to have more idea about what to expect from a play. This time the running backchat is directed quite pointedly at what is happening on stage. But there is also a disturbing racist undercurrent in some of the comments, and the four black kids in the audience of about 60 frequently look uneasy, particularly during the vitriolic 'Chocolate England' speech halfway through. There had been a hint that this might happen when Paul Moriarty, again recognised from *The Gentle Touch*, encountered some 'we hate blacks' abuse on his way to the dressing room before the performance started. Happily, it didn't surface in the discussion afterwards. However, although the play seemed to have been more widely understood than at Eastlea, it was again noticeable that most of those who spoke had to be pressed into connecting it up with issues like unemployment or racism and were much happier simply talking about how it confirmed their own experience of skinheads as 'nutters' full stop. In the end, they identify with

177

the character who rejects the racist stance of the rest of the band because he doesn't fit into this category – and not because of his leftish politics. Still, the overall impression among the cast is that the production is beginning to hit home.

But now there is a major hiccup. A youth worker from Hoxton Hall, the next stop on the tour, has contacted the Royal Court and asked them to pull out of the two dates there. The National Front has a high profile in the area and there have been threats to disrupt the performance. After some hectic toing and froing, they are persuaded to allow the shows to go ahead and, to everyone's relief, they pass without incident.

By the time the tour reaches Walthamstow Youth Club, out in E17, most of the early teething problems have been ironed out. The performances are tighter and the whole evening more closely structured to fit the expectations of the audience. These changes are reflected in the quality of the discussion that follows. There is a lot of talk about how the play captures the frustrations of being young in 1982 and about how unemployment and skinhead violence go hand in hand. One black youth goes right to the heart of Griffiths' concerns when he expresses an affinity with the problems faced by the skinheads in the piece. A number of whites in the audience are visibly shocked. Someone even enquires about Griffiths' own preferred hair-style.

When *Oi for England* opens to the general public this week, audiences at the Theatre Upstairs certainly won't simply be seeing a version of the original low-budget TV drama. It's now an altogether more immediate piece and the two-way exchange between cast and audience throughout the tour has helped to give its politics a much more incisive and credible edge. Plans for similar tours . . . are already well-advanced. Clearly any projects they do develop will have to build on the experience of the *Oi* tour, which shows, perhaps above all else, that although new audiences can be created, their needs have to be carefully structured into what is offered them. This probably means working closely with local communities and dramatising concerns specific to them – in this respect *Oi for England* could well prove just the beginning of an important move towards democratising theatre's traditional middle-class audience.[12]

A subsequent tour in South Yorkshire, again with the dialogue and setting 'localised', ran into controversy when the left-wing South Yorkshire County Council refused to fund the undertaking on the grounds that the piece might *promote* racism.[13]

Overall, though, the experiment can be said to have had positive political effects. It provided a model for a new kind of cultural exchange in which representations would circulate not in the once-and-for-all fixity of the networked transmission or the theatrical performance but in the changing spaces provided by specific communities and contexts; communities and contexts that would allow them to be continuously reworked and interrogated in the process of recirculation. In a sense, this was a personally chastening experience for Griffiths since it conclusively demonstrated that the radicalising effects of network television were limited. Much more limited than he had always believed: even after lengthy group discussions, the kind of 'recognitions' he sought from *Oi for England*'s audience remained at best inchoate. Yet at the same time what the experience also showed was that this was perhaps now the only way to reach a disaffected and frequently hostile youth audience on contemporary issues. In a study of media coverage of the 1981 riots published by the Broadcasting Research Unit at the British Film Institute at the same time as *Oi for England* was first transmitted, Howard Tumber noted that among 12–19 year-olds less than 10 per cent watched news bulletins.[14]

For Griffiths, however, despite initial talk of a further follow-up project, *Oi for England* does seem to have been something of a subcultural dead-end. Certainly it failed to issue in any widespread return to contemporary themes. On the contrary, not only was nothing more urgent to emerge: the project that would absorb Griffiths throughout the rest of 1982 was a six-part historical reconstruction of Scott and Amundsen's turn-of-the-century race for the South Pole, by far the most elaborate piece of period drama he had ever been involved in.

10 Postscript: 'Something to struggle for'

After completing *Oi for England* in early 1982 Griffiths began what was to be almost a year's writing on a new series of six films. Like 'Tory Stories' they were set in the past, but this time in those two decades – 1900-1920 – which seem to attract the writer so strongly. The subject is the race to the South Pole between Scott and Amundsen, which culminated in the latter's triumph and Scott's death in 1912. Griffiths had been sent a recent book about this at the end of 1980, a study by Roland Huntford which included much new historical information, particularly about the Norwegian expedition, and which had attracted some attention. Roland Joffé, who had worked with Griffiths on *Bill Brand*, together with producer Rob Buckler had bought the rights to the book, and approached Griffiths about a screenplay. He was impressed with the material but felt that he simply did not have the time. Nor could he really find a sympathetic politics within it. A year later Joffé asked him again; he re-read the book and this time agreed. He then miscalculated the time it would take him to complete it, and wrote through the second half of 1982, just as Britain was again acting out an imperial adventure, this time in the Falklands. A resonance is unmistakable in the final scripts, collectively called 'Judgement over the Dead', but with the title of the sixth echoing Margaret Thatcher's infamous cry during the Falklands War, 'Rejoice'.

The scripts are scrupulously detailed reconstructions of events leading up to the final expeditions, and then of occurrences on the polar journeys. The dynamic is the contrast between Scott and his team – ill-organised gentlemen amateurs – and the highly pro-fessional colleagues of Amundsen. Consequently there appears initially to be an odd disjunction between the symbol of Empire in the films and the representatives of that ideology today, who are the more dangerous precisely because they are so professional. Griffiths acknowledges this, but says his interest in dealing with the subject arose from other aspects, which *are* highly pertinent today. One is with the genesis and operation of historical myth, 'the way in which the past is mythologised in the moment of its making. In the case of Scott there is perfect material to hand, since he spent nine days at the end writing something like 30,000 words, addressing directly the problems of the expedition, whether it was worthwhile, whether it had been well organised, and systematically erasing all trace of disaster and catastrophe, which was part and parcel of British Empire thinking.'[1]

Even more important are what Griffiths describes as 'the real politics of the piece [which] are the politics of social organisation and leadership: collective leadership on the part of Amundsen . . . as against hierarchic, assumptive leaderships such as we have today and such as we had then in the British Empire. These are problems that I've been grappling with since *Occupations*, what is the relationship between leaders and led, do we need those terms in socialist culture and so on . . . That's what I'm after politically, showing forms of organisation – democratic, embryonically socialist on the one hand and authoritarian, post-aristocratic formations on the other'.[2] Only the finished production, which is to be made by Central Television, will show whether these meanings are created. Originally Roland Joffé was to direct, but now Philip Saville – director on *Boys from the Blackstuff* – will shoot the films.

As this book is written, Griffiths is scripting a further film for television, but is actively planning work in the theatre and the cinema as well. The present script, *Fatherland*, is the first of two to be made by Ken Loach, and is to be about a singer who comes out of East Berlin into the West. Commercial interests descend on him and threaten to corrupt his talent. Situated within the spy genre, it is, Griffiths says, 'basically a realist text, but not of the sort of social realism associated with Ken's work . . . I've mixed the time up a lot; in the present there are anticipations of other events and there are flashbacks, there are layers of time.' The other possible film with Loach may be about the comic Frank Randall and his life from 1929 to 1939. 'My worry,' Griffiths says, 'is that it probably demands a theatrical conception. And I've got enough problems with *Fatherland* at the moment. . . .'

Other plans for the stage include a one-person show for Gavin Richards from Belt and Braces, who was so effective in *Oi for England*. Griffiths' most ambitious idea for the theatre, however, originated during discussions about an adaptation for the Royal Shakespeare Company of Brecht's *Mother Courage*. The artistic terms laid down by the Brecht estate were totally unacceptable to Griffiths and the idea did not proceed but, as he recalls, 'during those discussions I saw a great play for the theatre . . . *Mother Courage* is based on a seventeenth-

181

century text by Jacob Grimmelhausen, an early German novelist . . . Brecht never invented a single play, he ripped everybody off, and good on him. So I thought if old Bert did it, why can't I? So I got a German text and struggled through it and saw that I could use that beautifully for a play set in the late 80s, in Europe, at the time of a theatre nuclear war.'

Lastly, Griffiths has begun to block out an adaptation for the cinema of the recent American novel by William Wharton, *A Midnight Clear*. Set in Northern Europe in 1944, it tells of an encounter between a group of American intelligence soldiers and a group of Germans. 'It's a new terrain in that it's not an overtly political one. It's one where I have to inflect a politics, a peace politics, from a book which smells it on every page but doesn't generate it into a central meaning.' There is also one other film project, a version of Orwell's *Homage to Catalonia*, which Griffiths has long wanted to attempt.

So despite his experiences on *Reds*, Griffiths wants to take on the powerplays of Hollywood again. 'If you don't mess with Hollywood again, on your terms, you say, O.K., it's theirs . . . I know the odds are truly and catastrophically stacked against you, but what do I do with the learning I've had on *Reds*? I've had a lot of very positive experiences with audiences over *Reds*, which lead me to suppose that progressive meanings were taken away from it as well as reactionary meanings. And it would be a smashing victory for a text-producer to get more progressive meanings taken away than reactionary ones. That wasn't the case with *Reds*, I suppose. But it's something to struggle for.'

Notes

1 Introduction: 'Intervening in society's life'

1. Trevor Griffiths, 'Countering Consent' in *Ah! Mischief: the Writer and Television*, ed. Frank Pike, London, Faber and Faber, 1982, p. 36.
2. Edward Braun, 'Trevor Griffiths' in *British Television Drama*, ed. George W. Brandt, Cambridge, Cambridge University Press, 1981, p. 56.
3. Trevor Griffiths, Preface to *Through the Night* and *Such Impossibilities*, London, Faber and Faber, 1977, p. 7.
4. Ibid., p. 9.
5. Ibid., p. 10.
6. Griffiths, 'Countering Consent', p. 39.
7. Ibid., pp. 39–40.
8. Ibid., p. 40.
9. Interview with Catherine Itzin and Simon Trussler, 'Transforming the Husk of Capitalism', *Theatre Quarterly*, Summer 1976, p. 44.
10. Trevor Griffiths, 'Lost Leader', *Quarto*, December 1980, p. 19.
11. David Edgar, 'Is Jimmy Porter Dead?', *Voices*, Channel 4 Television, 10 March 1983.
12. Raymond Williams, 'Problems of the Coming Period', *New Left Review*, no. 140, July–August 1983, pp. 7–18.

2 The Making of a Television Dramatist

1. First performed at The Stables Theatre Club, Manchester, 28 October 1970, directed by Buzz Goodbody.
2. *Theatrefacts*, no. 9, p. 2.
3. *Sunday Times*, 17 October 1971. Our emphasis.
4. *The Times*, 14 October 1971.
5. *Observer*, 17 October 1971.
6. Richard Hoggart, *The Uses of Literacy*, Harmondsworth, Penguin, 1969, p. 292.
7. Unpublished interview with the authors, 15 June 1983.
8. Ibid.
9. Ibid.
10. Trevor Griffiths, 'Lost Leader', *Quarto*, December 1980.
11. Raymond Williams, *The Long Revolution*, Harmondsworth, Penguin, 1965, p. 269.
12. Ibid., p. 269.
13. Interview with the authors, 15 March 1983.
14. Unpublished interview with John Wyver, summer 1981.
15. Ibid.
16. Sydney Newman in an interview with John Wyver, 'TV's dramaturge', *Time Out*, 6–12 April 1979.

17. Malcolm Hay, *Theatrefacts*, no. 9, p. 36.
18. Unpublished interview with the authors, 15 March 1983.
19. Ibid.
20. See, for example, Trevor Griffiths, 'Countering Consent' in *Ah! Mischief: the Writer and Television*, ed. Frank Pike, London, Faber and Faber, 1982, pp. 31–2.
21. Unpublished interview with John Wyver, summer 1981.

3 'Lessons to be learnt': *Occupations* and other dramas of revolution

1. Interview with Michael Billington, BBC World Service, reprinted in the *Listener*, 23 June 1983.
2. Ibid. Our emphasis.
3. An incident based on the evidence of the Sovnarkom decree between Fiat and the Soviet authorities ratified in November 1920.
4. David Caute chose a similar title for his novel *The Occupation*, a study of campus militancy, exploring conflicts between the Old and New Left, which also appeared in 1970.
5. Martin Jacques, 'Thatcherism – Breaking out of the Impasse' in *The Politics of Thatcherism*, ed. Stuart Hall and Martin Jacques, London, Lawrence and Wishart, 1983, p. 45.
6. *New Left Review*, no. 51, September–October 1968, pp. 1–2.
7. Ibid., pp. 56–7.
8. *Occupations*, London, Faber and Faber, 1980, pp. 58–9.
9. Quoted in Paulo Spriano, *The Occupation of the Factories*, translated by Gwyn A. Williams, London, Pluto Press, 1975, p. 54.
10. The best consideration of these factors is still to be found in Spriano, op. cit.
11. Spriano, op. cit., p. 18.
12. Interview with the authors, 15 March 1983.
13. *7 Days*, 3 November 1971.
14. From a reply to Nairn published in *7 Days* and reprinted as the introduction to the revised edition of the text published in 1980 by Faber and Faber, pp. 7–11. The new text, which contains substantial changes, had been reworked under the impetus of a Dutch-language production of the play by the socialist theatre group Sater.
15. Ibid., p. 11.
16. Unpublished interview with the authors, 15 June 1983.
17. John Willett, *The New Sobriety: Art and Politics in the Weimar Period*, London, Thames and Hudson, 1978, pp. 151–2.
18. Bertolt Brecht, *Writings on Theatre*, III, translated and quoted in Frederic Ewen, *Bertolt Brecht*, London, Calder, 1970.
19. Nigel Thomas, 'Trevor and Bill: On putting politics before News at Ten', *The Leveller*, November 1976, p. 12.
20. Nigel Andrews, 'A Play Postscript', *Plays and Players*, April 1972, p. 82.
21. From an interview by Catherine Itzin and Simon Trussler, 'Petrol Bombs through the Proscenium Arch', *Theatre Quarterly*, no. 17, 1975, p. 16.

22. Ibid.

23. From an unpublished interview with Karin Gartzke, quoted in Catherine Itzin, *Stages in the Revolution*, London, Eyre Methuen, 1980, p. 167.

24. Itzin and Trussler, 'Petrol Bombs through the Proscenium Arch', p. 18.

25. Introduction to *Apricots* and *Thermidor*, London, Pluto Short Plays, 1978.

26. Ibid.

27. Ibid.

28. Letter to Margaret Hare, dated 23 July 1971; included in the BFI collection.

29. Ibid.

30. Peter Calvocoressi, *The British Experience 1945–75*, Harmondsworth, Penguin, 1975, p. 74.

31. Letter, op. cit.

32. Malcolm Pitt, *The World on Our Backs*, London, Lawrence and Wishart, 1979, p. 12.

33. Trevor Griffiths, Preface to *Through the Night* and *Such Impossibilities*, London, Faber and Faber, 1977, p. 12.

34. Colin McArthur, *Television and History*, London, British Film Institute, 1978, p. 40.

35. Griffiths, Preface, op. cit.

36. Letter to the authors, 28 July 1983.

37. Interview with the authors, 29 June 1983.

38. Trevor Griffiths, 'Countering Consent' in *Ah! Mischief*, p. 37.

39. From an interview with Catherine Itzin and Simon Trussler, 'Transforming the Husk of Capitalism', *Theatre Quarterly*, Summer 1976, p. 40.

40. Ibid.

41. Interview with Pat Silburn, *Gambit*, no. 29, 1976, p. 31.

42. Itzin and Trussler, 'Transforming the Husk of Capitalism', op. cit., p. 42.

43. From an unpublished lecture by John McGrath given at King's College, Cambridge, Conference on Political Theatre, April 1978; quoted in Itzin, *Stages in the Revolution*, pp. 167–8.

4 'Now and in England': *All Good Men, Bill Brand* and Labourism

1. Quoted in the *Guardian*, 19 December 1973.

2. Cited in Edward Braun, 'Trevor Griffiths' in *British Television Drama*, ed. George W. Brandt, Cambridge, Cambridge University Press, 1981, p. 59.

3. *Daily Express*, 7 June 1976.

4. Graham Taylor and Nigel Grey, 'Brand of the Recent Future', *Streetlife*, 20 March–2 April 1976.

5. Interview with the authors, 29 June 1983.

6. Interview with Manuel Alvarado and Edward Buscombe for *Hazell: The Making of a Television Series*, London, British Film Institute, 1978; transcript in BFI library.

7. Interview with Alvarado and Buscombe, op. cit.

8. Taylor and Grey, op. cit.

9. Interview with the authors, 29 June 1983.

10. Trevor Griffiths, 'Countering Consent' in *Ah! Mischief*, op. cit., p. 34.

11. *The Listener*, 22 July 1976.

12. Trevor Griffiths, 'Countering Consent' in *Ah! Mischief*, op. cit., pp. 34–5.

13. David Edgar, 'On political theatre: part two', *Socialist Review*, May 1978, p. 36. Reprinted in *Theatre Quarterly*, no. 32, Winter 1979, pp. 25–33.

14. Taylor and Grey, op. cit.

15. Braun, op. cit., p. 77.

16. Alan Sked and Chris Cook, *Post-War Britain – A Political History*, Harmondsworth, Penguin Books, 1979, p. 351.

17. *The Leveller*, November 1976, p. 12.

18. Edgar, op. cit., p. 36.

5 'Taking the struggle further': *Comedians*

1. Nigel Thomas, 'Trevor and Bill: On putting politics before News at Ten', *The Leveller*, November 1976, p. 12.

2. *Daily Telegraph*, 1 October 1975.

3. Colin McArthur, *'Days of Hope'*, *Screen*, vol. 16, no. 4, Winter 1975–6. Reprinted in *Popular Television and Film*, ed. Tony Bennett et al., London, British Film Institute/Open University Press, 1981, p. 309.

4. McArthur, op. cit., p. 309.

5. Colin MacCabe, 'Realism and the Cinema: Notes on some Brechtian Theses', *Screen*, vol. 15, no. 2.

6. Colin MacCabe, *'Days of Hope* – A Response to Colin McArthur', *Screen*, vol. 17, no. 1, Spring 1976. Reprinted in Bennett (ed.), op. cit., p. 312.

7. Keith Tribe, 'History and the Production of Memories', *Screen*, vol. 18, no. 4, Winter 1977–8. Reprinted in Bennett (ed.), op. cit., pp. 325–6.

8. Sheila Rowbotham, 'Leninism in the Lurch', reprinted in *Dreams and Dilemmas*, London, Virago, 1983, pp. 122–3.

9. Interview with Pat Silburn, *Gambit*, no. 29, 1976, p. 31.

10. Interview with John Wyver, videotaped at the Institute of Education, London, 8 February 1983.

11. Interview with Catherine Itzin and Simon Trussler, 'Transforming the Husk of Capitalism', *Theatre Quarterly*, Summer 1976, p. 42.

12. Silburn, op. cit., p. 32.

13. Ibid.

14. Ibid., p. 33.

15. Ibid., p. 34.

16. Ibid., pp. 33–4.

17. The *Guardian*, 25 October 1979.

18. Trevor Griffiths, 'Countering Consent' in *Ah! Mischief*, op. cit.

19. Edward Braun, 'Trevor Griffiths' in George W. Brandt (ed.), *British Television Drama*, Cambridge, Cambridge University Press, 1981.

20. Quoted in W. Stephen Gilbert, 'In for Treatment', *Time Out*, 28 November–4 December 1975, p. 10.

21. Interview with Itzin and Trussler, 'Transforming the Husk of Capitalism', op. cit., p. 44.

22. Videotaped interview with John Wyver, op. cit.

23. Unpublished interview with Richard Eyre, 20 August 1983.

24. Ned Chaillet, 'Deeds', *Plays and Players*, April 1978, p. 24.

25. Interview with Richard Eyre, 20 August 1983.

6 'Mucking about with love and revolution': *Comrades* and *Reds*

1. The Broadway production of *Comedians* opened on 28 November 1976. Milo O'Shea played Eddie Waters; Jonathan Pryce continued in the role of Gethin Price, the part he played in the original Nottingham production.

2. Mick Eaton, 'History to Hollywood: Mick Eaton speaks to Trevor Griffiths', *Screen*, vol. 23, no. 2, July–August 1982, p. 61.

3. *Variety*, 26 March 1980.

4. Aaron Latham, 'Warren Beatty Seriously', *Rolling Stone*, 1 April 1982, p. 20.

5. Eaton, 'History to Hollywood', p. 65.

6. Latham, op. cit., p. 18.

7. John Orr, 'A Trail of Red Herrings', an interview in *AIP & Co.*, no. 30, January 1981.

8. Eaton, op. cit., p. 61. Our emphasis.

9. Orr, op. cit., p. 17.

10. Cited in Ed Buscombe, 'Making Love and Revolution', *Screen*, vol. 23, no. 2, July–August 1982, pp. 71–2.

11. Unpublished interview with Mike Poole, 5 January 1981.

12. All references to *Comrades* are to the manuscript and notes lodged in the BFI Trevor Griffiths collection.

13. Buscombe, op. cit., p. 73.

14. Ibid., p. 73.

15. Orr, op. cit., p. 16.

16. Eaton, op. cit., p. 64.

17. Ibid., p. 65.

18. Ibid., p. 62.

19. Orr, op. cit., p. 16.

20. Eaton, op. cit., p. 68.

7 'Working in a factory': *Sons and Lovers* and *The Cherry Orchard*

1. Stuart Burge, interview with the authors, 29 June 1983.

2. Mike Poole, 'The Classic Gets Some Class', *Time Out*, 30 January–5 February 1981, p. 16.

3. *Radio Times*, 10–16 January 1981; a fuller version of this article was published as the introduction to the *Sons and Lovers* screenplay, Nottingham, Spokesman, 1982, pp. 7–12.

4. Poole, op. cit., p. 16.

5. Ibid., p. 16.

6. Ibid., p. 16.

7. Interview with Mike Poole, 5 January 1981.

8. Trevor Griffiths, introduction to *Sons and Lovers* screenplay, pp. 11–12.

9. Interview with the authors, 29 June 1983.

10. Griffiths, op. cit., p. 12.

11. Mike Poole, 'Sons and Good Friends', *Time Out*, 27 February–5 March 1981, p. 58.

12. Letters, *Time Out*, 13–19 March 1981, p. 3.

13. Poole, 'The Classic Gets Some Class', p. 17.

14. Ibid., p. 17.

15. Nigel Andrews, 'A Play Postscript', *Plays and Players*, April 1972, p. 83.

16. Catherine Itzin and Simon Trussler, 'Transforming the Husk of Capitalism', *Theatre Quarterly*, Summer 1976, p. 37.

17. One of the present authors witnessed the main stages of this production. For a full account, see John Wyver, 'How "the Best Play of the Twentieth Century" took to the Air', *City Limits*, 9–15 October 1981, pp. 50–3.

18. Trevor Griffiths, introduction to *The Cherry Orchard* text, London, Pluto Press, 1978, p. vi.

19. Raymond Williams, *Drama from Ibsen to Brecht*, Harmondsworth, Penguin, 1968, p. 109.

20. Griffiths, introduction to *The Cherry Orchard* text, p. v.

21. Ibid., p. vi.

22. Ibid.

23. *Financial Times*, 14 March 1977.

24. David Hare, 'Ah! Mischief: The Role of Public Broadcasting' in *Ah! Mischief: The Writer and Television*, ed. Frank Pike, London, Faber and Faber, 1982, p. 47.

25. W. Stephen Gilbert, 'Closed Circuits', *Guardian*, 17 October 1981.

8 'A Tory Story': *Country*

1. Griffiths quoted in Jim Crace, 'A View of the Country', *Radio Times*, 17–23 October 1981, p. 13.

2. Quoted in W. Stephen Gilbert, 'Closed Circuits', *Guardian*, 17 October 1981.

3. Interview with John Wyver, videotaped at the Institute of Education, London, 8 February 1983.

4. W. Stephen Gilbert, op. cit.

5. Unpublished interview with John Wyver, summer 1981.

6. Trevor Griffiths, 'Countering Consent' in *Ah! Mischief*, p. 38.

7. Interview with John Wyver, summer 1981.

8. Mike Poole, 'Another Country?', *New Statesman*, 30 October 1981, pp. 33–4.

9 'Nothing more urgent': *Oi for England*

1. Stuart Cosgrove, 'Refusing Consent: The *Oi for England* Project', *Screen*, vol. 24, no. 1, 1983, p. 96.

2. Mike Poole, 'Mistaken Identities', *City Limits,* 16–22 April 1982, p. 38.

3. Dick Hebdige, *Subculture: The Meaning of Style,* London, Methuen, 1979, p. 55.

4. Poole, op. cit., p. 38.

5. Cosgrove, op. cit., p. 92.

6. Ibid., p. 93.

7. Poole, op. cit., p. 39.

8. Ibid., p. 38.

9. Ibid., p. 39.

10. Cosgrove, op. cit., p. 94.

11. Trevor Griffiths, Preface to *Through the Night* and *Such Impossibilities,* London, Faber and Faber, 1977, p. 7.

12. Mike Poole, 'Trying to get under the skins', *Guardian,* 7 June 1982.

13. See the *Guardian,* 8 October 1983, and the *Barnsley Chronicle,* 8 October 1983.

14. Howard Tumber, *Television and the Riots,* London, British Film Institute, 1982, p. 46.

10   Postscript: 'Something to struggle for'

1. Interview videotaped at the Institute of Education, London, 8 February 1983.

2. This and all other quotations in this chapter are from an unpublished interview, 8 September 1983.

Trevor Griffiths in Television

Adam Smith

Granada TV

First series tx: 23 January–10 April 1972.
Under the pseudonym Ben Rae, Trevor Griffiths wrote nine of the twelve transmitted episodes (although thirteen scripts were commissioned). Episodes six, seven and eight were written by Tom Gallacher.

Regular cast: Andrew Keir (*Adam Smith*), Brigit Forsyth (*Annie Smith*), Kara Wilson (*Helen Smith*), Tom Conti (*Dr Calvi*), Janet Munro (*Elizabeth Crichton*), David Leyton (*David Crichton*).
Designers: Colin Rees, Alan Price. *Directors:* Brian Mills, June Howson, Richard Martin. *Producer:* June Howson.

Second series tx: 17 September 1972–25 March 1973.
Episodes thirteen and fourteen are credited to Ben Rae; the subsequent four episodes are credited to John Hardiman and Susi Hush, although they appear to be closely based on Griffiths' scripts for these episodes.

Director (episodes thirteen and fourteen): Ray Menmuir. *Director* (episodes fifteen–eighteen): June Howson. *Producer:* June Howson.

Other writers in this series included C. P. Taylor, James MacTaggart, Barrie Keeffe and Peter McDougall.

The Silver Mask (from the series *Between the Wars*)

London Weekend Television

Adapted from a short story by Hugh Walpole.
Tx: 15 June 1973.

Joyce Redman (*Sonia Herries*), Joan Peart (*Amy Weston*), Anthony Roye (*George Weston*), Scott Antony (*Henry Abbott*), Tara Soppet (*Nora*), Zoe Wanamaker (*Ada Abbott*), Robert Lister (*Policeman*), John Rae (*Dr McArdle*), Charles Farrell (*Mr Edwards*), Margery Withers (*Mrs Edwards*).
Music: Denis King. *Designer:* John Clements. *Associate Producer:* Tony McLaren. *Producer:* Verity Lambert. *Director:* Alastair Reid.

All Good Men (Play for Today)

BBC1

Tx: 31 January 1974.

Bill Fraser (*Edward Waite*), Ronald Pickup (*Richard Massingham*), Jack Shepherd (*William*), Frances de la Tour (*Maria*).
Script editor: Ann Scott. *Designer:* Peter Brachacki. *Producer:* Graeme McDonald. *Director:* Michael Lindsay-Hogg.

Absolute Beginners (from the series *Fall of Eagles*)

BBC1

Tx: 19 April 1974.

Bruce Purchase (*Von Plehve*), Charles Kay (*Nicholas*), Patrick Stewart (*Lenin*), Lynn Farleigh (*Krupskaya*), Edward Wilson (*Martov*), Mary Wimbush (*Zasulich*), Michael Kitchen (*Trotsky*), Peter Weston (*Bauman*), Paul Eddington (*Plekhanov*), Svandis Jons (*Alexandrovna*), David Freeman (*Lieber*), Julian Fox (*Tupuridze*), Robert O'Mahoney (*Krasikov*), Raymond Witch (*Martinov*), Michael Hordern (*Narrator*).
Costumes: Daphne Dare. *Sound:* Derek Miller-Timmins. *Designer:* Allan Anson. *Producer:* Stuart Burge. *Director:* Gareth Davies.

Occupations   Granada TV

Tx: 1 September 1974.

Donald Pleasence (*Kabak*), Jack Shepherd (*Gramsci*), Natasha Parry (*Angelica*), Georgina Hale (*Polya*), Nigel Hawthorne (*Libertini*), Barry Stanton (*D'Avanzo*), John Steiner (*Terrini*), Richard Leech (*Valletta*).
Designer: Vic Symonds. *Producer:* Jonathan Powell. *Director:* Michael Lindsay-Hogg.

Don't Make Waves (from the series *Eleventh Hour*)   BBC1

Tx: 12 July 1975.
Written with Snoo Wilson, with songs by Kevin Coyne.

Script editor: Frank Hatherley. *Designers:* Jeremy Bear, Geoff Powell. *Producer:* Graeme McDonald. *Director:* Piers Haggard.

'Eleventh Hour' was a series of live plays, written, rehearsed and produced in one week. As far as can be ascertained no copy was made of *Don't Make Waves*, which now exists only in script form. No other credits are available.

Through the Night (Play for Today)   BBC1

Tx: 2 December 1975.

Alison Steadman (*Christine Potts*), Jack Shepherd (*Dr Pearce*), Tony Steedman (*Mr Staunton*), Thelma Whiteley (*Dr Seal*), Anne Dyson (*Mrs Scully*), Julia Schofield (*Anna Jay*), Dave Hill (*Joe Potts*), Andonia Katsaros (*Sister Warren*), Phylomena McDonagh (*Nurse O'Malley*), Sheila Kelly (*Staff Nurse Brenton*), Rebecca Mascarenhas (*Nurse Chatterjee*), Richard Wilson (*Registrar*), Patricia Leach (*Night Sister*), Wendy Wax (*Theatre Sister*), Sue Elgin, Angela Bruce, Anna Mottram (*Night Nurses*), John Rowe (*Anaesthetist*), Richard Ireson (*Dr Mount*), Jeillo Edwards (*Lucy*), Louis Cabot (*Porter*), Anna Wing (*Mrs Goodwin*), Jane Freeman (*Martha Paisley*), Rachel Davies (*Outpatients Sister*), Barbara Ashcroft (*Auxiliary*), Shirley Allen (*Tea-Lady*), Peter Lawrence (*Religious Visitor*), Kathleen Worth (*Mother*), Myrtle Devenish (*Woman Patient*), Jeanne Doree (*Joan*), Lucy Griffiths (*Agnes*).
Script Editor: Colin Tucker. *Designer:* Sue Spence. *Producer:* Ann Scott. *Director:* Michael Lindsay-Hogg.

Bill Brand   Thames TV

Tx: 7 June–16 August 1976.
A series in eleven episodes.

Series production team: *Designers:* David Ferris, Harry Clark. *Music composed by:* Jack Trombey. *Series Adviser:* Lewis Minkin. *Associate Producer:* Michael Harvey. *Executive Producer:* Stella Richman. *Producer:* Stuart Burge.

Episode one: **In**

Jack Shepherd (*Bill Brand*), Lynn Farleigh (*Miriam Brand*), Karen Silver (*Jane Brand*), Philip Cox (*Michael Brand*), Allan Surtees (*Alf Jowett*), Clifford Kershaw (*Frank Hilton*), John Barrett (*Albert Stead*), Cherie Lunghi (*Alex Ferguson*), Dave Hill (*Eddie Brand*), Anne Dyson (*Mrs Brand*), Harry Markham (*Mr Brand*), Jan Harvey (*Woman interviewer*), Colin Jeavons (*Bernard Shaw*), Carole Hayman (*Angie Shaw*), Alan Bowles (*Returning officer*), Nellie Hanham (*Lily Atherton*), Lynne Carol (*Elsie Wright*), Peter Ellis (*Pru*), Alan Luxton (*Martin*), Myrtle Devenish (*Mrs Watson*), Jeanne Doree (*Gladys*), Rosemary Frankau (*Liberal candidate*), James Drake (*Conservative candidate*).
Director: Michael Lindsay-Hogg.

Episode two: **You Wanna Be a Hero, Get Yourself a White Horse**

Jack Shepherd (*Bill Brand*), Lynn Farleigh (*Miriam Brand*), Karen Silver (*Jane Brand*), Philip Cox (*Michael Brand*), Richard Leech (*Waverley*), William Hoyland (*Sandiford*), Richard Butler (*Tom Mapson*), Frank Mills (*Paxton*), James Giles (*McNab*), Rosemary Martin (*Winnie Scoular*), Michael Atha (*Mosley*), Peter Copley (*Maddocks*), Stanley Dawson (*Ticket Collector*).
Director: Roland Joffé.

Episode three: **Yarn**

Jack Shepherd (*Bill Brand*), Anne Dyson (*Mrs Brand*), Lynn Farleigh (*Miriam Brand*), Dave Hill (*Eddie Brand*), Edith Carter (*Aunt Ethel*), Allan Surtees (*Alf Jowett*), Clifford Kershaw (*Frank Hilton*), James Garbutt (*Hughie Marsden*), Colin Jeavons (*Bernard Shaw*), Enid Irvin, Tommy Wright, William Hamilton (*Leighley E.C. Members*), Tom Harrison (*Bowers*), Walter Hall (*Swinson*), Richard Ireson (*Wellburn*), William Hoyland (*Sandiford*), Douglas Campbell (*Reg Starr*), Gary Roberts (*Wilkinson*), Albert Moses (*Pakistani*), Alan Badel (*David Last*), Alick Hayes (*Walton*), Ralph Nossek (*Pearson*), Nigel Hawthorne (*Browning*), Rosemary Martin (*Winnie Scoular*), Richard Butler (*Tom Mapson*), Richard Leech (*Waverley*), Geoffrey Palmer (*Malcolm Fraser*), Fred Feast (*Parfitt*), Peter Martin (*Bryant's gateman*), Karen Silver (*Jane Brand*), Philip Cox (*Michael Brand*).
Director: Michael Lindsay-Hogg.

Episode four: **Now and in England**

Jack Shepherd (*Bill Brand*), Lynn Farleigh (*Miriam Brand*), Bernard Atha (*Mr Hollins*), Allan Surtees (*Alf Jowett*), James Garbutt (*Hughie Marsden*), Anne Raitt (*Mrs Pilling*), Cherie Lunghi (*Alex Ferguson*), Alan Badel (*David Last*),

192

Louise Jervis (*Waitress*), Geoff Tomlinson (*Police Inspector*), Gary Roberts (*Wilkinson*), Albert Moses (*Pakistani*), Peter Martin (*Geoff*), Rona Anderson (*Mrs Marples*), Robert Hardy (*Mr Marples*), Richard Ireson (*Wellburn*), Peter Copley (*Cedric Maddocks*).
Director: Michael Lindsay-Hogg.

Episode five: **August for the Party**

Jack Shepherd (*Bill Brand*), Douglas Campbell (*Reg Starr*), Richard Butler (*Mapson*), Peter Howells (*Venables*), Rosemary Martin (*Winnie Scoular*), Lynn Farleigh (*Miriam Brand*), Karen Silver (*Jane Brand*), Philip Cox (*Michael Brand*), Cherie Lunghi (*Alex Ferguson*), Allan Surtees (*Alf Jowett*), Don Hawkins (*M.C.*), Colin Jeavons (*Bernard Shaw*), Carole Hayman (*Angie Shaw*), Peter Ellis (*Pru*), Alan Luxton (*Martin*), David Bradley (*Peter Malone*), Jan Harvey (*Woman interviewer*), Lynne Verrall (*Secretary*), Peter Jeffrey (*Maidstone*), Carol Drinkwater (*Pat*), Helen Rappaport (*Bonny Clark*), Jane Briers (*Christine Waite*).
Director: Roland Joffé.

Episode six: **Resolution**

Jack Shepherd (*Bill Brand*), Robert East (*Television director*), Rosemary Martin (*Winnie Scoular*), Gary Roberts (*Wilkinson*), Allan Surtees (*Alf Jowett*), Gerald James (*Morgan*), Clifford Cox (*Garner*), James Walker (*Lane*), Fred Feast (*Parfitt*), James Maxwell (*Robert*), Don McKillop (*Jim*), Alan Badel (*David Last*), Peter Davidson (*Renshaw*), Ray Smith (*Moores*), George Waring (*Wiltshire*), Geoffrey Palmer (*Frear*), Arthur Lowe (*Watson*).
Producer/Director: Stuart Burge.

Episode seven: **Tranquillity of the Realm**

Jack Shepherd (*Bill Brand*), Karen Silver (*Jane Brand*), Philip Cox (*Michael Brand*), Lynn Farleigh (*Miriam Brand*), Ann Pennington (*Clare Cranston*), William Hoyland (*Sandiford*), Douglas Campbell (*Starr*), Peter Howell (*Venables*), Cherie Lunghi (*Alex Ferguson*), Rosalie Crutchley (*Mrs Martin*), Richard Leech (*Wormley*), Michael Macowan (*Latey*), Richard Morgan (*Labour MP*), Michael Gover (*Wale*), Alex Scott (*Bealey*), Malcolm Terris (*Henson*), Basil Henson (*Hinchcliffe*), David Henry (*Mace*), Neville Barber (*Conservative MP*), Gary Roberts (*Wilkinson*), Albert Moses (*Pakistani*), Bernard G. High (*Police sergeant*).
Director: Roland Joffé.

Episode eight: **Rabble**

Jack Shepherd (*Bill Brand*), Cherie Lunghi (*Alex Ferguson*), Eileen Kennally (*Irene*), Allan Surtees (*Alf Jowett*), James Garbutt (*Hughie Marsden*), John Barrett (*Albert Stead*), Ian Liston (*Young Socialist*), Ken Kitson (*Policeman*), Mike Henson (*Postman*), Alan Badel (*David Last*), Duncan Faber (*Call boy*), Dave Hill (*Eddie Brand*), Barrie Fletcher (*Barman*).
Producer/Director: Stuart Burge.

193

Episode nine: **Anybody's**

Jack Shepherd (*Bill Brand*), Alan Badel (*David Last*), Geoffrey Palmer (*Frear*), Stephanie Cole (*Marjorie*), Peter Copley (*Maddocks*), Rosemary Martin (*Winnie Scoular*), James Giles (*McNab*), Richard Butler (*Mapson*), John Nightingale (*Corbishley*), Richard Beale (*Preen*), Hugh Martin (*Blackwell*), Doreen Mantle (*Edna James*), Martin Fiske (*Armfield*), John Woodnutt (*Brent*), Anthony Woodruff (*Bullock*), Godfrey Quigley (*Kersley*), John McKelvey (*Wilks*), Peter Howell (*Venables*), William Hoyland (*Sandiford*).
Director: Roland Joffé.

Episode ten: **Revisions**

Jack Shepherd (*Bill Brand*), Rosemary Martin (*Winnie Scoular*), Douglas Campbell (*Reg Starr*), James Giles (*McNab*), Peter Davidson (*Renshaw*), John Pennington (*Charlie Wade*), Alan Badel (*David Last*), John Woodnutt (*Brent*), Peter Howell (*Venables*), John Barrett (*Albert Stead*), Ian Liston (*Young Socialist*), Lindsay Campbell (*Police Inspector*), Bernard Gallagher (*Walter Marland*), Phil McCall (*Gus Lynch*), Ray Smith (*Moores*), Godfrey Quigley (*Kersley*), Geoffrey Palmer (*Frear*), Jean Boht (*Edna Copple*), John McKelvey (*Wilks*), Peter Copley (*Maddocks*), Allan Surtees (*Alf Jowett*), Lynn Farleigh (*Miriam Brand*), Dave Hill (*Eddie Brand*), Anne Dyson (*Mrs Brand*), Bill Tasker (*Stan*).
Producer/Director: Stuart Burge.

Episode eleven: **It is the People who Create**

Jack Shepherd (*Bill Brand*), Karen Silver (*Jane Brand*), Jonathan Pryce (*Jamie Finn*), Rosemary Martin (*Winnie Scoular*), William Hoyland (*Sandiford*), Douglas Campbell (*Reg Starr*), Alan Partington (*Priest*), Colin Douglas (*Gallimore*), Avril Marsh (*Researcher*), Salami Coher (*Mboya*), Willie Payne (*Enoma*), Angela Easterling (*TV presenter*), Peter Copley (*Maddocks*), Peter Howell (*Venables*), Sharon Duce (*Sian*), Adelaida Arias (*Aya*), Miranda Bell (*Cleo*), Susan Glanville (*Dink*), Allan Surtees (*Alf Jowett*), Constance Chapman (*Mrs Wainwright*).
Director: Roland Joffé.

Comedians (Play for Today)   BBC1

Tx: 25 October 1979.

Jonathan Pryce (*Gethin Price*), John Barrett (*Caretaker*), James Warrior (*Phil Murray*), Derrick O'Connor (*George McBain*), Linal Haft (*Sammy Samuels*), David Burke (*Mike Connor*), Bill Fraser (*Eddie Waters*), Edward Peel (*Ged Murray*), Ralph Nossek (*Bert Challenor*), Moti Makan (*Mr Patel*), Mike Henson (*Concert secretary*).
Make-up artist: Norma Hill. *Studio sound:* Norman Bennett. *Lighting:* Dave Sydenham. *Designer:* Paul Joel. *Director:* Richard Eyre.

Tx: 14 January–25 February 1981.
By D. H. Lawrence.
A dramatisation by Trevor Griffiths.

Series production team: *Music:* John Tams. *Designer:* Chris Pemsel. *Script editor:* Betty Willingale. *Producer:* Jonathan Powell. *Director:* Stuart Burge.

Episode one

Eileen Atkins (*Gertrude Morel*), Tom Bell (*Walter Morel*), Ian Kirkby (*William Morel, as a child*), Cindy Wooley (*Annie Morel, as a child*), Glyn Cook, Craig Napier (*Arthur Morel, as a child*), Geoffrey Burridge (*William Morel*), Amanda Parfitt (*Annie Morel*), Myrtle Devenish (*Mrs Kirk*), Muriel Lawford (*Washerwoman*), Mollie Guilfoyle (*Mrs Anthony*), Wilfred Grove (*Israel Barker*), Anna Wing (*Mrs Bower*), David Allister (*Mr Heaton*), Jacquie Cassidy (*Girl at door*), Kevin Stoney (*Mr Braithwaite*), John Quarmby (*Mr Winterbottom*), Brenda Peters (*Barmaid*).

Episode two

Eileen Atkins (*Gertrude Morel*), Tom Bell (*Walter Morel*), Karl Johnson (*Paul Morel*), Geoffrey Burridge (*William Morel*), Amanda Parfitt (*Annie Morel*), Bobbie Brown (*Gypsy Western*), Leonie Mellinger (*Miriam Leivers*), Jonathan Church (*Pit boy*), Wilfred Grove (*Israel Barker*), Mark Rockley (*Arthur Morel, as a child*), Kenneth Keeling (*Mr Jordan*), Caroline Cartlidge (*Waitress*), John Tams (*Mr Poppleworth*), Hilda Braid (*Polly*), Janet Hardy (*Girl at Jordan's*), Caroline Hutchison (*Fanny*), Anne Dyson (*Emma*), Gail MacFarlane (*Connie*), Ben Silburn (*Boy fighting Arthur*), Elizabeth Choice (*Landlady*), Richard Ireson (*Doctor*), Jean Boht (*Mrs Leivers*), Peter Davidson (*Mr Leivers*), David Neilson (*Edgar*), Bob Middleton (*Maurice*), Steven Holt (*Geoffrey*), Mark Nightingale (*Hubert*).

Episode three

Eileen Atkins (*Gertrude Morel*), Tom Bell (*Walter Morel*), Karl Johnson (*Paul Morel*), Leonie Mellinger (*Miriam Leivers*), Lynn Dearth (*Clara Dawes*), Jean Boht (*Mrs Leivers*), Peter Davidson (*Mr Leivers*), David Neilson (*Edgar*), Bob Middleton (*Maurice*), Steven Holt (*Geoffrey*), Mark Nightingale (*Hubert*), Amanda Parfitt (*Annie Morel*), Mark Rockley (*Arthur Morel*), Stephen Finlay (*Leonard*), Theresa Ratcliff (*Alice*), Deirdre Lee (*Kitty*), Janine Duvitski (*Beatrice*).

Episode four

Eileen Atkins (*Gertrude Morel*), Tom Bell (*Walter Morel*), Karl Johnson (*Paul Morel*), Leonie Mellinger (*Miriam Leivers*), Lynn Dearth (*Clara Dawes*), Jean Boht (*Mrs Leivers*), Peter Davidson (*Mr Leivers*), David Neilson (*Edgar*), Bob Middleton (*Maurice*), Steven Holt (*Geoffrey*), Mark Nightingale (*Hubert*), Amanda Parfitt (*Annie Morel*), Stephen Finlay (*Leonard*), Geoffrey Andrews (*Preacher*), Dave Hill (*Mr Limb*), Maureen Morris (*Miss Limb*), Mark Rockley

(*Arthur Morel*), Janine Duvitski (*Beatrice*), Charles Rea (*Postman*), John Tams (*Poppleworth*), Gail MacFarlane (*Connie*), Jack Shepherd (*Baxter Dawes*), Mary Wimbush (*Mrs Radford*).

Episode five

Eileen Atkins (*Gertrude Morel*), Tom Bell (*Walter Morel*), Karl Johnson (*Paul Morel*), Leonie Mellinger (*Miriam Leivers*), Lynn Dearth (*Clara Dawes*), Caroline Hutchison (*Fanny*), Hilda Braid (*Polly*), Anne Dyson (*Emma*), Gail MacFarlane (*Connie*), Cherith Mellor (*Mildred*), Elizabeth Rider (*Gladys*), Madoline Thomas (*Tearoom lady*).

Episode six

Eileen Atkins (*Gertrude Morel*), Tom Bell (*Walter Morel*), Karl Johnson (*Paul Morel*), Lynn Dearth (*Clara Dawes*), Ann Heffernan (*Sarah Bernhardt*), Mary Wimbush (*Mrs Radford*), Jack Shepherd (*Baxter Dawes*), John Joyce (*Bar acquaintance*), Vince Eager (*Chucker-out*), Tony Kilbane (*Young clerk*), Kenneth Keeling (*Mr Jordan*), Richard Ireson (*Doctor*), Amanda Parfitt (*Annie*), Michael Turner (*Dr Jamieson*), Jeni Ktori (*Nurse*), Mark Rockley (*Arthur Morel*), Stephen Finlay (*Leonard*).

Episode seven

Eileen Atkins (*Gertrude Morel*), Tom Bell (*Walter Morel*), Karl Johnson (*Paul Morel*), Leonie Mellinger (*Miriam Leivers*), Lynn Dearth (*Clara Dawes*), Jack Shepherd (*Baxter Dawes*), Amanda Parfitt (*Annie*), Roberta Thayne (*Nursing sister*).

The Cherry Orchard   BBC1

Tx: 13 October 1981.
By Anton Chekhov.
English version by Trevor Griffiths
from a translation by Helen Rappaport.

Bill Paterson (*Lopakhin*), Frances Low (*Dunyasha*), Timothy Spall (*Epikhodov*), Paul Curran (*Firs*), Suzanne Burden (*Anya*), Judi Dench (*Madame Ranevsky*), Harriet Walter (*Varya*), Frederick Treves (*Gayev*), Anna Massey (*Charlotte*), David Rintoul (*Yasha*), Wensley Pithey (*Pischik*), Anton Lesser (*Trofimov*), Richard Vanstone (*Passer-by*), David Blake Kelly (*Stationmaster*).
Senior cameraman: Geoff Feld. *Sound:* Richard Partridge. *Lighting:* Howard King. *Designer:* Susan Spence. *Producer:* Ann Scott. *Director:* Richard Eyre.

Country (Play for Today)   BBC1

Tx: 20 October 1981.

Piers Flint Shipman (*Andrew Oliphant, son*), Leo McKern (*Sir Frederic Carlion*), Deborah Norton (*Faith*), Wendy Hiller (*Lady Carlion*), Madoline Thomas (*Nanny*), Donald Eccles (*The Dean*), James Fox (*Philip Carlion*), Eliza

Buckingham (*Margaret Harcourt*), Frederick Treves (*Matthew Harcourt*), Edward Hicks (*Teddie Harcourt*), Tamzin Neville (*Elizabeth Harcourt*), Jill Bennett (*Alice Carlion*), Julian Wadham (*Robert Carlion*), Suzanne Burden (*Lindsey Carlion*), Richard Durden (*Guy Wheldon*), Anbone Tennant (*Nigel Wheldon*), Tim Seely (*Andrew Oliphant, father*), Joan Greenwood (*Dollie van der Biek*), Frank Mills (*Ashford*), Bryan Coleman (*Edward Carlion*), Richard Vanstone (*Hop picker*), Alan Webb (*Sir Piers Blair*), David Neville (*James Blair*), Malcolm Storey (*Inspector*), Ralph Nossek (*Mr Joseph*), Penelope Wilton (*Virginia*).
Sound recordist: John Pritchard. *Film editor:* David Martin. *Designer:* Geoff Powell. *Lighting cameraman:* Nat Crosby. *Producer:* Ann Scott. *Director:* Richard Eyre.

Oi for England   Central TV
Tx: 17 April 1982.

Adam Kotz (*Finn*), Neil Pearson (*Napper*), Richard Platt (*Landry*), Ian Mercer (*Swells*), Gavin Richards (*The Man*), Lisa Lewis (*Gloria*).
Designer: Ann Croot-Hawkins. *Director:* Tony Smith. *Producer:* Sue Birtwistle.

Bibliography

Plays

Sam, Sam, in *Plays and Players*, April 1972.
Occupations and *The Big House*, Calder & Boyars, 1972.
Lay By (with others), Calder & Boyars, 1972.
The Party, Faber and Faber, 1974.
Comedians, Faber and Faber, 1976.
All Good Men and *Absolute Beginners*, Faber and Faber, 1977.
Through the Night and *Such Impossibilities*, Faber and Faber, 1977.
Apricots and *Thermidor*, Pluto Press, 1978.
The Cherry Orchard, Pluto Press, 1978.
Deeds (with others) in *Plays and Players*, May and June 1978.
Occupations (revised text), Faber and Faber, 1980.
Country: A Tory Story, Faber and Faber, 1981.
Sons and Lovers, Spokesman, 1982.
Oi for England, Faber and Faber, 1983.

Other Writings, Interviews and Criticism

Nigel ANDREWS, 'A Play Postscript', *Plays and Players*, April 1972, pp. 82–3.
Peter ANSORGE, 'Current Concerns' (interview with Griffiths and David Hare), *Plays and Players*, July 1974, pp. 18–22.
Peter ANSORGE, 'Trevor Griffiths' in *Disrupting the Spectacle*, Pitman 1975, pp. 63–6.
M. BARNES, 'The Plain Face of Politics', *Sunday Times*, 8 August 1976.
Merete BATES, 'Interview with Trevor Griffiths', *Guardian*, 6 November 1970.
Michael BILLINGTON, 'Trevor Griffiths', *Guardian*, 20 February 1976.
Edward BRAUN, 'Trevor Griffiths' in *British Television Drama*, ed. George Brandt, Cambridge University Press, 1981, pp. 56–81.
Edward BUSCOMBE, 'Making Love and Revolution', *Screen*, July–August 1982, pp. 71–5.
Stuart COSGROVE, 'Refusing Consent: the "Oi for England" Project', *Screen*, January–February 1983, pp. 92–6.
Elizabeth COWLEY, 'Bill Brand is Out to Get his Own Way', *TV Times*, 5–11 June 1976, pp. 13–15.
Jim CRACE, 'A View of the Country', *Radio Times*, 17–23 October 1981, pp. 11–13.
J. CROALL, 'From Home to House', *Times Educational Supplement*, 25 June 1976, pp. 18–19.
Stephen DIXON, 'Joking Apart', *Guardian*, 19 February 1975.
Mick EATON, 'History to Hollywood – Interview with Trevor Griffiths', *Screen*, July–August 1982, pp. 61-70.
David EDGAR, 'Political Theatre', *Socialist Review*, April and May 1978; reprinted in *Theatre Quarterly*, Winter 1979, pp. 25–33.
W. Stephen GILBERT, 'In for Treatment', *Time Out*, 28 November–4 December 1975, pp. 9–10.
'Brand X', *Time Out*, 4–11 June 1976, p. 7.

198

'Closed Circuits', *Guardian*, 17 October 1981.

Leonard GOLDSTEIN, 'Trevor Griffiths, "The Party" and the Left v Radical Critique of Bourgeois Society' in *Political Developments on the British Stage in the Sixties and Seventies*, Rostock, 1976.

T. GOULD, 'One Brand of Hero', *New Society*, 5 August 1976, p. 300.

Trevor GRIFFITHS, 'In Defence of "Occupations"', letter to *Seven Days*, 1971; reprinted as the introduction to *Occupations*, Faber and Faber, 1980.

'Author's Preface' in *Through the Night* and *Such Impossibilities*, Faber and Faber, 1977, pp. 7–12.

'Introduction', *The Cherry Orchard*, Pluto Press, 1978.

'Lost Leader' (on Kenneth Tynan), *Quarto*, December 1980, p. 19.

'A novel Lawrence', *Radio Times*, 10–16 January 1981, pp. 84–6; reprinted in its full form as the introduction to *Sons and Lovers*, Spokesman, 1982.

Jonathan HAMMOND, 'Trevor Griffiths' in *Contemporary Dramatists*, ed. James Vinson, St James's Press, 1977, pp. 327–9.

Malcolm HAY, 'Theatre Checklist No. 9', *Theatrefacts*, no. 9, 1976, pp. 2–8, 36.

Ronald HAYMAN, 'Trevor Griffiths – Attacking from the Inside', *The Times*, 15 December 1973.

Adrian HODGES, 'The Telephone Calls from Beatty that Change Two Men's Careers', *Screen International*, 27 February 1982, p. 12.

Albert HUNT, 'A Theatre of Ideas', *New Society*, 16 January 1975, pp. 138–40; reprinted in Paul Barker (ed.), *Arts in Society*, Fontana, 1977.

Catherine ITZIN and Simon TRUSSLER, 'Transforming the Husk of Capitalism', *Theatre Quarterly* vol. VI no. 22, 1976, pp. 25–46.

Catherine ITZIN, *Apricots* and *Thermidor*, introduction to the texts, Pluto Press, 1978.

'Trevor Griffiths' in *Stages in the Revolution – Political Theatre in Britain since 1968*, Eyre Methuen, 1980, pp. 165–75.

Peter LENNON, 'The People Speak', *Sunday Times*, 7 December 1975.

Jim McGUIGAN, 'Four Years that Shook the Movie World', *New Socialist*, March–April 1982, p. 37.

Rod McSHANE, 'Hollywood leans Left?', *Time Out*, 26 February–4 March 1982, pp. 14–15.

J. MORRIS, 'Reviews: "Bill Brand"', *Red Letters*, no. 3, 1976, p. 14.

Graham MURDOCK, 'Radical Drama, Radical Theatre', *Media, Culture and Society*, no. 2, 1980, pp. 151–68.

John ORR, 'A Trail of Red Herrings', *AIP & Co*, no. 30, January 1981, pp. 11–18.

Mike POOLE, 'The Classic Gets Some Class', *Time Out*, 30 January–5 February 1981, pp. 16–17.

'Sons and Good Friends', *Time Out*, 27 February–5 March 1981, p. 58.

'Another Country', *New Statesman*, 30 October 1981, pp. 33–4.

'Mistaken Identities', *City Limits*, 16–22 April 1982, pp. 38–9.

'Trying to Get Under the Skins', *Guardian*, 7 June 1982.

Dennis POTTER, 'Prickly Pair', *New Statesman*, 8 February 1974, p. 198.

Christopher PRICE, 'Haggard Odysseus', *The Listener*, 22 July 1976, p. 85.

Peter PRINCE, 'Soft Centre', *New Statesman*, 12 December 1975, p. 766.

Pat SILBURN, 'Gambit Interview', *Gambit*, no. 29, 1976, pp. 30–6.

Ken SWALLOW, 'Enabling Perception to Occur', *Liberal Education*, no. 45, Spring 1982, pp. 6–14.

Dick TAVERNE, 'Bill Brand and I', *New Statesman*, 30 July 1976, pp. 140–1.

Graham TAYLOR and Nigel GREY, 'Brand of the Recent Future', *Streetlife*, 20 March–2 April 1976, pp. 22–3.

James THOMAS, 'Strictly his own Brand', *Daily Express*, 5 July 1976.

Nigel THOMAS, 'Trevor and Bill – On Putting Politics before News at Ten', *The Leveller*, no. 1, November 1976, pp. 12–13.

Robin THORNBER, 'Oi Hits a Cultural Brick Wall', *Guardian*, 8 October 1982.

Paul TICKELL, 'Red, White and Blue: The Politics of Colour', *New Musical Express*, 17 April 1982.

Kenneth TYNAN, 'Party Piece', *Sunday Times*, 16 December 1973, pp. 82–7.

Brian WINSTON, 'Public and Private Medicine', *The Listener*, 11 December 1975, p. 798.

Janet WOLFF, 'Bill Brand, Trevor Griffiths and the Debate about Political Theatre', *Red Letters*, no. 8, 1976, pp. 56–61.

Janet WOLFF, Steve RYAN, Jim McGUIGAN and Derek McKIERNAN, 'Problems of Radical Drama: The Plays and Productions of Trevor Griffiths', in *Literature, Sociology and the Sociology of Literature*, University of Essex, 1977, pp. 133–53.

John WYVER, 'How "The Best Play of the Twentieth Century" Took to the Air', *City Limits*, 9–15 October 1981, pp. 50–3.

'Winning the Peace', *City Limits*, 16–22 October 1981, pp. 49–51.

'Countering Consent: An Interview with Trevor Griffiths' in *Ah! Mischief: The Writer and Television*, ed. Frank Pike, Faber and Faber, 1982, pp. 30–40.

The Trevor Griffiths Special Collection

The British Film Institute Library possesses an important archive of Griffiths manuscripts, donated by the author. The collection is of foremost importance for any research on the writer; hence our decision to supplement the bibliography with a catalogue (prepared by Ian MacDonald) of the documents in the collection.

Unproduced scripts

The Love Maniac: Manuscript; typescript draft, with amendments; typescript draft, after amending, dated 30 May 1968.
Dropping Out: Manuscript, with title page and three others typescript, marked 'Draft 1'.

Radio script

Jake's Brigade (i.e. radio version of *The Love Maniac*): Radio script.

Television scripts

Adam Smith episode 1: New schedule; pink script dated 6 September 1971, with manuscript amendments.
Adam Smith episode 2: Rehearsal script dated 25 August 1971, with manuscript amendments; another rehearsal script with amendments; camera script dated 7 September 1971.
Adam Smith episode 3: Rehearsal script with some amendments.
Adam Smith episode 4: Rehearsal script with some amendments.
Adam Smith episode 5: Rehearsal script with some amendments, dated 31 August 1971.
Adam Smith episode 10 (transmitted as 9): Rehearsal script dated 3 November 1971.
Adam Smith episode 11 (transmitted as 10): Rehearsal script dated 23 December 1971; rehearsal script dated 23 December 1971, with some manuscript amendments.
Adam Smith episode 12 (transmitted as 11): Rehearsal script dated 23 December 1971.
Adam Smith episode 13 (transmitted as 12): Rehearsal script dated 12 April 1972, with some manuscript amendments; pink script.
Adam Smith episode 15: Rehearsal script dated 13 June 1972; pink script.
Adam Smith episode 16: Pink script dated 5 April 1972; photocopied script; pink script (rewritten), dated 30 May 1972; rehearsal script dated 13 June 1972.
Adam Smith episode 17: Pink script; photocopied script; pink script (rewritten); rehearsal script dated 13 June 1972.
Adam Smith episode 18: Pink script; photocopied script; pink script (rewritten); rehearsal script dated 13 June 1972.
The Silver Mask: Manuscript; six pages of notes; camera script; photocopy of Hugh Walpole's story; typescript draft.

All Good Men: Camera script.

Absolute Beginners: Manuscript; four cards of notes; camera script; rehearsal script; 44 rewrite pages; typescript draft.

Occupations: Pink script dated 16 November 1973.

Such Impossibilities: Manuscript; typescript draft; various notes.

Don't Make Waves: Rehearsal (?) script.

Through the Night: Manuscript; rehearsal script; camera script; amended pages for script; various correspondence.

Bill Brand episode 1: Manuscript; rehearsal script with amendments.

Bill Brand episode 2: Manuscript; rehearsal scripts with amendments.

Bill Brand episode 3: Manuscript; rehearsal scripts; camera script.

Bill Brand episode 4: Manuscript; rehearsal scripts with amendments.

Bill Brand episode 5: Manuscript; typescripts, one dated 'Revised 8 Sept. 75'; rehearsal script with amendments.

Bill Brand episode 6: Manuscript; rehearsal script; camera script.

Bill Brand episode 7: Manuscript; rehearsal scripts with amendments; camera script.

Bill Brand episode 8: Manuscript; rehearsal script with amendments; camera script.

Bill Brand episode 9: Manuscript; first typescript draft; camera script.

Bill Brand episode 10: Manuscript; typescript draft.

Bill Brand episode 11: Manuscript; rehearsal scripts with amendments; fifteen substitute pages.

Comedians: Rehearsal (?) script, with some amendments.

Sons and Lovers (ATV): Various schedules; scripts for various locations; rehearsal scripts for episodes 4–6, with some amendments.

Sons and Lovers (BBC): Rehearsal scripts for episodes 1–6. Reconstructed scripts for new episodes 4, 6 and 7; various amendment pages; various schedules; various camera scripts; manuscripts for episodes 1–6; draft typescripts.

The Cherry Orchard: Manuscript; typescript literal translation from the Russian by Helen Rappaport, with some manuscript notes; two rewrite pages for TV version; camera script; rehearsal script.

Country: Draft typescript; shooting script.

Oi for England: Manuscript; rehearsal script; camera script.

Film script

John Reed, aka *Comrades*, aka *Reds*: Research notes; manuscript – loose; manuscript, collated material, marked 'April 77'; typescript draft marked 'Original unamended 1st draft (pp. 1–73)'; typescript draft pp. 1–54; step outline marked 14 January 1979; first typescript draft.

Trevor Griffiths: Film and Videocassette Availability in Britain

The following films and videocassettes are currently available for rental in Britain:

Title	Producer	Format	Available from
Bill Brand, episodes 1, 6, 7 and 10	Thames TV	Videocassette	BFI, 127 Charing Cross Road, London WC2H 0EA
Comedians	BBC TV	Videocassette	BFI
Country	BBC TV	16mm film and videocassette	BFI
Fall of Eagles: (Absolute Beginners)	BBC TV	Videocassette	BFI
Oi for England	Central TV	Videocassette	Concord Films Council 201 Felixstowe Road, Ipswich
Reds		16mm film	Rank Film Library P.O. Box 20, Great West Road, Brentford, Middlesex